nettl's elephant

Bruno Nettl

Foreword by Anthony Seeger

University of Illinois Press

Urbana, Springfield, and Chicago

nettl's elephant

· ·

On the History of Ethnomusicology

Library
Quest University Canada
3200 University Boulevard
Squamish, BC V8B 0N8

© 2010 by the Board of Trustees
of the University of Illinois
All rights reserved
Manufactured in the United States of America
1 2 3 4 5 C P 6 5 4 3 2
∞ This book is printed on acid-free paper.

Library of Congress Cataloging-in-Publication Data
Nettl, Bruno, 1930–
Nettl's elephant : on the history of ethnomusicology /
Bruno Nettl ; foreword by Anthony Seeger.
p.   cm.
Includes bibliographical references and index.
ISBN 978-0-252-03552-4 (cloth : alk. paper) —
ISBN 978-0-252-07742-5 (pbk. : alk. paper)
1. Ethnomusicology—History. I. Title.
ML3799.N38   2010
780.89—dc22   2009046708

Photographs by Nick Mann

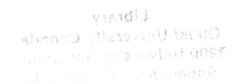

For Stefan Fiol

Contents

I. Central Issues in a Grand History

II. In the Academy

III. Celebrating Our Principal Organizations

IV. A Collage of Commentary

Foreword

Anthony Seeger

I was invited to write this introduction to a book that already had an eloquent introduction by an author who needed no introduction. I could
not resist the offer because I had so much enjoyed reading the manuscript that I felt a twinge of regret when I finished the last essay—What?
Nothing more? I felt as I did as a child on Christmas Day after I had un-
wrapped my last present: I had a great pile of exciting things, but the joy
of discovering the unknown was at an end. Lucky reader, you get to open
them all for the first time!

This is a brilliant book by a renowned author who has for decades
shaped thinking in the field on which he reflects in these essays. The
volume is elegantly structured. The chapters move from a reflection on
the grand history of ethnomusicology to discussions of the field within its
institutional contexts and then to evaluations of the principal organizations in the field (the two essays on the ICTM and SEM are structured in
wonderfully parallel ways). It concludes with some delightful short pieces

on a variety of topics, each of them shedding new light both on usually neglected literature and on the author himself. The last, appropriately, is a conversation between two German musicologists about the definition of music; Nettl's couches his answer in some of the things he learned from Blackfoot, Iranian, and South Asian musicians.

Bruno Nettl is a living legend in the field of ethnomusicology. He participated in many of the events and processes he describes in these essays, and his own life history is part of the movement of European musicologists to the United States and profoundly shaped the musicology of this country. The essays are very well and clearly written, are documented with citations ranging over the centuries and in several languages (I wish I were half as widely read), and usually contain fascinating perspectives on historical writings, as well as the most recent bibliography in the field.

Professor Nettl has published many volumes over the years, several of which have dealt with similar kinds of questions—especially his masterful *Study of Ethnomusicology: Thirty-One Issues and Concepts*. Some of those issues and concepts inevitably reappear here, along with observations based on his research among the Blackfoot, in Iran, and in South India. In the present essays, however, he consistently focuses on history and inserts his own experience and observations into the topics he addresses. This is, to borrow from the language of psychology, a group of essays written in the eighth of Erik Erickson's stages of life. They are reflective and integrative considerations of meaning and purpose written from a perspective of wisdom and renunciation (in the sense that the author writes these essays not to slay dragons and win a princess but rather to reflect on what the prince, the princess, and the dragon have in common). He rarely takes "sides" but often shows how apparently warring perspectives are really not so different after all. This rare and gentle approach leaves the readers to decide which—if any—of the perspectives is that of demons and ignoramuses.

Written largely for oral delivery, the chapters are clear and approachable. They distinctively and significantly contribute to an understanding of the history of ethnomusicology in the twentieth century within the context of population movements, wars, philosophy, and the author's own life. No other author could write with such authority and personal experience about ethnomusicology. Nettl repeatedly uses the apt metaphor of an arrow and a circle. The essays keep coming back to certain of his personal experiences as the son of an immigrant musicologist, a young scholar involved in the formation of professional organizations, and a decades-long participant-observer in the field's central debates. Yet each essay also has its arrow, or specific direction, and usually hits the mark to make a profound point.

Professor Nettl is an author of considerable wit as well as erudition, as anyone knows who has heard him give lectures or tell stories or received his holiday e-mails. The essays are fun to read partly because he often uses "throwaway" lines—frequently placed at the end of paragraphs—to make his most profound statements or critiques, doing so without the fanfare and self-congratulation so common in our field but rather with humor or apparent (but not real) unconsciousness. Watch for them.

It is especially appropriate that the University of Illinois Press should publish this book. In spite of insistent offers of positions elsewhere, Professor Nettl has been loyal to the University of Illinois and taught there for decades. Largely because of him (and of course the colleagues he recruited and the students they attracted), the University of Illinois has helped shape ethnomusicology and musicology over the past fifty years. He has even made the Illinois School of Music the subject of an ethnographic study, *Heartland Excursions*. Tony Bennett may have "left his heart in San Francisco," but Bruno Nettl clearly planted his in Champaign-Urbana. Many presses would have loved to publish this book; it is a fitting tribute to the author's loyalty to his institution that the University of Illinois Press is doing so.

You can dive into this book and read it from beginning to end or dip your toe in to check the temperature at any point. I enjoyed the thoughtful chapter sequencing, extremely rare in a collection of essays, and wish you joy, insight, and productive thoughts as you read. Later histories of ethnomusicology will be written partly about your responses to the ideas herein.

Introduction

Histories, Narratives, Sources

Elephants

Why should I, a student of ethnomusicology, title a book "Elephant" when it is obviously about music research and not about elephants? I'll explain. But first, please consider: if you didn't have some advance information, would you have guessed the content of books titled "*Heartbeat of a People*," "*The Black Cow's Footprint*," "*In Township Tonight*," or "*Moving away from Silence*"? They are all classics in ethnomusicology. So why not "Elephant?"

This is a collection of essays and lectures written beginning in the mid-1980s, a time when elephants came to play a major role in my life. Most of my friends know that that's when I began to collect elephants—a maximum of two inches tall, since we live, after all, in a modest home. It all started as a convenient Father's Day or birthday suggestion (for the man who has everything), but as the little statues multiplied, I came increasingly to

associate this collection with the nature of ethnomusicology. I've now got about 150, and like the musics with which ethnomusicologists are concerned, they come from many nations and cultures, they have old and modern and hybridized designs and shapes, they include works of "folk" art and "high" art, and they show the subjects in different moods, positions, and attitudes. In parallel to the ethnomusicological studies I'll be discussing in these pages, they provide a variety of interpretations of what it means to be an elephant (or, for ethnomusicology, to study musical culture). One specimen, constructed entirely of nuts and bolts, represents modern technology; another, made out of a starfish, is a metaphor for our field's interdisciplinary nature. Then, in the late 1980s, looking for a name for a private publishing venture, my wife, Wanda, and I—going, so to speak, public with our collectanea—came up with "Elephant & Cat."

To me, the elephant symbolizes history. In the late 1980s, I began to take a special interest in the history of my field, perhaps because I was becoming one of its "old men" who had been present when the very word *ethnomusicology* began to be used, and I came to feel close to the iconic pachyderm. No zoologist, I admire elephants for their sensitivity to sound, their senses of smell and taste, and their sophisticated social organization, all associated with what is recognized as an incredible memory. And so, setting out in these pages to deal with the history of my field, I logically choose the elephant as emblem. Having at times claimed that ethnomusicology asks music's most fundamental questions, I must also suggest that when music lovers make generalizations about the world of music and musicianship, the issues emanating from ethnomusicological insights are often the "elephant in the room."

Have I justified my title? There's more. One of the characteristics of ethnomusicology has been its decades-long search for identity, evident in the large amount of space that its literature devotes to questions of disciplinary definition, and I see the scholars who argue about and try to explain the precise nature of ethnomusicology as a modern version of the blind men of fable who examine an elephant and, feeling its legs, trunk, tusks, and tail and hearing its voice, provide a variety of interpretations of its nature.

Finally, there is Ganesh, the elephant-headed Hindu deity, remover of obstacles, good-humored patron of letters and scholarship, who often looks as if he had just told a funny story. Like Ganesh, I'd like to avoid being unpleasantly critical and occasionally to be light-hearted and even humorous; like the super-sensitive African elephant, I hope I got things right with sensitivity to context; and I hope that my collection of essays, like my collection of elephants, may give the reader a sense of the diversity of the issues and questions that ethnomusicologists have confronted.

Histories

"Ethnomusicology today is an area of study caught up in a fascination with itself." That may be the most widely quoted sentence written by the oft-quoted Alan P. Merriam (1964:3), one the most influential leaders of this field from 1955, when the Society for Ethnomusicology was founded, until his death in 1980. What he said is still true half a century later. Merriam suggested that this fascination stemmed from the sudden and rapid growth of the field in the ten or fifteen years before he wrote. It had to do, as well, with the need for all these new scholars and students to give themselves an identity and to define their discipline. Almost fifty years later, however, professional ethnomusicologists, along with members of related fields to whom aspects of ethnomusicology are helpful, continue to be engrossed not only by the work in which they are engaged—that's to be taken for granted—but also by the nature of their field as a whole. What have we, not as individuals but as a group of scholars with a degree of homogeneity, been trying to accomplish?

Thus, if novelty was the principal motivation for this concern in the 1960s, forty-some years later, as the field acquired maturity, the need for identity and definition, the interest in the scope, methods, and goals of ethnomusicology (to recapitulate the title of Guido Adler's trailblazing 1885 article about musicology), continues to be a subject of debate in publications, on Internet conversations, and at conferences. The subjects of these discussions in recent years have ranged from technology to ethics; from the changed nature of the musical world to different notions of the appropriate subject matter for humanistic scholarship; and from the relationship of ethnomusicology to other kinds of music research to its association with studies of society, biology, and the hard sciences. Often one comes on references to the history of ethnomusicology as a basis for interpretation, criticism, and justification.

I have no statistics, but an exceptionally large number of research studies—articles, chapters, books—begin with some reference to the history of the field and the place of the study at hand in it. The considerable number of books dealing with ethnomusicology as a field of research devote significant space to its history. Only a few publications deal entirely or substantially with this history, however, and this collection of essays makes no attempt to present a history of the whole. It is thus appropriate, by way of acknowledgment and appreciation, to mention the works that seem most important in their inclusiveness. They include the initial portion of Jaap Kunst's celebrated survey, especially the third edition (Kunst 1959); a lengthy statement by Artur Simon (1978); the introduction to Helen Myers's edited volume *Ethnomusicology: An Introduction* (1992); the only book devoted entirely to the field's history, by Mervyn McLean, *Pioneers of Ethnomusicology* (2006); and the capsule treatment in *Précis d'ethnomusicologie* by Simha Arom and Frank Alvarez-Péreyre (2007). And there are lots of other publications—too many—that might be mentioned here, though some will appear as references in the ensuing essays.

At this point, my purpose is not to summarize these publications or to attempt a critique. Instead, I would like to suggest that in writings, but even more in oral presentations—and further, in classrooms and informal conversations—one may encounter several narratives of the history of ethnomusicology, narratives that generally do not disagree much about the facts but that provide contrastive interpretations and emphases, focusing on different domains of thought or activity as being significant or central. These narratives are the main subject of my discussion in the following paragraphs.

Narratives

So then, how did ethnomusicologists see the history of their field? What are its overall characteristics, its defining events, its landmarks; what is its shape? What stories do they tell themselves and one another?

The closest to a universally accepted narrative, particularly in American publications, presents two dichotomies. The first divides the history into two main periods, one usually labeled "comparative musicology" and dominated by European, mainly Germanophone scholars who engaged, principally, in analytical and historical studies of recordings and artifacts with emphasis on comparison of various kinds, and the other, beginning around 1950 and marked by the adoption of the term *ethnomusicology*, dominated by American scholars who were first concerned with the study of non-Western contemporary musical cultures from a number of perspectives. The other dichotomy divides the second of these periods into two movements. One is labeled, for convenience (though not quite accurately) "anthropological," and it sees ethnomusicology as a subdivision of sociocultural anthropology and thus emphasizes the definition "the study of music in culture." The other, associating itself academically with the field of music, has as its hallmark the study of non-Western musical performance and the concept of bimusicality as a principal entrée into a foreign musical system. Although I believe that the importance of these two dichotomies in history may have been overstated, this seems to be the most widely accepted interpretation of the way the field has developed, described in major publications including those by Myers (1992 and 1993:3–12) and McLean (2006)—and mentioned in lots of others. And they provide the principal construct of the nature of ethnomusicology in Kerman's (1985) portrayal of the discipline of musicology.

This version of the history posits a mainstream that begins in central Europe and moves to North America, ignoring various movements elsewhere in the world that may also have played a part. To the extent that these are not ignored, they are often co-opted; in the last few decades, ethnomusicologists throughout the world, even in Asian and African cultures, have viewed themselves part of this history, adhering to it as a mainstream and referring to pre-1950 European scholars such as Erich M. von Hornbostel and his school and to post-1950 North American and British scholars such as Alan P. Merriam, Mantle Hood, and John Blacking as their models. Essentially, this narrative sees ethnomusicology coming from a single root that gradually developed a number of branches.

A second narrative of the history provides a contrasting view. Here, ethnomusicology has its beginning more or less simultaneously in many places—indeed, each culture may have its own proto- or early ethnomusicology—but as international communication and globalization (which began long before the term was introduced) became dominant in the world, these movements coalesced into one or maybe a few strands. The argument that ethnomusicological activities and their predecessors, working essentially without mutual contact, began in various parts of the world was made by Stephen Blum (1991:6–10), who lists antecedents or scholars in ethnomusicology working in the nineteenth century in several Asian nations and in all parts of Europe. Blum's narrative can be sustained if ethnomusicology is defined substantially as the study of traditional and folk musics. The adherents of the first, "mainstream" view of history may object to this definition and to this interpretation of the history. By way of resolution, one may suggest that the variety of historical narratives may be traced to the variety of definitions of ethnomusicology.

Mervyn McLean, author of the only book-length history of ethnomusicology (2006), presents a modified version of this interpretation, proposing the simultaneous origins and the eventual joining of a European and an American school.

Other narratives of the history are derived by privileging certain domains or activities as most essential or central. To some, the history of ethnomusicology is to be seen most explicitly in the history of the world's technology essential to music-making but also, importantly, in the history of the technology that enables and supports research (e.g., recording technology). Fundamental to both branches are certain technologies that have become so established that we tend to take them for granted, but they must surely be mentioned in this context: musical notation and music printing. All musical life changed substantially as a result of their development, but the basic character of early ethnomusicology, which involved the recording of traditional music on paper, was first made possible by the invention of notation and its dissemination by printing.

Nonetheless, what is most emphasized in the various accounts of ethnomusicological history—and, incidentally, ought to be stressed more in conventional history of music and musical life—is the invention of recording, for this changed the musical culture of the world's societies and also made ethnomusicology, in the sense in which it is practiced today, possible in the first place. Recording goes back to the late nineteenth century, and its almost incalculable effect on listeners—not just in the developed nations of the world (see Gronow 1978)—goes back to the early twentieth century. I won't try to rehearse the many changes, which one may or may not wish to regard as "progress," through the twentieth century, the different media of recording and reproduction and the increasingly available personal recording devices and techniques, from disks, wire, and tape to digitalization, from sound to video, and lots more. Throughout the course of these developments, change in musical culture and in ethnomusicological method have gone substantially hand in hand. So, one of the important narratives of ethnomusicological history shows culture change, as influenced or determined by technological advances, accompanied by parallel changes in ethnomusicological method and technology (see Kunst 1959:1–45; Hood 1963b:240–59).

There is a somewhat contrastive narrative that emphasizes the history of the relationships between investigator and the people and the music being investigated. Perhaps more broadly, one could call this the history of fieldwork (which still ought also to include considerations of the technical devices used in fieldwork). But surely central to the conception of a history of fieldwork is a fundamental change in the relationship to the people who are, in effect, our sources, change symbolized by the progression of terminology for the host as "informant" to "consultant" and eventually more commonly to "teacher." There are other important kinds of changes: from the fieldworker always as a student of what may be interpreted as the exotic to the fieldworker investigating his or her own culture and from the concept of traditional cultures as homogeneous (in which each "informant" would be equally representative) to emphasis on the individuality of the teacher. There is, further, growing awareness of the ways in which an investigator affects a host culture and the issues subsumed under the term *ethics*. This narrative—"the history of ethnomusicology is the history of fieldwork"—is illustrated in the introduction to the second edition of *Shadows in the Field* (Barz and Cooley 2008), which tells this story, and also by several chapters of the work that show how field experience changed the attitudes of the authors. Barz and Cooley's work portrays the history of fieldwork as progressing from naive to sophisticated but as continuing to confront ethical challenges. Helen Myers's general history of the field (1992:3–17), too, tends to look at the history of fieldwork as the discipline's most distinguishing feature.

A further narrative suggests that the history of ethnomusicology is best interpreted through understanding the changing identities of the investigators. One central feature in this story is the enormous increase in the number and influence of female scholars beginning around 1960 (although they were hardly absent before that) and, somewhat related, the increased sensitivity to a variety of gender identities and sexual preferences among ethnomusicologists and in the host cultures. Also, we may note a somewhat smaller but significant increase in scholars representing various minorities in North America (and somewhat less, in Europe) and further, the increased participation of scholars from many Asian, African, Latin American, and other nations and cultures. Aside from the implications of these changes for society at large, the gradually altered composition of the ethnomusicological population also resulted in important changes in the subject matter(s) addressed and the theoretical and methodological underpinnings. Several of the major works, particularly coming from the perspective of gender studies, relate this narrative (see, e.g., Koskoff 1987, Moisala and Diamond 2000, Solie 1993).

A narrative contrasting with these anthropologically oriented narratives, found in a number of European publications, associates the history of ethnomusicology more closely with the developments of systematic musicology—acoustics, organology, classification systems, measurements of various sorts—than with sociocultural anthropology. This aspect of the history is emphasized, for example, by A. Schneider (2006), Sachs (1962:5–15, 1959:7–10), and Arom and Alvarez-Péreyre (2007). It's an approach found also in the account of ethnomusicology given in some works dealing with musicology as a whole (e.g., Haydon 1941). The currency of this interpretation of history decreased in the late twentieth century, as the majority of ethnomusicologists devoted themselves less and less to studies that relate their methods to those coming from the hard sciences, but by the same token it may be revived as considerations of evolution and cognitive studies play an increased role.

A number of narratives try to follow the course of what may appear to be central concepts in ethnomusicological thought. One such narrative follows the notion that the entire field is identified by the quest for a central question: what is it that ethnomusicologists are trying to do; what basic question do they wish to answer, or with what principal task are they concerned? I have found this approach to history largely in informal conversations that compare "earlier times" with the recent or present. Such a narrative is touched on by Rice (1987, 2003), and I'll round it out. Early scholarship began with the purpose of preservation followed quickly by the reconstruction of history. After 1950, the central purpose was stated by Merriam as the study of music in culture. This was initially based on a three-pronged model of music—ideas, behavior, sound—and followed by Rice's own central question: "How do people historically construct, socially maintain, and individually create and experience music?" (Rice 1987:473); later, it was explained via a fourfold model of music as art, social behavior, symbol, and commodity (Rice 2003:166).

Alan Merriam (1977) built a narrative of the history of definitions. Presenting a chronology of definitions (some of them, to be sure, taken somewhat out of context and not necessarily intended by their authors as formal definitions), Merriam begins by translating Guido Adler's (1885:14) account, a "comparison of musical works—especially the folksongs—of various peoples of the earth for ethnographical purposes" (in Merriam

1977:199), goes on to quote several dozen statements, and ends with Elisabeth Helser, who in 1977 defined ethnomusicology as "the hermeneutical science of human musical behavior" (in Merriam 1977:204).

In the history of science, the principal landmarks have sometimes been identified as "paradigms," a term of art coined by Thomas Kuhn in *The Structure of Scientific Revolutions* (1970). Paradigms, in this context, are conceptual structures in which a majority of scientists (in a given area) share an understanding or agree on what to take as established facts or methods. Attempts have been made to see the history of scholarship in various humanistic fields along the same lines, but with only modest success. There seems to be a belief that there should be something like paradigms that would mark critical points in the history of ethnomusicology but little agreement on what they might be and whether they ought to be shared understandings on method and approach or on facts about the nature of music and society. Perhaps the turning point from "comparative musicology" to "anthropology of music," and the subsequent bifurcation to "anthropology" and "musicology" as point of departure—the "narrative" first broached in this chapter—might qualify as paradigm shifts. Ruth Stone (2008:1–4) discusses the history of ethnomusicology as a series of paradigms but also suggests that leading figures, such as Anthony Seeger, believe that concentration on the paradigm building might deprive the field of much of its desirable diversity.

The typical narrative of the history of ethnomusicology is positive; we have made progress and are getting better. But there is the occasional dissenting voice, and there are certainly scholars and conversations that are sharply critical of what has happened. One can summarize and group some of them, but in general, they see ethnomusicologists as having at some point turned in the wrong direction or abandoned earlier established principles. Some have seen the history of the field as gradually encompassing more and more of the musical world, encroaching on the purview of historical musicology and abandoning its devotion to "traditional" musics. Kerman (1985:168–81) maintained that "Western music is just too different" from others to be subsumed in the same intellectual scope. The implication is that ethnomusicologists have not done well in their contemplation of Western art and popular music. Alexander Ringer (1991) takes an essentially opposite view, criticizing a history that begins with scholars who see themselves as students of the whole of (well, non-Western) music moving gradually to an increased degree of specialization that separates the world's musics from one another and inhibits a holistic view of music.

A different critical narrative sees ethnomusicologists continuing to avoid dealing with practical problems that result from the variety of interactions among the cultures of societies whose music is studied and among scholars from a variety of societies and backgrounds, with a large body of literature pointing out these issues and warning of consequences. The social and intellectual results of gender discrimination are significant in this narrative (Frisbie 1991; Herndon 2000). This kind of criticism may be expressed colloquially as "we may have made progress, but not nearly enough."

The critical narrative most concerned with specific methods involves the abandonment and neglect of comparative study and comparative methods. Stated in many publications, but perhaps most forcefully by McLean (2006:314–16), Grauer (2006) and A. Schneider (2006), this criticism asserts that at some point, ethnomusicology turned away from its most powerful and promising tool for finding answers to certain central questions. It contradicts the optimistic tone of the most widely accepted narrative (mentioned first in this chapter), in which the change from a principally "comparative" musicology devoted to analysis of music to a study of music in individual cultures is presented as the great step forward that provided the field's salvation.

Just as many nations and regions have developed individual approaches to ethnomusicology in the course of the twentieth and twenty-first centuries, some of them have also provided their own interpretations of the history of the field. Thus, Isabel Wong (1991) sees the history of Chinese ethnomusicology as heavily following political developments, while Tang Yating (2000:67) suggests that the basic outline of Western disciplinary history, which Chinese scholarship followed, consisted of successive introductions of comparative musicology, folkloristic approaches, the study of individual non-Western traditions through analysis and practice, and anthropology of music.

Ethnomusicologists see their history in many different ways; they subscribe to a number of different narratives. The diversity of ethnomusicological narratives may be due to the variety of disciplinary associations enjoyed by the people who work in this field, the diversity of their backgrounds and ultimate purposes. It may be due to the variety of definitions that have been used to identify ethnomusicology, as illustrated by Merriam (1977)—a variety that has only increased in the thirty years since Merriam's article was published. Merriam was frustrated throughout his career by the absence of a unified identity, purpose, and methodology and expressed a wish, in publications, symposia, and roundtables, to set this matter straight. Late in his career—sadly cut short by his premature death—he seemed to make his peace with this diversity of definitions, saying, with some degree of prescience and a bit of world-weariness, "I have no doubt that new definitions of ethnomusicology will continue to be proposed and they, too, will reflect the growing maturity of the field and its practitioners" (1977:198).

Sources

The history of my field of study has been of special interest to me for many years, but this interest has increased as both the field and I myself have aged, and it has been, since the mid-1980s, the subject of some publications and a good many lectures of mine. I am pleased to offer here a number of these essays and lectures, hoping to provide a personal perspective with some data but more interpretation. This is by no means a history of the field—it is in no way comprehensive. It speaks principally to issues, events, and literature with which I have been involved, or that relate to my own areas of research.

Included here are studies that have been published previously, as well as invitational lectures and papers presented at conferences, between 1988 and 2008. In contrast to the previous section of this chapter, which discussed the ethnomusicological population's own views of its history, these essays, in the aggregate, attempt to provide my personal perspective. Moreover, as I was a senior citizen at the time of writing these pages, having taken a course in ethnomusicology as early as 1948 and having been introduced to recordings of gamelan, of maqams and ragas, as early as 1935, I experienced a good deal of this history myself. I therefore beg the reader's indulgence for introducing a personal and autobiographical tone into several of the essays.

I have been trying hard to walk a fine line between two purposes. On the one hand, this volume was from the beginning conceived as a retrospective, a collection of materials previously published or presented orally, the published ones usually in not very accessible venues. Thus one might expect these to be reprinted faithfully as they first appeared, "warts and all." On the other hand, many imperfections of these publications were obvious from the beginning, and many others were later pointed out by the scholars who read the versions in this manuscript for the publisher. Also, since the time most of these pieces were written, much has happened that would make me rewrite or thoroughly revise what I had said, perhaps to start totally "from scratch." Each of these publications and papers was originally intended to stand alone and thus contained its own statements of context and points of departure. Putting them together in a collection necessitated cutting out sections of some to reduce the most offensive redundancies. At the same time, since I wished to present each chapter as something that may be read independently, with its own coherence, I found that I had to provide certain pieces of information and some bits of discussion in more than one essay. Trying to compromise, I have made some essential revisions and some corrections, a number of deletions, and a few additions that seemed mandated by recent events. In those that were presented as lectures and not published subsequently, I have tried to add the most essential bibliographical references and to refer the reader to more comprehensive treatments.

Except for some needed editing and editorial rewriting, however, the materials here appear in close to their original form. As a result, you may encounter some incidents, such as the founding of the Society for Ethnomusicology, or the 1950 meeting of IFMC, or Alan Merriam's struggle with the field's identity, and some characters, such as George Herzog, E. M. von Hornbostel, Curt Sachs, and John Blacking, several times, periodically emerging to greet you like long-lost acquaintances. For these moments of reiteration and redundancy, I apologize.

Let me say a bit about the contents and indicate (with thanks for permission to reprint) the sources of the individual chapters. The first section, "Central Issues in a Grand History," presents five perspectives to interpret the whole of my subject. The first essay (chapter 1), "The Seminal Eighties," was originally written in 1985 to celebrate the centennial of both Guido Adler's statement (1885) setting forth his outline of musicology and Alexander John Ellis's (1885) article that in effect set forward the principle of relativism in the comparison of non-Western musics. Adjusted for publication in my book *Encounters in Ethnomusicology* (Warren, Mich.: Harmonie Park, 2002), 19–31, and lightly revised further for these pages, it suggests that—significantly for all that was to come in the ensuing century—the creation of a comprehensive musicology at that moment was related to, and perhaps the result of, prevailing currents and trends in European and North American politics and intellectual life. If the most conventional narrative of our history suggests a German beginning in the 1880s and a major revolution in America shortly after 1950, chapter 2, "Look at It Another Way" (a revised version of a talk prepared for the Universidade Nova de Lisboa in 2009), proposes that the development of ethnomusicology may also be interpreted as resulting from the growth of moderately independent national schools and a few individuals who worked at first quite alone to develop traditions of scholarship in their native nations. "Speaking of

World Music" (chapter 3) combines excerpts of a lengthy essay, "A History of Histories," prepared originally in 2007 for an as yet unpublished *Cambridge History of World Music* (edited by Philip V. Bohlman) with portions of a lecture on teaching world music courses given at the University of Illinois for music education students in 2007. Beginning by examining the role of college texts in the growth of the "world music" concept, it then reaches back to the idea of a world music as it evolved in the work of a few prominent scholars beginning in the late eighteenth century.

"A Tradition of Self-Critique" (chapter 4), written in 2006—originally for a Festschrift for Beverley Diamond (*Music Traditions, Cultures, and Contexts* edited by Robin Elliott and Gordon Smith and published by Wilfrid Laurier University Press in early 2010)—argues that since the late 1800s the history of ethnomusicology has been characterized by leading scholars' criticism of the field as a whole and of its principal direction and their belief that its major task is to correct received wisdom and conventional beliefs. Chapter 5, "Revisiting Comparison, Comparative Study, and Comparative Musicology," whose title is self-explanatory, was written in 2006 and first published in a special issue of the University of Hamburg's *Jahrbuch für Musikwissenschaft* no. 24, edited by Albrecht Schneider and titled *Systematic and Comparative Musicology: Concepts, Methods, Findings* (Frankfurt: Peter Lang, 2008), 295–314.

The second section, "In the Academy," historically relates ethnomusicology to other disciplines and fields of study. "Ethno among the Ologies" (chapter 6), a lecture prepared for an anniversary celebration in the Department of Ethnomusicology and Folklore of Indiana University in 2003, describes some ways in which the history of ethnomusicology interrelates with the developments of historical musicology and of folklore. "On the Concept of Evolution in the History of Ethnomusicology" (chapter 7) was first prepared for a conference on evolutionary musicology at Seewiesen, near Munich, in 2004, and attended largely by biological scientists. Then, revised and titled "Response to Victor Grauer: On the Concept of Evolution in the History of Ethnomusicology," it was published in *World of Music* 48, no. 2: 59–72, as a contribution to a symposium based on a paper by Grauer. It contemplates the role of the concept of evolution (sometimes interpreted incorrectly) in the history of ethnomusicology and comments on ethnomusicological notions of the origins of music, the course of universal music history, and the ability of musical systems to develop adaptive mechanism for survival.

Chapter 8, "The Music of Anthropology," prepared originally as a lecture given at the Department of Anthropology at the University of Illinois in 1992, with excerpts published later in my professional memoir (Nettl 2002a:62–68), looks at the role music plays in sociocultural anthropology—the thought and teaching of sociocultural anthropologists who, when holistically presenting culture as a concept, may or may not include music as one of the domains.

In discussing the history of their field, many ethnomusicologists speak as if their principal professional organizations were virtually identical to the discipline, with the character of ethnomusicology finding a precise parallel in the nature of the Society for Ethnomusicology (SEM) and perhaps of the International Council for Traditional Music (ICTM). My third section, "Celebrating Our Principal Organizations," presents three invitational papers given at anniversary conventions of these two organizations. All have been slightly expanded, in part to speak to criticisms of my presentations. Two of them (chapters 9 and 10) were delivered as keynote papers for the ICTM's fortieth and fiftieth anniversaries, presented in (then) East Berlin (1987) and Nitra, Slovakia (1997), respectively, and published in the *Yearbook for Traditional Music* (Nettl 1988, 1998). The third, "We're on the Map" (chapter 11), was the lead paper in a panel at the fiftieth anniversary of SEM in Atlanta, 2005, in which members of different generations of scholars spoke to their individual perceptions of the history of the society, and published in *Ethnomusicology* 50, pp. 179–89.

Chapter 9, "The IFMC/ICTM and the Development of Ethnomusicology in the United States," suggests that this organization served as a counterweight to the Society for Ethnomusicology in the field's development in the United States. "Arrows and Circles" (chapter 10) looks at the history of the ICTM as a combination of forward motion and change, on the one hand, and as a process continually returning to the principles prominent at the time of its founding, on the other. Chapter 11, "We're on the Map," recalls the founding of the Society for Ethnomusicology and its early years and debunks three not really justified beliefs or "myths" that form part of the widely held informal narrative of the society's history.

The last section, "A Collage of Commentary," consists of short essays that do not narrate segments of history itself but make excursions into events, activities, and ideas that I believe have historical significance. Chapter 12, "Recalling Some Neglected Classics in Musical Geography," prepared for a memorial volume for Tullia Magrini and dedicated to her (*Antropologia della musica nelle culture mediterranee: Interpretazione, performance, identità*, edited by Philip V. Bohlman and Marcello Sorce Keller with Loris Azzaroni [Bologna: CLUEB, 2009], 29–38), takes the widespread use of geographical distribution in the history of ethnomusicology as a point of departure and comments on a number of scholars and publications that have been largely neglected in our narration of this history. "Minorities in Ethnomusicology: A Meditation on Experience in Three Cultures" (chapter 13), prepared for a meeting of the ICTM Study Group on Minorities (published in *Voices of the Weak,* edited by Zuzana Jurková [Prague: Slovo 21, 2009], 12–23), asks whether the field of ethnomusicology is in fact largely devoted to minorities and, conversely, whether the concept of "minority" is appropriate for a field interested in the very music thought to be the principal expression of "the people" as a whole. Delivered in my birthplace of Prague, it touches on the way in which my family musically negotiated membership in several minorities and on the differential concept of minorities in musical life in my experience of Native American and Iranian cultures, and it also suggests that the concept of "minority" may be helpful in interpreting new developments such as "medical ethnomusicology."

"Riding the Warhorses" (chapter 14) was an offering in a conference held at the University of Illinois in 2007 and titled "Canons in Musical Scholarship and Performance." It contemplates the concept of canons in the musics of the world and their varying functions and then discusses the construction and use of canons in the education of ethnomusicologists as factors in their research.

I beg the reader's special indulgence for my inclusion of the last two essays, because they even more directly reflect my personal experiences than do the preceding chapters. More specialized in their original intent, they look at history in quite contrastive ways. Chapter 15, "A Stranger Here? Free Associations around Kurt Weill," quoting from the title of Kurt Weill's famous song "I'm a Stranger Here Myself," is a response to an invitation to write about this famous composer from an ethnomusicological perspective in the *Kurt Weill Newsletter* (21, no. 2 [Fall 2003]: 6–10). Using a personal encounter with Weill and his music in 1949 as background, I try to show how ethnomusicology can usefully comment on some of the musical and social events that characterized Europe and America in the middle of the twentieth century.

"Music—What's That?" (chapter 16) came from a 2004 conference that celebrated the birthday of the distinguished German music historian Hans Heinrich Eggebrecht (1919–1999), a man whose World War II record has recently come under critical scrutiny. My paper took as point of departure *Was ist Musik?* (Wilhelmshaven: Heinrichshofen, 1985), a book by Carl Dahlhaus and Eggebrecht, who debated ten fundamental questions about music. My contribution speaks to these questions from an ethnomusicological perspective. Delivered and published in German

("Was ist Musik? Ethnomusikologische Perspektive," in *Musik—zu Begriff und Konzepten,* edited by Michael Beiche and Albrecht Riethmüller [Munich: Franz Steiner Verlag, 2006], 9–18), I'm presenting here my own translation of the paper into English.

As this collection begins with an essay centered on Guido Adler's precedent-setting article of 1885, it seems appropriate to close by focusing on this book by Dahlhaus and Eggebrecht (1985), which was published as an offering for the hundredth anniversary of that article.

Considering that ethnomusicology is a small subdivision of one of two fields that are themselves relatively small within the academy—musicology according to some, and to others, sociocultural anthropology—the amount that has been written about its history is actually astonishing. Inviting us to engage in this discourse, Alan Merriam, in an essay titled "Ethnomusicology Revisited" (Merriam 1969:225), wrote: "We badly need histories, and particularly histories of ideas, in ethnomusicology. . . . Far too few of us, for example, know what von Hornbostel really did." I am not sure whether Merriam's criticism of the absence of historical concern before he wrote that article was justified, but he certainly would have been pleased with the efforts of many, later on, who insisted that historical context is essential for proper understanding of the literature written in any period. I cannot claim here to reply to Merriam specifically by shedding any new light on the activities of our father figure Erich M. von Hornbostel, but I do hope that these essays provide some insight into what happened in the history of his discipline—and in some cases, why.

Thanks

I am happy to have the opportunity of thanking at least a few of the individuals and institutions that have been helpful to me in constructing and editing this compilation. I am grateful, first of all, to the publishers and editors of the books and periodicals in which a number of these essays originally appeared, for permission to completely or partially reprint, sometimes with and sometimes without revisions. Without their kind cooperation, this volume could never have been produced. The last six months of my work on this book were done while I had the honor of holding a Mellon Distinguished Emeritus Fellowship, for which I was nominated by the chancellor of the University of Illinois at Urbana-Champaign.

I am especially grateful for good advice and encouragement from, among many others, Judy McCulloh, Anthony Seeger, Philip Yampolsky, Michael Bakan, Phil Bohlman, Steve Blum, Tom Turino, and my editor at the University of Illinois Press, Laurie Matheson. I wish to thank Bruce Bethell, scholar and copy editor extraordinaire, and Cope Cumpston, art director at the University of Illinois Press, for developing designs truly unique in a conventional academic book. I am indebted to Jessica Hajek for help with the index. I am grateful to Wanda for help with proofreading and editing and—as always—thank her much more for having lived with me through the years during which these essays were written and seen me through yet another project.

These essays come from a number of published sources, and a good many were presented as lectures, so I have benefited from comments, questions, and criticisms given before and after publication and contributed by so many colleagues, friends, and students that I can't possibly construct—or reconstruct—a list. Many thanks to all.

Central Issues
in a Grand History

1

The Seminal Eighties

Historical Musicology and Ethnomusicology

Adler's Paradigm

This is a narration, and perhaps more, an interpretation, of what may be considered the beginnings of musicology as a coherent discipline and of its subdivision ethnomusicology. In 1885, Guido Adler (1885, 3), the man often credited with giving musicology its start, began his most influential article by asserting, "Die Musikwissenschaft entstand gleichzeitig mit der Tonkunst" (Musicology began simultaneously with music). Did he define *Tonkunst* as "music," or did he mean "art music"? Either way, this origin occurred very, very long ago.

Since Adler's time, music historians have declared several moments of creation: 1703, the publication date of Sébastien de Brossard's *Dictionnaire de musique;* 1732, when Johann Walther's famous first dictionary of music appeared; 1768, the publication year of Jean-Jacques Rousseau's *Diction-naire de musique;* 1776, the year in which Burney's and Hawkins's histories of music were published; and 1863, when Friedrich Chrysander published the first volume of the *Jahrbücher für musikalische Wissenschaft,* (Chrysander 1863–69), maybe the first periodical that looks remotely like the *Journal of American Musicology,* or *Musikforschung,* or *Music and Letters.* But most typically, the beginning of musicology is assigned to the 1885 publication of the *Vierteljahrschrift für Musikwissenschaft* and especially to Adler's article because it lays out, in ways that have never been totally abandoned by music scholars in the Western world (and those elsewhere influenced by this tradition), the structure and fundamental function of this field.

My father, Paul Nettl, considered himself a disciple of Adler, having served for a time as his assistant, and thus frequently mentioned his name. He would allude to Adler's great accomplishments—and sometimes also to his stiff-necked irascibility, which was probably responsible for many of his administrative successes: founding and supervising the *Denkmäler der Tonkunst in Österreich;* publishing a major compendium of music history, the *Handbuch der Musikgeschichte* (1930); and developing a Ph.D. program that produced a generation of the most influential music historians. When my father assisted him in the 1920s, Adler was already over seventy years old but still going strong, and in 1927 he asserted Vienna's hegemony as a musicological center by hosting an international centennial congress commemorating Beethoven. Paul Nettl was proud of his association with Adler, who like himself had been born to a Jewish family in a German-speaking community in the Czech lands (the little town of Eibenschütz, in southern Moravia, in 1855) and had held the celebrated musicology chair in Prague when my father was still a little kid.

Some sixty years later it was time for another centennial, this one in a small town well into the countryside of Lower Austria outside Vienna, a region dotted with churches and monasteries. There I attended—in a funny-looking hotel in a reconstructed medieval granary and thus comically named "Alter Schuttkasten," (Old Granary)—a conference about Adler and the consequences of his article of 1885. Taken for granted in the 1930s, when Adler worked as a historian uncovering great music (and also some of the minor music) of that grand music history of Austria, the article began to stand out increasingly as Adler's most significant accomplishment because it stated, in unprecedentedly broad perspective, that musicology should encompass all kinds of research on music. I believe it was this holistic approach to the field that set musicology apart from other disciplines among the humanities, and although most living musicologists have perhaps never read that article, it has always been the cornerstone of the field. To many, it qualifies as the moment at which musicology began.

In Adler's world, there was no doubt that the true music was the music of Western culture and that the truest music was the art music of eighteenth- and nineteenth-century Austria and Germany and maybe Italy and France. Eventually Adler came to be considered the leader of paradigmatic conservatives among music historians, despite his interest in Wagner and his book on the (then) recently deceased Mahler (Adler 1916). What he says here and there about non-Western music shows that he saw it in a somewhat Darwinian style, as music representing an earlier stage of development far outstripped by European accomplishments. But in 1885, barely thirty years old, Adler was a kind of firebrand, bringing to the world of scholarship a vision of a new field—musicology—and approaching his task with a wide scope that was not soon if ever shared by scholarship in the other arts.

The importance of the 1885 article rests in the way it lays out the field of musicology. Let me remind you of the structure it imposes. There are two major divisions, historical and systematic, each with subdivisions. Historical musicology includes paleography, taxonomy, the study of chronology (in music, theory, and practice), and, as a kind of annex, the history of musical instruments. Systematic musicology includes theory—the bases of harmony, rhythm, and melody; aesthetics; music pedagogy; and, again as a kind of curious annex, something called "*Musikologie*," defined as "comparative study for ethnographic purposes." There are several auxiliary sciences whose inclusion persuades us that Adler regarded musicology as closely related to other fields. It's important, by the way, to point out that the kinds of considerations appropriate to ethnomusicology are not found exclusively under "*Musikologie*." Adler's discussion of his chart places non-Western and comparative study, and music's relationship to the rest of culture, also within other aspects of the systematic branch of musicology (particularly aesthetics) and in the historical branch as well.

The classes given in Adler's article stayed around for a long time, for example, in his methodological handbook (1930) and in the textbook *Introduction to Musicology*, by one of his North American students, Glen Haydon (1941). Other outlines have been proposed (see especially C. Seeger 1977, 125–27). Despite some internecine strife and a lot of attitudes, however, musicology has remained for over a century a single field in which most individuals recognize that the rest, however far-flung their musical interests, are colleagues. It continues to be thus defined in dictionaries of music.

Well, the division of a holistic musicology into such categories has perhaps become old hat, but a hundred years ago it must surely have been a new thing. There were parallel stirrings elsewhere also: in Russia, in France, even of a sort in the United States. Adler had predecessors, too, most obvious among them Friedrich Chrysander, who for a few years beginning in 1863 published his *Jahrbücher für musikalische Wissenschaft*, in whose preface he asserts that this *"Wissenschaft"* has several branches: history, aesthetics, theory, folk music scholarship (including intercultural comparison), and the presentation—for practical musicianship—of newly discovered works. This periodical soon disappeared for lack of support, but Chrysander tells the reader that however many concerns are represented among scholars involved with music, they have much in common and ought at least to share a periodical.

In 1884, however, Chrysander, by then about fifty-nine and the distinguished biographer and editor of Handel's works, and Philip Spitta, by then about forty-five and the great biographer of Bach, joined with the youthful Adler (who was living in Vienna but getting ready to go to Prague to assume the chair of musicology) in founding the new *Vierteljahrschrift für Musikwissenschaft*. There was no fly on the wall, but I like to imagine the older, established scholars permitting Adler, with his youthful energy and enthusiasm, to be the principal architect of this venture while also leaving him most of the work. Anyway, Adler's view of the field as encompassing all imaginable kinds of musical study seems to have dominated this journal throughout the ten years of its life. His own article leads the others and is presented as a kind of position paper for what follows. In some ways, it reads like the work of a seasoned scholar, stating its points with authority and even majesty. At the same time, to lay out a field with courage and conviction, from scratch, may have been the characteristic approach of a young man.

So far I've presented the founding of musicology as a function of the "great man" theory of history—acts of courage and conviction. But as an ethnomusicologist I'm much more inclined to look for cultural forces. Why should this periodical and its seminal article come about, and its impact stick, particularly in 1885 and in the German-speaking lands? Actually, the kind of grand entry that musicology experienced in the 1880s didn't occur in a vacuum. This was a time when much was being done with a lot of courage and conviction, if not always with ethical conscience and good judgment. The notion of a grand vision for a new discipline and the publication of a periodical exhibiting this broad scope seem to fit beautifully into the 1880s, a period when thinking big, innovation, looking at the whole world, and looking at the whole nation were all very prominent in the minds of European intellectuals, and maybe most so in those of Germany and Austria. To illustrate the context in which Adler was working, let me list at random a few of the things that were happening in 1885, as well as just before and after that year.

Maybe most significant for the development of the concept of ethnomusicology was the beginning, in 1884, of a series of conferences where European powers carved up the continent of Africa for themselves in thoroughly cavalier fashion. In the United States, where ethnomusicology would take root most vigorously, this era saw unrest on the labor front and large-scale emigration from Eastern and Southern Europe; it was also the last period in which a group of Native Americans, in this case the so-called Plains Indians, used violence to oppose white domination, and it included the Ghost Dance movement, which culminated in the infamous massacre at Wounded Knee in 1890. The 1880s were a period of great technological innovation, too. The short period of 1884–86 saw the development of a practical phonograph, electrical devices in general, agricultural machinery, the single-cylinder engine, coated photographic paper, the rabies vaccine, cameras, the fountain pen, and fingerprinting. The notion of comfort for all was presaged in 1885 or thereabouts by the discovery of gold in the Transvaal, the introduction of golf to America, the opening of the first subway in London, and—in quite another way—the initial publication of the *Oxford English Dictionary*. I've mentioned only a few events, but enough perhaps to give something of the flavor of European thought and social relations of the time. More specifically, I suggest that the history of musicology in the 1880s can be understood through three related themes of the period.

First, European society was at this time ready to take on the world and devour it in various ways—politically and culturally, but also intellectually and aesthetically. People tended to think big during this period. Huge scholarly endeavors, incredibly ambitious schemes of invention, and vast projects in the arts are typical, paralleling the insupportably grand and, in retrospect, intolerable political, social, and military schemes. Second, there was an increasing interest in the concept of nationalism—something, to be sure, going back over a hundred years—a nationalism that involved understanding the cultural heterogeneity as well as unity of one's own nation. Taking on the world was to some extent a function of the growing nationalism of the time—particularly, at that late date, the nationalism of Germany and the United States, both new participants in the colonial activities in which Britain, France, Spain, and the Netherlands were seasoned veterans. And third, a result perhaps of the first two, there appeared an interest in the relationships among cultures as Europe, devouring the world and trying to digest it in ways compatible with the notions of nationalism, also had to absorb and reinterpret its variety. Taking on the world and doing the impossible; collecting and utilizing one's own national heritage; and seeing what the world was made of, how one could make use of it, and how it came to be—these are three major themes of the 1880s. Arousing admiration as well as dread, they are ultimately the wellsprings of musicology as it was fashioned by Adler. Let me comment on each, illustrating briefly from the musicological literature of this seminal age.

Thinking Big

It is easy to see how someone like Edison (who thought he was up to solving all mechanical and electrical problems), Ranke (who was confident of being able to present the whole history of the world), or Wagner (who presented central questions of human history in a confluence of all performative arts at unprecedented length) could be seen as a paradigm of an era in which people seemed to say, "Let's grab the whole world"—or maybe, less politically and militarily, an era that said, "Let's learn everything about the world," "Let's not be afraid to think big," and also, with supreme self-confidence, "We *can* find out everything." In the world of politics and economics and even the arts, musicology was (and is) a humble byway, but here too the concept of thinking big asserts itself. The establishment of musicology as a holistic field taking on all intellectual problems concerning music, as outlined by Adler, clearly fits the pattern, and it was at this time that the tradition of publishing complete collections such as the *Gesamtausgaben* of Bach, Handel, and Mozart, as well as comprehensive editions such as *Denkmäler* and collections of national folk songs, really took off. Other publications, too, contributed to this notion of comprehensiveness.

Take, for example, Victor Mahillon's (1880–1922) celebrated five-volume catalog begun in 1880, of the instrument collection of the Royal Conservatory of Brussels. The collection had some 3,500 specimens, and Mahillon developed a taxonomy (derived from an old Indian system) that eventually led to the now-standard classification of Hornbostel and Sachs published in 1914. Mahillon divides the instrument groups into European and non-European and gives a great deal of detail about many items, including scales, details of structure, and cultural context and interest. It's a marvel of care and love, but the point I want to make here is that Mahillon conceived of this as a work in which all imaginable instruments might have a place—a work that encompassed the whole world of instruments. In the area of instruments, Mahillon was taking on the whole world.

The idea of establishing a kind of framework into which one might place all phenomena of a particular class within musical culture, from all societies, for the purpose of comparative analysis was to become a hallmark of later ethnomusicology. Chronologically the first example of this kind of framework was the practice devised by Stumpf, Hornbostel, and Abraham (in many of their joint publications—see, e.g., vol. 1 of *Sammelbände*, 1922–24) for describing, in similar terms, a great variety of the world's music. More to the point, as this tradition was continued—and more analogous to Mahillon's plan—was the approach of Mieczyslaw Kolinski (e.g., in 1965a and b), who in the 1950s and 1960s promulgated outlines for the comparative analysis of melodic contour, scale and mode, rhythm, and tempo; these outlines gave space to all extant and imaginable musics. Clearly related, too, is the analytical component of Alan Lomax's "cantometrics" (first articulated in 1968), which tries to enable the analyst to create a profile of any imaginable musical style. There are also the first attempts at defining a universal, not culture-specific way of classifying the songs (folk songs and perhaps hymns) in a large collection, first in a rather simple-minded plan by Oswald Koller (1902–3), followed by a more sophisticated approach by the Finnish scholar Ilmari Krohn (1902–3), whose system was later adopted and thoroughly modified, with much success, by Béla Bartók (1931) in his fundamental book on Hungarian folk songs.

If the idea of taking on the world is reflected in musical scholarship, one would expect to find something like a world ethnography of music. After all, if Leopold von Ranke could claim to present a true history of the world (even though it turned out to be that of Europe to 1500), one might expect that someone would have attempted a history of world music. There isn't really enough data to accomplish that even today, and there certainly wasn't in 1885, and anyhow, the concept of music would have been quite narrow back then. Still, the first large attempt at a comprehensive history of Western music, by August Wilhelm Ambros (1862), merits consideration.

Ambros is worthy of a digression in any event, for he belongs to the "thinking big" movement. A musical polymath—composer, scholar, aesthetician, early Czech-German-Bohemian musical nationalist—who spent his life in Prague, he was born in 1816 and thus belongs to the generation of Schumann, Mendelssohn, and Wagner; he was near the end of his life (in 1876) by the time the great Czech nationalists Smetana and Dvořák were transforming musical life in Prague. Ambros was arguably the first person to hold a designated full professorship in musicology at a European university, having in 1869 been appointed professor of history of music and art at the German-speaking branch of the University of Prague (and thus forever justifying my native city's claim to a place in the early history of musicology), and so he gets a few lines on these pages even though he doesn't quite fit my theory, given that publication of his comprehensive *Geschichte der Musik* began in 1862. His appointment no doubt resulted in part from this great project.

Ambros, like Ranke, didn't get far in the chronology—he left off with Palestrina, in volume 3 (1868). But his history is an astonishing work considering the modest amount of data then available, and it bids fair to be an ancestor of ethnomusicology. Ambros wrote not only music history in the narrow sense but also cultural and contextual history. It's amazing, also, to find the first volume devoted entirely to non-Western music and ancient Europe: twenty pages on China, forty on India, thirty on the Islamic Middle East, and some four hundred on Egyptians, Hebrews, Mesopotamians, and Greeks. It was not an easy read, even for the reader of Ambros's time, as he clearly knew when he famously said in his preface (xix), "Die Wissenschaft hat zu Zeiten das Recht, langweilig zu sein" (scholarship has the right, occasionally, to be boring). But he was determined to put together everything as he saw it and as it could be made available to him.

Since limited data ruled out any meaningful attempt at a comprehensive world music history in the 1880s, as well as any proper description of the contemporary musics of the world, we may look for the thinking-big principle in works that say everything about a given subject, and so we're led to Theodore Baker's published dissertation *Über die Musik der nordamerikanischen Wilden* (On the music of North American savages [1882]), the first comprehensive book on Native American music. Born in New York in 1851, Baker went to study music in Leipzig, where he earned a Ph.D., and eventually returned to the United States to become an editor and lexicographer, finally retiring in Germany. The dissertation was written in German and is usually mentioned as being of only historical interest, but it antedated the earliest tribal monographs on American Indian music and the first general works on ethnomusicology and is impressive in its inclusiveness. There are chapters about the various elements or structures of music, such as poetry, tonality, melodic form, rhythm, recitative, and instruments—an organization one might find in work from the 1950s. Especially interesting is Baker's introduction to music in Indian culture, because it gives a viewpoint not really very different from one we might express today, albeit with different terminology. In contrast to some later students, Baker does not denigrate Native Americans and takes their music seriously, pointing out that it has a long history, is closely related to social life, and shares in certain cultural universals.

I also find myself impressed by Baker's sophistication in his description of performance practice—done, I remind you, before the advent of field recording. Dividing this section into components rather in the manner of Lomax's cantometrics, but with fewer categories, Baker discusses consonants and vowels and their treatment, range, general quality of voice, aspects of singing style—slide, growl, portamento—and ornamentation. He was sensitive to issues of performance practice almost fifty years before the subject became au courant in musicology.

This sympathetic approach to the music of Native Americans occurred, it's important to note, at a time when Indians were at the forefront of white American consciousness. On the one hand, they were subject to an early, brutal form of systematic "ethnic cleansing," receiving, both officially and unofficially, harsh treatment from white Americans. But the American body politic also began to view Native American concerns as a challenging issue and the cultures as worthy of serious study. In the 1880s, the reservation system was finally being imposed on the Plains Indians, and tribes were being forcibly moved, decimated by disease and starvation, and murdered by military and civilians. They saw their lands taken and redistributed. Nevertheless, in 1881, while Baker was writing in Leipzig, Helen Hunt Jackson (1881) published an influential book, *A Century of Dishonor,* that aroused concern over the problems of Native Americans and stimulated the founding of the Indian Rights Association, which lobbied successfully for liberalized legislation. And Franz Boas (1888) published his first large monograph, *The Central Eskimo.* Baker's dissertation, possibly a curiosity to his fellow students at the University of Leipzig, fits well into the beginnings of white Americans' serious concern for Native Americans and their cultures.

But if we are looking for the truly quintessential practitioner of "thinking big" in this incunabular period of musicology, it has to be Hugo Riemann, a towering figure who in literally dozens of volumes during his long career managed to write about virtually everything musical. Born in 1849, he reached his peak in the 1880s. His massive output is downright frightening, though not totally uncharacteristic of German scholars of the time, who were industrious (and didn't have to wash their cars or take out the garbage), had excellent training in background and memory, and were supremely self-confident. Today, in the era of peer review and computer-generated editorial fussiness, such productivity is virtually inconceivable, and we readers may marvel—perhaps gratefully—that times have changed so. Riemann's work includes histories, compilations, reference works, editions, theory texts, and monographs and articles in musicology. His publications from the 1880s include about ten books on theory or theory texts (though his landmark history of music theory was not to appear until the next decade), a couple of books on notation, and two major encyclopedic efforts. His music encyclopedia was published in two massive volumes in 1882 and has been repeatedly re-edited (although by now the contents have turned over completely). It was first written entirely by one man, yet in length it rivals the later team-produced efforts such as the early editions of the Grove dictionary. He also published an encyclopedia of the opera (Riemann 1887), which, though it of course omitted many later operas now in our standard repertoire—Puccini, Strauss, Berg—seems to have an entry for every opera known or discovered by then and an entry on every operatic subject, to say nothing of composers. Hardly useful any more, it must have been a gold mine for the opera buff of a century ago. But in Riemann's oeuvre these two works are almost drops in the bucket.

Spending his career in Leipzig and not personally associated with Adler, Riemann lived an Adlerian life, devoting himself to studies in both the theory and history of music and often dealing with perception and theoretical universals. He also dipped into ethnomusicology—in a theoretical fashion—extending to all music an eighteenth-century concept of rhythmic symmetry (called *Vierhebigkeit*) based on physiology that explained everything in a fundamentally quadruple metric structure and examining tonality in folk music. He was one of those people who evidently think that nothing worth doing is too difficult or too much work. During the 1880s and the few decades that followed, he wasn't unique in his efforts. Think of all the folk songs Béla Bartók collected from Hungarians, Slovaks, Romanians, Bulgarians, Serbs, and Turks between 1900 and 1914, just in his spare time. Or think of Thomas Edison, a man who rarely slept, and his hundreds of inventions. Or think, for that matter, of Franz Boas, the founder of American-style anthropology, with his dozens of publications in all branches of anthropology, who ultimately made possible the importation of European comparative musicology.

It really was a time when people in Western culture thought they could do everything, conquering all worlds, physical, social, and intellectual. Was this a sign of their courage, or should we see it more as an indication of incredible immodesty, bravado, and greed? Were these great men heroes or the intellectual by-products of a society of bullies? I'm telling you about the grand accomplishments of these early musicologists, but I see an uncomfortable analogy between Adler's dividing up the world of music for a unitary musicology and the European powers dividing up Africa into a unitary colonial system in the same year; or between Riemann's incredible concentration, indefatigable work habits, and wish to contribute something to every branch of music and the twentieth-century Germans' self-confidence as would-be military conquerors of the world. But no, Riemann—zany theories and all—surely wouldn't have recognized himself in this parallel, and Adler, dictatorial to his assistants and students, would have been horrified to find himself seen as a general or field marshal. He himself, dying peacefully (I believe) in 1941 in Vienna, barely, perhaps because he was then eighty-five, escaped perishing in the Holocaust.

Celebrating the Nation

The development of national consciousness is a major theme for students of nineteenth-century history, but it plays a special role in the ideology that led to the development of musicology. If one took on the world, it was in a sense on behalf of one's nation, and one of the palpable values of early musicological literature was love and admiration of nation—usually one's own, but the concept of "nation" could also be celebrated by looking outward. The move toward publishing series of scores of major or even minor works that in some sense represented the nation (series typically titled *Denkmäler* or *Monuments* or *Monumenta*) is typical, as is the publication of comprehensive collections of folk songs with a national focus, as well as the development of a national orientation to the writing of music-history books. Musical land-grabbing sometimes accompanied political and military action. Thus, the Austrian *Denkmäler* includes works by composers usually associated with Bohemia (Biber, Hammerschmidt), Italian composers brought to Vienna or Prague mainly as a result of opera commissions (Cesti, Monteverdi), and composers whose works happened to be included in manuscripts found on Austrian territory or even territory arguably not properly Austrian, such as the works of Renaissance Dutch composers discovered in manuscripts at Trent. So, certainly, issues of nation played an important role in the early development of musicology.

The conception of folk song as a defining element of nation was already set forth in works by August Wilhelm Herder in the early nineteenth century; by then, the "nationhood" of ethnic groups such as Czechs, chafing under the hegemony of empires, began to be recognized in the collecting of folk songs, as was the negotiation between nation and region in the coalescing "second empire" of Germany. But in the last decades of the century, the movement intensified. To illustrate, let me mention two important figures, Ludwig Erk and Franz Magnus Boehme, who produced (together and individually) collections of *Volkslieder* (folk songs) and *volksthümliche Lieder* (songs in a folklike vein) of Germany. These collections use a debatable concept of folk music; land-grabbing of a sort is evident in the inclusion of Low German, Dutch, and Scandinavian examples; and the presentation of songs in chronological order by source is also noteworthy not only because it provides something of scholarly value but also because it suggests the significance of the German nation as a long-enduring unit (for which one can make a better case with folk songs than with political history).

The collections by Erk and Boehme (1893–94) play a major role in the history of folk-music scholarship, but as a group they show that the German concept of folk music was one of emotional wealth, historical depth, geographical breadth, and cultural relevance. Interestingly, as part of this "program" of presentation, at the moment of ethnomusicology's most seminal publications, Boehme (1886) published *Geschichte des Tanzes in Deutschland*. Like many scholars of the time, Boehme was not a member of the academic profession. He was involved in many aspects of music—as composer, editor, choral conductor, and collector and editor of folk songs—at times making his living teaching elementary school in Weimar, Dresden, and smaller towns of central Germany. He is best known for the folk-song collections, but the subtitle of his book on dance, translated as "a contribution to German history of customs, literature and music," has to warm the heart of the historian of ethnomusicology, as must its basic tenet: that scholarship on dance has a special relationship to musicology (more special than, say, its relation to the history of theater or athletics). I say this because in its publications since the 1950s, the field of ethnomusicology has always reserved a special place for dance.

Boehme's history of dance in Germany is rather comprehensive, with chapters on various early periods. Some chapters also deal with problems the art of dance has had in establishing itself as respectable. The subjects ranged broadly: evaluation and preaching about dance from the Middle Ages to the modern era, official prohibitions of dance, foreign dances in Germany in the sixteenth century, old German ritual dances that have been maintained into the nineteenth century, types of folk dances still in use today, social dance in Germany, dance music and dance musicians, and the preservation of old folk dances in modern children's games. It's a true if early contribution to the anthropology of dance in that it thoroughly examines society's attitudes toward dance; it treats on an equal footing the genres of dance that might be called artistic, popular, and folk; and it pays a lot of attention to intercultural issues in its study of the relationship between German and non-German dances. It has its light moments, too. Boehme exposes the attitude of his time (but only his?) when, defending the art of dance, he nevertheless criticizes the then-current state of affairs:

> Our social dancing is too fast, unattractive, and even dangerous to the health. The good old slow dances of earlier times, perhaps old-fashioned and pedantic but at least not unhealthy, are everywhere scorned and indeed hardly known; or the rapidity of our lifestyle has transformed them into galloping tempo in order to satisfy humanity, that living steam engine. (Boehme 1886, 1:31; my translation)

I don't know how widespread this kind of attitude may have been in the 1880s. When I noticed it a hundred years later, it sounded very familiar.

Boehme's book leads me to explore two ideas. First is the development of folk-music collecting and scholarship in Europe—related, as I said, to the growth of nationalism—through the nineteenth century and on, in a strand of intellectual history quite separate from the "comparative musicology" that was looking at non-Western music. Well, why should European scholars interested in East Asian and African music also be interested in the folk music of their own nations (or vice versa) or feel they have a lot in common? I don't have an answer, but there were occasions when the two groups got together, as in 1932, when Bartók, folk-song collector par excellence, and Hornbostel, Lachmann, and Sachs, leaders of German-style comparative musicology, all (as interestingly described in Racy 1991) attended the Cairo Congress on Arabic Music and met with Middle Eastern musicians and scholars and with interested composers such as Alois Hába of quarter-tone fame.

Nonetheless, the conception of ethnomusicology as a field in which students of both non-Western and folk musics had a stake, with books and courses that included both, didn't come about until the work of George Herzog, who put them together in his survey of research (1936b) and in his courses, such as the one I took with him titled "Folk and Primitive Music." In the nineteenth century, folk-music research was largely a matter of national orientation and interest, and each nation eventually came to have its most prominent folk-music collector or collectors—for example, Bartók (1931) for the Hungarians, but much earlier, K. J. Erben (1862) for the Czechs, O. Kolberg (1991) for the Poles, and Erk and Boehme

(1893–94) for the Germans. Attitudes differed. Bartók looked for what he judged truly authentic and eliminated what seemed foreign, urban, or precomposed. Erk and Boehme looked for early written sources of songs that seemed folkish, included non-German tunes and texts if a relationship could be found, and were generally inclusive (or maybe expansive). But surely in the 1880s, the stream of folk-music scholarship was becoming a tributary leading to a larger ethnomusicology.

Further, the fact that Boehme undertook to write a history of dance of all sorts in Germany is also significant to the early history of ethnomusicology. The world of dance in twentieth-century America strove for recognition as an independent art, and dance remains separate in performance and teaching. It cooperates with music, of course, but also with theater, visual art, and disciplines concerned with physiology. My daughter Rebecca, dancer, choreographer, and a professor of dance in my university, wouldn't be inclined to consider attaching her department to the School of Music. But in historical and ethnographic research it has been different. Ethnomusicologists since the 1950s have considered dance to fall within their field's boundaries. The International Folk Music Council, founded in 1947, included dance scholars and teachers among its governing board from the beginning and has always had representatives of dance on its program committees, to say nothing of paper sessions on dance or of folk dancing in the evenings. In 1958, the first year its journal appeared, the Society of Ethnomusicology began having an associate editor responsible for dance; this practice continued until 1972. Since then, the field of dance research and ethnochoreology has established itself in curricula and organizations. But the literature of ethnomusicology, of which Boehme's book may be considered an early exemplar, continues to have much about dance and dancing.

Comprehending the "Other"

If two of the themes of 1880s Europe that informed musicology were the discovery and conquest of the world and the understanding of one's national culture, it follows almost logically and inevitably that a third theme, combining the first two, would lead to a concern with understanding the world that has been politically or intellectually conquered, contemplating the interrelationship of its cultures and their components. Juxtaposition of nation and world led inevitably to a need to confront and relate to the cultural "other," and this need was the most direct inspiration for the development of ethnomusicology. Thus, if one wishes to argue about a date for the beginnings of musicology as a whole, claiming 1732 or 1776 or 1863 as a worthy rival to 1885 as the field's proper commencement, I find it most persuasive to assign the beginnings of *ethno*musicology to no decade other than the 1880s. It was in this decade that landmark publications and other events heralding the principal issues and paradigms of later ethnomusicology first appeared: intercultural studies in music, fieldwork, the study of music in culture, comparative organology, attention to analytical problems—all of these surfaced almost simultaneously.

Still, these landmarks could arrive only in an atmosphere sympathetic to a holistic view of musicology, and a holistic musicology could exist only if it included pursuit of the cultural "other." Never mind that this pursuit moved, at first, in peculiar and probably wrong-headed directions. I'm inclined to suggest that the various kinds of historical study that had been carried out before the 1880s *required* the appearance of something leading to ethnomusicology in order to develop into a discipline that could indeed properly be called *musicology* rather than simply the history of music. Interestingly, the same kind of development did not take place in other humanistic fields such as art history, whose practitioners—perhaps for the better, in their view—relegate the anthropological study of art to departments of anthropology, the psychology of art to psychology, the physical components of art to the sciences, and the contemplation of vernacular genres such as commercial art to departments of advertising.

The comprehensive approach to musicology promulgated by Adler is superbly illustrated by the amazing variety of subjects in the first volume (1885) of the *Vierteljahrschrift für Musikwissenschaft.* Immediately following Adler's seminal article is one by Friedrich Chrysander on an unexpected subject: "Über die altindische Opfermusik" (On ancient Indian sacrificial music), an analysis, on the basis of Sanskritic and other Indological literature, of the Vedic chants. It takes issue with Sir William Jones, the great Sanskritist who in 1792 had written the first Western study of Indian music. Chrysander's essay is followed by Philip Spitta's comprehensive study about Sperontes's *Singende Muse an der Pleisse,* a 1736 collection of popular or vernacular music of Leipzig; an article by George Ellinger on Handel's "Admetus" and its sources; and a piece by Paul Graf Waldersee about Vivaldi's violin concertos as arranged by Bach. Mathis Lussy's article on the relationship between meter and rhythm sets out problems in analysis of the use of time that are still with us and, as is particularly significant, criticizes theorists for emphasizing harmony and neglecting rhythm. There is a large critical review essay by Carl Stumpf, the leading psychologist whom we'll shortly meet as the "grandfather" of ethnomusicology, about

British approaches to the psychology of music, dealing in large measure with origin theories and summarizing contributions by Herbert Spencer, James Sully, Charles Darwin, and Edmund Gurney. Then there is an early article by Franz Xaver Haberl on the life and works of Dufay. In sum, the *Vierteljahrschrift* published articles on the methodology of the field, theory, psychology of music, sources, processes (the arrangements by Bach), biography, popular music, and non-Western music. You can see why this quarterly, with a scope broader than that of any periodical today, is often properly regarded as the centerpiece of a period in which musicology as a discipline began.

But I return to the third intellectual characteristic of the 1880s—the confrontation of the cultural "other"—and thus to the beginnings of ethnomusicology as a way of studying the relationships among cultures. Three events of the decade are especially noteworthy. One, Carl Stumpf's article about the music of the Bella Coola Indians, appeared in 1886, in the second volume of the *Vierteljahrschrift*. Hardly the first study of a tribal or non-Western repertory, it is often seen as a seminal work in ethnomusicology—principally, it seems to me, because it establishes a procedure for describing "a" music that Stumpf himself used for various cultures (as eventually Hornbostel, Abraham, and others did, too) and that became for a time a paradigm of description. Actually, though greatly modified and expanded, it dominated as a method until ethnomusicologists, in tandem with the ascendancy of the "new ethnography" of the 1950s, came to believe in the greater efficacy of following a culture's own way of presenting its music and of developing for each music a method of description appropriate to itself.

In America, Stumpf (1848–1936) is actually better known to historians of psychology than to musicologists: his many publications are largely about psychology, perception, and psychoacoustics, following in the footsteps of Hermann Helmholtz (1821–94). After 1886, however, he continued working with his student Hornbostel, publishing transcriptions and analyses of collections of recordings, writing an early synthesis on tribal music (1911), founding and guiding the Berlin Phonogrammarchiv, and revealing in a series of articles his conviction that the psychology of music and comparative musicology have a lot to say to each other. Some consider him the originator of ethnomusicology, but that's a title we've bestowed on several. It's important to note, however, that the close association of psychoacoustics—that is, what we now (in America) call "systematic musicology"—to ethnomusicology has always been maintained in Germany and Austria (and other parts of Europe). This association, largely lacking in the North

American tradition, goes back to Stumpf and to his student Hornbostel (see Hornbostel 1904–5, 1986), whose influence determined its continued maintenance in the work of such scholars as Franz Födermayr (1971), Walter Graf, and Albrecht Schneider (1976, 2006).

Stumpf's Darwinian view of the music of nonliterate peoples as a frozen stage in normal evolution is not dissimilar to Adler's and is reflected in much later scholarship, related to the approaches of cultural evolutionists of many stripes. His article about the Bella Coola (Stumpf 1886) would hardly be helpful to anyone today but still merits a moment of celebration as a historical milestone. Four areas of method in this article are worth mentioning: (1) It is centered on a set of transcriptions that are presented in the text; (2) it includes an element-by-element discussion of the musical style; (3) unlike most others writing even a few decades later, Stumpf describes in detail how he gathered his data, interviewed, and transcribed; and (4) in a harbinger of the interest in reflexivity that came a century later, he discusses his relationship to Nutsiluska, his principal consultant and singer. Near the end of his essay, Stumpf contemplates the cross-cultural views held by himself and Nutsiluska, imagining their contrastive reactions to Bach's B-minor Mass and thus interestingly—though maybe naively—examining the specialness of Western culture, which colonizes and holds hegemony over other cultures but also looks at them with a relativistic perspective.

Stumpf's transcriptions were made from live performances, but the second major event leading to the development of ethnomusicology in the 1880s is so obviously essential that one need hardly mention it. It is the first field recording of American Indian music—and of any non-Western music—made in 1890 by Walter Fewkes. A biologist by training, Fewkes worked throughout his life in several disciplines—ethnology, archeology, zoology—and his contributions to ethnomusicology were only a small part of his oeuvre. Interested in Native Americans from several viewpoints, he undertook to test the usefulness of the phonograph, developed some ten years earlier, for field research. In 1890, Fewkes recorded songs of the Passamaquoddy of Maine and the Zuni of Arizona. The technique spread like wildfire, of course; soon, despite the difficulties of the cylinder technology, anthropologists, missionaries, and tourists were recording music in many parts of the world. By 1901, important archives had already been established in Vienna and Berlin.

I don't have to talk about the importance of recording in the history of music and musicology, but adopting field recording as a central data-gathering technique is not something that was "natural" or "inevitable." One might, for example, have concentrated on gathering commercial and other prerecorded publications, as these began to play a major role in many of the world's societies before 1910. That we opted for field recording gave us a vast store of recordings that were in many ways authentic, though because they were often especially elicited, their representativeness of ordinary musical life is not always clear. That we ignored the commercial recordings (because they were "commercial," hence impure and polluted in some way) kept us ignorant of much that was going on in the world's music one hundred years ago. Since those early decades, ethnomusicologists—maybe even more than music historians—have turned their attention to the uses of old recordings.

It's no surprise that musicology participated in the development of technology in this exceptional period. And so, the third event of the 1880s to which I want to call attention draws on both technological and intellectual developments of the time. If the true centerpiece of one end of our musicological table was the 1885 article by Adler, we must place next to it Alexander John Ellis's (1885) article "On the Musical Scales of Various Nations," a work often described as the first major piece of writing providing a comparative study of musics. In contrast to Adler, the young firebrand, Ellis (1814–90) was by 1885 a senior citizen and a prominent figure in British intellectual life who had made major contributions to psychology, physiology, acoustics, and mathematics and had played a role in the preparation of the *OED*. In this 1885 study, Ellis introduced the cents system as a device for the universal measurement of intervals. He examines a number of tone systems and tunings, exhibiting the universe of scales; importantly, he approaches this variety with an essentially relativistic attitude, not a normative or evolutionist stance. His orientation has characterized ethnomusicology ever since.

The works and careers of A. J. Ellis and Carl Stumpf were complementary but also parallel. Both contributed mightily to their home disciplines from which they came to music, and both became fascinated by three explicitly musical aspects of non-Western musical cultures: perception, scale, and pitch—and less, it must be noted, by rhythm or form. For neither scholar could one say that the substantive contributions are still usable, but each provided an idea that set us moving in directions that were long followed: in Stumpf's case, the systematic comprehension of a musical style on the basis of a statistical description of a set of recordings, and for Ellis, the nonjudgmental, relativistic comparison of the world's musics.

Each of the three events or publications (Adler 1885; Stumpf 1886; Ellis 1885) seems to me to presage the new approach to ethnomusicology as the study of interrelationships of musical cultures through intensive field study, technology, and comparative research. Now, when we look back at those publications by Stumpf, Ellis, Boehme, and Baker, we're inclined to think, "Wow, those people really had naive ideas about the world's cultures and about music"; "Ouch, how primitive their technology was"; and even, "What condescension their writing betrays." After all, much has been learned since their time. But it is important to read the work of each period in the context of its own society, culture, worldview, and state of knowledge. I have to confess that I admire the scholars of the 1880s because they began to move us toward our present location while they worked with little in the way of models or precedents. If we have vastly overtaken them, that is as it should be.

Again considering the *musicological* profession, the 1880s were really the period in which its course was determined for the next century: it would include all types of research on music, including what later came to be known as ethnomusicology. By the early 1900s, many scholars were at work, their accomplishments worth remembering, but in determining the relationship of ethnomusicology to the rest of musicology, two heroic figures stand out: Adler and Ellis—or, perhaps more properly, their two heroic articles of 1885. Adler and Ellis had rather different perspectives on their work. Adler, the innovative junior scholar, was unequivocal and knew where he was going. He began by thinking big: "All peoples who can be said to have music have a system of musical thought, even if this is not always a fully developed musicological system" (1885, 3). Ellis, the experienced man of letters, wiser and thus more tentative, began, "The title of this paper was meant to be 'On the Musical Scales of *All* Nations.' 'All' is a big word, and I have had to withdraw it." But significantly he concludes by declaring that "the Musical Scale is not one, not 'natural,' . . . but very diverse, very artificial, and very capricious" (1885, 527). Both men's statements move us toward an appreciation of music as a universal phenomenon and toward a culturally pluralistic view of music. In his own way, each of these two men outlined methods whereby his aims could be carried out, and both looked to a future in which their approaches would be followed. It is because of their concern with general principles of research, basic assumptions, and method that they deserve to be celebrated as the principal representatives of the seminal 1880s in the history of musicology.

$$2$$

. . . .

Look at It Another Way

. . . .

Alternative Views of the History

The Conventional View

I have often been asked how I got into ethnomusicology. I am tempted to give a complicated answer in which I try to explain the various definitions that our field experienced over time and to say something about its rather outré history, but what I should really say is simply that in college I took a course whose subject matter seemed interesting on its own, and particularly interesting because it presented the "other" side of music—"other" in the sense of opposition to the conventional subject matter of college music study. It helped, of course, that it was taught by a person who was recognized as an authority, in part because of whom he had studied with. And so, a member of a family heavily involved in Western art music, I was able to both continue in a family tradition and rebel against it.

But that vignette of a few weeks' events is a kind of microcosm of the way the history of ethnomusicology is often interpreted. It is seen as derived from and dependent on standard (i.e., "historical") musicology but also opposed to it and involved in correcting its false assumptions. Further, the interpretation focuses on a central lineage of scholars, an interacting school of teachers, disciples, and students, often seen as a kind of "mainstream." That lineage consists of a generation in the late nineteenth century, centering on the psychologist Carl Stumpf, often referred to as the field's grandfather, so that his pupil, Erich M. von Hornbostel, could be labeled its father. Hornbostel had a number of students and disciples, several of whom, because of the political events in Germany and Central Europe, immigrated to Israel (then Palestine), Scandinavia, and particularly North America, and it was the North American immigrant George Herzog who became the most influential in continuing the previously mentioned mainstream. I was fortunate to study with Herzog for several years, and thus I and some of the other students who worked with me may consider ourselves to be in this central line as well.

Now that's a very simplified sketch of the history. Stumpf worked under the influence of and in concert with British and American scholars such as Alexander John Ellis and B. I. Gilman. Hornbostel's students also worked with other scholars, particularly Curt Sachs. Herzog had been heavily influenced by Hungarian folk-song scholarship before he came to Hornbostel; afterward, he went on to finish his Ph.D. under Franz Boas and, after that, came to be significantly associated with American folk-song scholars such as Phillips Barry. The mainstream wasn't by any means straight and narrow.

The history of ethnomusicology, though a small field, is a pretty complicated affair, especially since ethnomusicologists have all along acted like the blind men confronting the elephant, trying to fashion a definition of their field agreeable to all its members, an objectively valid description of its extant character and ultimate goals. The scheme of a mainstream on whom scholars in many disciplines depend is helpful and has been widely adopted or cited (e.g., Myers 1992, 1993; McLean 2006; Arom and Alvarez-Péreyre 2007), but it omits consideration of central events, influential persons and approaches, and most important, two (at least) of the field's significant characteristics.

It thus seems helpful to try alternative ways of looking at our history. I'd like to explore two. First, I wish to take as a point of departure Stephen

Blum's (1991, 4–9) essay contending, in part via elaborate charts, that activities reasonably construed as ethnomusicological came into existence in many parts of the world during the nineteenth century. Thus, the world of ethnomusicology consists of a group of larger and smaller national and regional schools, many of them, incidentally, subjects of essays in Myers's (1993) volume titled *Ethnomusicology: Historical and Regional Studies*. Further, the history of ethnomusicology is replete with heroic figures who pursued their scholarly endeavors in isolation, sometimes with the goal of bringing to their nations what they hoped would be the social, musical, and political benefits of ethnomusicological activities. They became culture heroes of their nations and their field. Let me provide a small group of illustrative examples.

The Francophone World

Do (and did) different cultures practice different kinds of ethnomusicology? This is a complicated question, given that intercultural relations lie at the foundation of ethnomusicological thought. Some scholars might insist that all ethnomusicology is Western-based—for good, as a product of the grand Western traditions of scholarship, or for not so good, as an accompaniment to and result of colonial exploitation. Moreover, the scholars in a number of nations and culture areas, when they give an account of the history of their field, inevitably refer to the school of Hornbostel and his lateral and chronological associates as the center of that field. Still, it seems to me that looking at national or regional or ethnically determined schools of scholars can give us important insights.

Seeing so much said about ethnomusicology in the German- and English-speaking worlds makes one ask automatically about ethnomusicology in the French-speaking nations. It is curious that French scholarship on non-Western music is not accorded a prominent place in the history of ethnomusicology, since it includes one of the earliest ethnographic accounts (Amiot 1779) about Chinese music and the earliest transcriptions and ethnographic notes about Native Americans (by the Jesuit fathers, appearing in the eighteenth-century *Jesuit Relations* [Society of Jesus 1959]). These are predecessors of ethnomusicology, to be sure, and so is the inclusion of global perspectives in the voluminous work of the Francophone Belgian scholar and musician François-Joseph Fétis (1784–1871). Also noteworthy among nineteenth-century scholars was Victor Mahillon (1841–1924), the legendary curator of the museum of musical instruments in Brussels, whose arrangement of the catalog of the collection (1880–1922) provided a model for the later widely adopted Hornbostel-Sachs (1914) classification. Julien Tiersot (1837–1936), a musicologist who contributed to historical studies as well as the collection and interpretation of folk music, regarded Fétis as the founder of comparative musicology. A bit later, a prominent figure was Rodolphe d'Erlanger (1872–1932), an authority on Arabic music, especially its history as evident in treatises, many of which he translated (Erlanger 1930–59).

In many nations, scholars whose work preceded and led to ethnomusicology in the more specific sense made major contributions. Let me identify a few of their successors working through the middle of the twentieth century—and I'll mention for each figure one or two major works, citing where possible English translations. Jacques Chailley (1910–99; see Chailley 1961) was a prominent music scholar, a historian who, in publications that approached music from the perspective of historian, theorist, and composer, always tried to place Western music in a global context. Claudie Marcel-Dubois (1913–89) was a major figure in European folk-music research and one of the leaders of the International Folk Music Council soon after it was founded (see Marcel-Dubois 1941, 1946), and André Schaeffner (1895–1980; see Schaeffner 1936) founded and directed the Department of Ethnomusicology at the Musée de l'Homme in Paris from 1929 to 1965. Schaeffner's bibliography shows an interest in non-Western music, musical instruments, and Western music history. In the generation of Schaeffner, I should also mention Marius Barbeau, a French Canadian who was the principal leader in developing the study of French-Canadian folk music as well as research in First Nations music of the West Coast. He shared characteristics of his French colleagues, including a great breadth of disciplinary interest; he contributed to several humanistic fields and was strongly interested in transcription and preservation (see Jessup, Nurse, and Smith 2008).

This is hardly even a thumbnail sketch of the population of French ethnomusicologists. Of Francophone scholars working between 1955 and the recent past, we should include (again with at least one major work listed) Bernard Lortat-Jacob (1987, 1995), Simha Arom (an immigrant to France; see Arom 1985), Hugo Zemp (1971, 1979), and Gilbert Rouget (1970, 1985), as well as, perhaps, Amnon Shiloah, trained in France but residing in Israel (1979, 1992), and Jean-Jacques Nattiez (1990, 1999), born in France but residing in Canada.

There are many more, an illustrious group of scholars. But can I characterize them as a school, one contrasting with the German-and-Anglophone mainstream? They worked in many cultures but concentrated on the French and on Africa. They were involved in organology. They deal with broad issues—trance (Rouget), ethnographic experimentation (Lortat-Jacob), semiotics (Nattiez), Jewish and Arabic traditions everywhere (Shiloah), music theory in tribal societies (Zemp), and the nature of rhythm and the problems of transcription (Arom). But most important, they had broad interests that usually went far from the study of non-Western and traditional musics. They were also music historians, theorists, and composers. They avoided separating the European from the non-European, and they tried to find ways of looking at music as a unitary phenomenon rather than interpreting the world of music as a series of discrete musics.

Latin America

I'm not sure whether it makes sense to identify a Latin American school of ethnomusicology, given the size and diversity of the area. Regional and national distinctions get in the way. Moreover, the cultural configuration of Central and South America contrasts with that of other continents. Ethnomusicologists working in Europe drew sharp distinctions among "art," "folk," and "popular musics" and until recently restricted themselves to the "folk." Working in Africa, they stuck with music that could arguably (though surely not in fact) be considered devoid of Western influence; they did the same in most of Asia. North Americans looked at folk songs of European-derived groups, at all African American music in aural tradition, and at all music of Native Americans except what might have been created by Native American students at Juilliard. Latin America produced genres and contexts at variance with this situation. The people who might be regarded as "native" are a majority there, but they have for many generations participated in aspects of Western culture, such as Christianity and the Spanish and Portuguese languages, producing music that adapts older indigenous traditions to central elements of Western music, such as harmony and certain instruments.

Latin America comprises a group of societies that has produced a large number of music scholars; I offer only a small sample. Carlos Vega (1898–1966), of Argentina, researched the folk traditions of his and other Latin American countries and was among the first to promulgate an ethnomusicological role in the study of popular music (Vega 1966). Vega's student Isabel Aretz (1991), also of Argentine origin but active throughout most of her career in Venezuela, similarly focused almost exclusively on Latin America but took an interest in the traditions of a number of its nations and in the history of ethnomusicology in Latin America. Mario de Andrade (1893–1945; see Andrade 1936), considered the founder of Brazilian ethnomusicology, collected and wrote about a great variety of traditions and tried to be an activist in urging the use of folk and indigenous traditions in the development of Brazilian art music. Fernando Ortiz (1881–1969), a Cuban scholar who was also known as a lawyer, government official, diplomat, and ethnographer, concentrated on many aspects of Cuban musical culture, but his greatest achievement was his five-volume ethnography of Afro-Cuban musical instruments (Ortiz 1952–55). If these scholars can be considered both as representative and as leaders, one might characterize Latin American ethnomusicologists as being concerned with the music of their own continents, concerned with preservation and documentation, taking on political issues impinging on musical life, and avoiding narrow specialization. Interestingly, Vega, Aretz, and Andrade (and many others) were also composers.

Much research on Latin American cultures, especially in the decades since 1960, has been carried out by scholars residing abroad, in North America or Europe. Some of them have certainly been enormously influential in Latin America itself. I mention only three: Robert Stevenson, who wrote voluminously about the pre- and postconquest history of music in Inca and Aztec territory (e.g., Stevenson 1960); Gerard Behague, who became the leading scholar of Latin American music residing in North America; and Anthony Seeger, who brought modern anthropological approaches to the study of small societies (see A. Seeger 1987). Again, there are many more whom I have no time to mention, but I wish to point out, finally, that in a generation who completed their studies in the 1980s and 1990s, in North America and Europe, one finds a large number of scholars of Latin American (or Hispanic American) background heavily involved in research in Latin American musical cultures.

Iran

For a third example of a national school of ethnomusicology, I turn to Iran, where the point of departure is again different, because the traditional music of Iran—and also, presumably, the intellectual life accompanying music—has itself been an object of ethnomusicological research by others. I don't wish to parse the complicated relationships among the ethnicities of cultures to be investigated and of the population of scholars. Let me accept, as a kind of "national school" of Iranian ethnomusicology, all scholarship on Persian music carried out by Iranian scholars, whether trained or self-identified as ethnomusicologists, and also research by non-Iranians who have specialized in the music of Iran (see Massoudieh 1976).

Many theorists and musicians have written treatises about Persian music (see Massoudieh 1996), but the first to contemplate Persian classical music from an at least partially international perspective was Ali-Naqi Vaziri, who was also a prominent modernizer and educator of musicians and of the public (see Khoshzamir 1979). The most prominent modern historian of Persian music was Vaziri's student Ruhollah Khaleqi (1955–60), and he was succeeded by the French-trained physicist Mehdi Barkechli (1960, 1963), who established a tradition of modern scholarship and who published works on the *radif* and on the nature of Persian scales and the theories of which they were a part. Barkechli was followed, in the 1960s, by the German-trained Khatschi Khatschi (1962); Hormoz Farhat (1990), a composer who studied ethnomusicology at UCLA; and Mohammad Taghi Massoudieh (1968, 1978), originally a violinist, who studied ethnomusicology at the University of Cologne with Marius Schneider and Josef Kuckertz—among others. Other important Iranian scholars of the late twentieth century include Dariouche Safvate (see Caron and Safvate 1966), whose principal scholarly connections were to France, and Mohammad-Reza Darvishi. With the exception of Darvishi, whose main contributions have been in the area of organology (2001–5), the central work of all these scholars has been to preserve, analyze, and interpret the *radif*, the basic repertory shared by all classical Persian musicians and used as basis for improvisation and composition. Each of the scholars mentioned presented a personal interpretation of the *radif*. Very little attention was paid to the social role of music, rural folk music, urban popular music, and issues such as modernization and Westernization. Moreover, the Iranian scholars as a group took little interest in other Asian or further non-Western musical traditions.

A group of non-Iranian ethnomusicologists, too, contributed to the study of Persian classical and other traditional music, significantly interacting with the Iranian scholars. This group includes, besides myself, the American-trained Ella Zonis (1973), Margaret Caton (1983), Stephen Blum (1969), the French scholar Jean During (1984), and the Japanese scholar Gen'ichi Tsuge (1970). The contributions of these foreign researchers are not markedly distinct from those of the Iranians themselves. Although the group included people who worked more broadly in Iran and also studied non-Iranian musics, they too were concerned most with the classical music and the *radif*. So, if there is a national school of ethnomusicology in Iran, it would have to be characterized thus: it was heavily focused on the *radif* and the classical system; it consisted of Iranians and foreigners who represented American, French, and German training and approaches; and the Iranians and foreigners creating it seemed to work cooperatively along similar lines with congruent purposes.

During the era of Ayatollah Khomeini, from 1979 to around 1990, musical activities and, to a degree, musical scholarship seemed to be restricted in Iran, although publications continued to appear abroad. After 1990, scholarship seemed to grow in quantity, quality, and esteem; sources (such as recordings of the *radif* by earlier masters) began to be made available; journals such as the excellent *Mahoor Music Quarterly* began to appear; and a greater variety of approaches to research, by a number of younger scholars, began to be followed.

Culture Heroes

Given all this, if there are phenomena that one could label national schools in the history of ethnomusicology, they differ considerably in all respects. We can, however, pursue a related way of seeing what happened in the history of ethnomusicology outside the framework of the widely recognized mainstream and national and regional schools—namely, by recognizing individuals who worked, usually in isolation, and developed the field or made unique contributions where there was a vacuum. Some of them never had significant followers; in important instances, they came, in retrospect, to be known as the "fathers" or "mothers" of the discipline in their homes. There are surely many who would qualify for inclusion here, but again, let me give you just a sampling.

I'll start with two people who, though living in the West, worked somewhat in isolation yet made great individual contributions. Maud Karpeles (1885–1976) was the founder, or at least the driving force behind the development, of something that became almost an analogue to a national school—the International Folk Music Council. The IFMC, to some extent an outgrowth of the English Folk Song and Dance Society, was founded after World War II as an organization welcoming all kinds of interest in Western folk music, gradually expanded to take interest in the folk traditions of non-Western societies, and eventually came to encompass the study of all music (well, more or less omitting Western classical traditions). Maud Karpeles was the longtime secretary general of the organization, which she sometimes seemed to run with an iron hand, but she was determined to include scholars from all nations, including those from strongly opposing blocs. She found ways to make it possible for scholars from Eastern and Western Europe, from North and South America, and eventually from the rest of the world to cooperate and collaborate even where the governments under which these scholars lived, and their own attitudes, made cooperation difficult. Perhaps more than anyone else, she was responsible for helping a kind of worldwide version of ethnomusicology (I don't think she ever liked that term) to exist from 1950 to 1980. When I say that she worked in isolation, I don't mean that she didn't have hundreds of colleagues and associates; rather, in her determination to make the IFMC—later the ICTM—prosper, she was far ahead of the rest.

And another scholar who worked in an isolated project was Barbara Krader (1922–2006), an American folklorist and scholar of East European musical cultures who devoted herself most to establishing and maintaining contacts between ethnomusicologists in the Western nations, particularly those belonging to NATO, and those of Eastern Europe, of the Warsaw Pact. Her labors in that direction included providing and publishing bibliographies, writing articles and giving talks in the United States about what she knew of research in Russia and Eastern Europe, introducing people to one another at the occasional international conferences, and simply writing to individuals she knew to apprise them of notable work by their Iron Curtain counterparts. Barbara Krader fulfilled this role in the 1960s living in the United States and Canada and after 1970, in Berlin (see Krader 1993). The importance of her activities as a mediator was made clear to me in 1988, in the time of "perestroika," under Party Secretary Gorbachev. A small conference of eight American and about ten Soviet ethnomusicologists (a term differently defined by the two sides) was held in Riga, Latvia (then in the USSR). It was a friendly meeting, and we all learned from one another, but the hero of the occasion was Barbara Krader, for she had made it possible in the first place.

If there is anyone who can be said to have invented African ethnomusicology, it has to be J. H. Kwabena Nketia (b. 1921). Of course, European scholars and (largely white) scholars in South Africa, such as Percival Kirby and Hugh Tracey, had produced voluminous research on African music, but Nketia, first studying composition in the United Kingdom, promulgated the idea that African music ought to be studied by African scholars and that an institution oriented toward African culture would be most appropriate for developing its scholarship, documentation, preservation, and propagation. As the longtime director of the Institute of African Studies at the University of Ghana, in Legion (accepting the position in 1965), and of other institutions in Ghana, he trained many Ghanaian, other African, and non-African scholars in an approach that included conventional scholarship and preservation, thus exerting enormous influence on the subsequent development of ethnomusicology in sub-Saharan Africa. Of his many publications, I'll cite only one of his most specialized (1954) and his least specialized (1974); I'll also point out his influence as an often imitated composer whose style combined nonexperimental Western and African traditions. He truly deserves the title "father of African ethnomusicology."

José Maceda (1917-) is a culture hero in the Philippines, known widely even among people who have no professional association with music. "The father of Philippine ethnomusicology" may be too narrow a title, for he was enormously active also as a composer, performer, and national leader. A concert pianist and composer working in France and the United States, he undertook ethnomusicological studies relatively late, completing a Ph.D. at UCLA at age forty-six. His publications cover a broad area (see, e.g., Maceda 1986), but his most intensive research involved the music of traditional instrumental ensembles. In the Philippines, he developed the study of local and native traditions and built a center for the study of Asian musics at the University of the Philippines, in Diliman. His work has been continued very intensively by his disciple Ramon Santos.

Several East Asian nations also developed ethnomusicology under the leadership of prominent individuals who initially worked alone. Lee Hye-ku (b. 1909), the father of Korean music research, with a vast bibliography, was eventually followed by a large school of Korean scholars, many trained in North America and Europe, and by a truly astonishingly large group of Western Korea specialists who feel that, to an extent, they are following in his footsteps. There are not nearly as many Vietnamese ethnomusicologists, but their leader, long working in isolation and spending most of his life living in exile in France, was Tran Van Khe (b. 1921). The fact that Vietnamese music is known outside Vietnam is largely due to his activities (Khe 1967).

The situation in Japan has been quite different; scholarship on Japanese music has been a part of that culture for centuries. Arguably, however, the first researcher to associate himself with Western ethnomusicologists is Shigeo Kishibe (b. 1912), who was principally a historian of Japanese traditional music (see Kishibe 1966) but also contributed to Chinese and other Asian music history. Younger Japanese scholars regard him as a paternal figure. I wish also to mention Koizumi Fumio (1927–83), who may more properly be considered the first Japanese ethnomusicologist. Koizumi undertook study using the methods of American and European ethnomusicologists, having studied at Wesleyan University and, in contrast to earlier scholars, did not limit his interest to Japanese and Western musics but undertook fieldwork in India, Iran, and West Africa.

Most of the scholars mentioned here might have been—or are—ambivalent about using the term *ethnomusicologist*. They associate it with undesirable characteristics. They feel that it suggests their music is in a different class, not worthy of the kind of attention "real" musicologists give to the world's "real" (Western) music; they don't like being labeled students of merely ethnic music. And when told that the *ethno-* is intended to indicate the study of music in culture from an anthropological perspective, they conclude that "ethnomusicology" is the study of music interesting only for what it tells about culture, not for its intrinsic value. Many of them prefer to be called "musicologists." I have a hard time disagreeing with that perspective. Nonetheless, among scholars in Europe and North America, it is the ethnomusicologists who wish to associate with them, who welcome them, who know something about their studies and their music. It's hard to avoid some ambivalence, but I feel that we ethnomusicologists in Europe and North America—and particularly we in the English-speaking world—need these scholars as colleagues and models.

This is no more than a small random sample of national or regional schools and of individuals who could be considered founding culture heroes in ethnomusicology working in isolation. It would be tempting to sketch Scandinavian, East European, Israeli, Hispanic, and Chinese—and for that matter, African American and Australian—schools, and it would have been fun to express respect for and admiration of many other scholars whose careers exhibited leadership under difficult circumstances. Failing that, though, I hope what I have said provides an alternative way of looking at the history of ethnomusicology, one that admits of more diversity than does the conventional concentration on a mainstream.

3

Speaking of World Music

Then and Now

Where did the term *world music* come from? It seems to me to be relatively new, although some notion of a connection between "world" and "music" must be very old. By the 1980s, however, most Americans who talked about music understood the term to designate music in which sounds from various and often contrastive cultures are combined, mixed, and fused. The implication is that there are lots of musics in the world, and that they have a lot to do with one another, that they are compatible and can be combined or "fused." But while this kind of world music would include lots of different kinds of sounds, the term means essentially a specific kind of music, a category like classical music, folk music, and maybe church music or dance music. The study of this kind of world music is and has been since the late 1980s a significant sector of ethnomusicological research.

33

One might think that the term was developed to help record stores classify their products, that they needed a way to group LPs and CDs that would guide their customers. Incidentally, in my town's record departments, neither "world music" (devoted largely to various fusions) nor "international music" (devoted to African, Asian, Latin American, and "Celtic") genres included Native American music, which had its own section next to country music. Looking at the taxonomies of musics in Western culture through the lens of record stores seems to be a fascinating enterprise.

But I first ran into the term *world music* in the 1960s, when the distinguished music program of Wesleyan University began using it, in preference to the conventional term *ethnomusicology*, to mean a curriculum in which, theoretically, all the music in the world could be studied. In the academic world it continued with that kind of meaning into the twenty-first century, as a designation for textbooks and course surveys that are, at least in the sense of sampling, about the world's musical systems and cultures—well, perhaps excluding Western art music, which usually doesn't get into those books and courses because it has books and courses of its own. So music was divided into the West, and its "real" music, and "the rest," or world music.

The term may be relatively new, then, but the idea of world music as music of the whole world has been around much longer—maybe forever. It lurks in the background whenever we see explorers, travelers, and missionaries over many centuries using the term *music* to designate not only Western but all kinds of exotic phenomena (see Harrison 1973) and in the concepts of a "harmony of the spheres" and of music as a "universal language," which led to our concern, as ethnomusicologists, with "universals." But a world music that is simultaneously an indivisible entity and a group of phenomena with only limited compatibility—that seems to me to be most closely associated with developments in Western academic practice in the late twentieth century, a kind of practice that has its background in European musical thought going back to the eighteenth century. So I'd like here to contemplate two temporally distinct concepts—world music in the last fifty years, as a field of general education in (mainly) American colleges and universities, and world music as it was understood (though not in that term) in European thought beginning in the nineteenth century.

World Music, Textbooks, and Education after 1960

When ethnomusicologists began to teach courses at American and European universities, they were expected to have a reasonable command of representative musics of the world. Indeed, the most prominent of the earliest ethnomusicologists—such as Carl Stumpf and Erich von Hornbostel (see *Sammelbände* vol. 1)—while not espousing "world music" as their area of expertise, individually undertook the study of a variety of diverse non-Western musics. And it's conceivable to consider works such as Lachmann's brief summary in Bücken's (1927–31) multivolume compendium or Sachs's (1943) attempt at a prehistory of Western music as world-music surveys. Nonetheless, world music as a category of college courses that made serious attempts at a responsible sampling seems to me to go back to the 1960s, and while looking at a "whole" world of music may seem the most logical of conclusions resulting from communication, colonialism, and exposure, it also seems to me to have come about because ethnomusicologists were being trained and needed jobs and had to develop a "product," a standardized type of course they could be counted on to handle. As a result, the period beginning around 1965 in American higher education may be the period of the world-music survey. But it may also be coming to an end. When I began teaching at the University of Illinois and was assigned a course titled "Music of the World's Cultures," which was to include material from virtually all continents, some faculty members considered this a very specialized kind of course. People like me were expected to be sufficiently broad generalists to know something about all musics. (Good luck!)

As time progressed and data accumulated, individuals were less inclined to be generalists of such a broad kind but instead moved to greater geographical and topical specialization. The typical menu of college courses since about 1985, while still including the "world-music survey," has moved its center of gravity to a narrowed geographic and, more important, topical focus.

So let me begin my survey of textbooks with an effort in which I participated, Prentice-Hall's History of Music series, edited by H. Wiley Hitchcock, consisting at first of six volumes covering the standard periods in Western music history plus one survey of American art music and two volumes on the rest of the world, by William Malm (1967) and myself (Nettl 1965). Devoting two volumes to "the rest" was the result of rather stiff negotiations between the publisher, who proposed one volume, and the ethnomusicologists, who insisted on a volume per continent or something of that sort. How to divide the world into two volumes was left to Malm and me, and we have never been totally happy with our result; while we tried to make our individual areas of expertise the point of departure, we ended up dividing the world into non-Western elite classical traditions and—again—the rest. I certainly wouldn't defend this arrangement today, but it reflects the way many ethnomusicologists saw the world of music in the 1960s. The organization of both volumes is geographical, a chapter for each culture area or major nation.

An emphasis on non-Western and nonclassical traditions as associated with notions of world peace, ecology, "greenness," and sustainability began in the 1970s, and it's still around, but it resulted early on in an important text by David Reck (1977) with the suggestive title of *Music of the Whole Earth*. Although its examples come from many cultures and world areas, Reck's work differs from the Prentice-Hall volumes in its arrangement by broad formal principles such as rhythm, polyphony, instruments, and en-sembles, always related to general aesthetic principles and demonstrated with references to visual art, literature, and sometimes social organiza-tion. With its many and varied illustrations, Reck's work somehow gives the impression of a coffee-table book, but it has served as a textbook to introductory courses on world music.

Somewhat later, a book by Pantaleoni (1985) followed a similarly id-iosyncratic approach, with a lot of visual representations, uniquely treat-ing melody, rhythm, harmony, and form, with detailed examples of each element from a number of cultures. A work of a totally different sort, O'Brien (1977), surveyed the world in a mere one hundred pages, with emphasis on instruments and general principles of musical construction. The notion of a "world" of music doesn't come up in that text; rather, in an approach with which most later authors would prefer not to be associ-ated, O'Brien stressed the dichotomy of "Western" and "non-Western," suggesting that non-Western musics are a homogeneous body contrasting with European music.

While Reck's and Pantaleoni's books give the impression of a rather uni-fied and integrated world of music, Elizabeth May's (1980) appropriately titled *Musics of Many Cultures* emphasizes diversity. The book is a collection of essays by recognized authorities on about twenty musical cultures, some surveying their subject musics and others concentrating on special prob-lems, such as recent developments and trends. The value of having each culture described by a specialist is offset by a certain unevenness: some essays assume prior knowledge on the reader's part, and others do not; some essays emphasize musical approaches, and others, cultural ones.

In the 1990s and the early twenty-first century, a good many other texts appeared, almost all accompanied with CDs carefully integrated with the text, demonstrating the increased importance of world-music courses in American institutions as they began to be used to satisfy "world-culture" general education requirements and expectations of multicultural understanding in music education. But the ideal of comprehensive coverage in a world-music textbook, clearly unattainable in its full sense from the beginning, began to be replaced by several variations of this theme.

A widely used work, *Worlds of Music,* edited by Jeff Titon (1984), consists of several chapters by authoritative scholars (the numbers have increased with each ensuing edition, the fifth appearing in 2008) that touch on various cultures, including those of Afghanistan, Ghana, and South India and indigenous cultures in North America—and each going into considerable detail. *Excursions in World Music* (Nettl et al. 2007, first published in 1992) provides one chapter on each of ten world areas, each chapter concentrating on a culture in which the author had field experience and illustrating the importance of the world area in question by carefully exploring an outstanding genre, instrument, or musician.

Soundscapes, by Kay Kaufman Shelemay (2001a), with an unusually large number of examples, mentions the musics of many of the world's societies but concentrates on the North American experience and on recent developments. Arranged topically, the book reveals its emphasis on contemporary events and concerns in its chapter titles—"Music and Migration," "Music and Memory," "Music and Identity," "Music and Politics," and so on, with each chapter marshaling material from a variety of contexts to demonstrate its points. *World Music: A Global Journey,* by Miller and Shahriari (2006), surpasses other works from this period in the attempt at global coverage, giving something from virtually everywhere, while also trying to introduce the reader to certain approaches of ethnomusicological research.

Michael Bakan's (2007) *World Music: Traditions and Transformations* is divided into two major parts, suggesting a course that begins by explaining and demonstrating general principles and then studies in detail a number of genres from eight cultures (in which the author has differing amounts of experience). The first part consists of chapters about such topics as rhythm, pitch and melody, texture, and instruments but also on the concept of music, while the ensuing chapters tell about specific genres, often tied to instruments such as the West African kora or the Balinese beleganjur gamelan, and include a section on modernization and interaction with musics from elsewhere.

Although perhaps closest to Bakan's work, *Music: The Cultural Context,* by Robert Garfias (2004), looks at world music from a different perspective. It emphasizes what the title suggests but does so in two large sections, the first titled "The Cultural Context" and the second, "The Structure of Music." Both sections approach their subjects topically, provide examples from the many cultures in which Garfias has done fieldwork (including European and North American), and bring the reader brief, page-long introductions to many issues. Intended as a textbook (and evidently used by Garfias in his classes), it does not follow the customs of undergraduate textbook writing but seems, rather, to be directed to a more advanced readership. This characteristic perhaps explains why it was published in Japan rather than by a North American publisher.

The concept of textbooks with options of various sorts, such as the use of modules that allow an instructor freedom in course construction, has become widespread in American educational publishing. In world music, the most prominent example is a series of short books titled "Experiencing Music, Expressing Culture," begun by Oxford University Press in 2004 and consisting at that time of two general introductions by the series editors, Patricia Shehan Campbell and Bonnie Wade, and fifteen books on individual cultures. Each volume, a survey of some 150 pages with a CD, is intended as a module. Included are books by such well-known authors as Timothy Rice (on Bulgaria), Ruth Stone (on West Africa), and Thomas Turino (on the Andes). The teacher of a typical course may use the two general books and perhaps four or five area surveys. This series develops further the concept that even in introductory, integrated courses on world music, the detailed insight of specialists is needed.

The world-music survey as text for a course seems to be largely a North American phenomenon. Similar books are uncommon in other languages, and some American texts have been translated into Spanish, Portuguese, and Chinese. It's interesting to examine one significant exception that, unlike most American surveys, makes a valiant effort to present all the world's music, in all periods of history, under one umbrella. Peter Fletcher's *World Musics in Context* (1997) is—if a bit uneven—an account of all areas of the world in both music history and musical ethnography by one author writing from a single perspective. Following a somewhat idiosyncratic approach that emphasizes history, Fletcher proposes a number of different origins of music, but the structure of early development as he characterizes it suggests the development of diverging traditions from common (not completely specified) roots. Thus, a strand of history begins in Egypt and Mesopotamia and diverges into (a) European and African and (b) South (and central) Asian branches. European art music is seen not as culmination but as only one, quite specialized development. For Fletcher, the history of the world's musics is one of ever-increasing diversification.

A composer, conductor, and educator, Fletcher intended this book as a contribution to music education, a field that has had to define its own conception of world music in both theoretical and practical ways. Secondarily, Fletcher's book is directed to a general but educated public. His approach as an educationist is clear, however, and leads me to mention briefly the role of world music in American primary and secondary education. The main thrust of the history of music education since 1970 or so, in the United States and elsewhere, has been the expansion of subject matter. It's probably correct to assume that in most systems of music teaching, pupils and student-musicians were taught what was considered the student's (or maybe the teacher's) own culture; music teaching consisted of, on an individual basis and in the classroom, passing on a defined heritage. (Never mind that the teachers' and the pupils'—or their parents'—definition of the heritage may have differed.)

Around 1970, music educators as a professional group began to recognize the diversity of the world's music and thus to participate in the interest in multicultural education. Two contrasting thrusts could be identified, both expanding the curriculum from the emphasis on Western classical (or classical-derived) music from 1720 to 1920. On the one hand, recognizing the cultural diversity of the pupils, educators wanted to offer them exposure to their "own" music. For example, one teacher told me that she had a large number of children from India in her class and thus felt obliged to teach Indian music. On the other hand, instructors felt the need to teach all pupils something about the music of the world, emphasizing those they did not already know. I believe the first thrust was the alternative more frequently chosen. What concept of history underlies these changes in orientation? The traditional Western approach looked at the art-music tradition as something from a grand past that should be preserved and nurtured; "normal" music was music composed long ago, and music composed recently must prove itself worthy. The multicultural approach suggests that what is being taught is not music of earlier times—of the Stone Age or the Asian Middle Ages, as Curt Sachs's presentations often suggest—but the contemporary music of distant societies or of the people—members of minorities—in the class. The emphasis is on the notion that the world's musical diversity is a present-day phenomenon.

Much of the cross-cultural content of music taught in schools might not easily be recognized in its original home as the culture's normal music. Thus, gamelans in American schools might include some instruments only remotely like those of the Javanese or Balinese originals. A "world music" concert by a sixth-grade choir might include songs of African, Caribbean, French, Chinese, and Central Asian origins, all of them arranged for diatonic scales with piano accompaniments using functional harmony. The purpose here, then, may be not so much to introduce students to the diversity of the world's musical sounds but rather to persuade them that all the world's people have music that can be comprehended—that all the world's musics have a lot in common.

The concept of world music in Western culture has a history that sometimes coincides but sometimes conflicts with the mainstream course of ethnomusicology. This history has progressed largely on the shoulders of a small group of scholars who, marveling at the world's musical diversity as well as its unity, tried in various ways to develop a view of music by reconciling these opposing yet complementary concepts.

Luminaries in Early "World Music" History

We've looked at one side of the world-music concept in twentieth-century academia. But as I've said, what we've done with that concept in recent decades has a long prehistory. I believe that some concept of world music was essential to the development of ethnomusicology. Nonetheless, the idea that something one might call "world music" differs from "music" pure and simple got a major impetus in the late eighteenth century, when the European world began to recognize the existence of the "rest." And notions that led to our courses on "world music" began—though with different terminology—to be developed gradually by a number of thinkers, scholars, musicians, a few of whom I would like to mention here. I see them as heroic figures of a sort. They gave us, either as their principal aim or perhaps just incidentally, to other more specialized purposes, a view of the music of the world that combines unity and diversity. If *heroism* is the right word, their heroics consist of the comprehensiveness of their knowledge given the available data and of their willingness to follow the difficulties of comparative method, to draw broad conclusions from what is often a spotty sample. In contrast to some of their contemporaries, they saw the world of music not as a single, universally valid system but as a group—maybe a plethora—of contrastive musics, the products of greatly varied cultures. Some of these "heroes" could unabashedly be called ethnomusicologists; others are historians, composers, philosophers, or folklorists. As a group, they constitute a discernible strand in the history of ethnomusicology.

THE TIMES OF CHARLES BURNEY AND JOHANN GOTTFRIED HERDER   The 1770s constituted a major period in the history of musicography. In the same year, Charles Burney (1776–89) and John Hawkins (1776) published the two earliest influential histories of Western music. Burney's, thought by some to be the less scholarly and more popularizing, has always received more attention. It sees music as a general feature of human culture but in its excellent and proper form as specific to certain peoples. It contains no mention of India or China, let alone African or indigenous North American cultures, but there is a large section—about 20 percent of the total work—devoted to "ancient" music, with chapters on Egyptian, Hebrew, and Greek music, all of these presented as complex systems. Burney does opine on the origins of music, asserting that "the art or practice of music cannot be said to have been invented by any one man, for that must have had its infancy, childhood, and youth, before it arrived at maturity" (1776–89, 164). He adds, "the first attempts must have been rude and artless: the first flute, a whistling reed, and the first lyre, perhaps the dried sinews of a dead tortoise" (165). There is a concept of music as something that developed gradually, but it wasn't true music until it had a conceptual body of theory and, so Burney implies, at least a rudimentary system of notation.

Further, Burney, rather in concert with both modern evolutionists and Native American mythology, suggested that the origins of song are "coeval with mankind. . . . This primitive and instinctive language . . . is still retained by animals" (1776–89, 165).

In contrast to Burney, Johann Gottfried Herder, in his *Stimmen der Völker* (1807 [1778–89]), may have been the first to propose that each people has its own music—that there is such a thing as a style of folk song, *"Volkslied,"* peculiar to each people, though these styles exhibit some internationally shared characteristics. Not the first to notice musical diversity, Herder may nevertheless have been the first who prominently made the point and suggested a term.

Burney and Herder thus represent two viewpoints that have divided music scholarship (though not necessarily scholars, some of whom try to mitigate the conflict): (1) all peoples have a distinct music, or (2) all music is part of a single development leading to—well, is it Bach, Mozart, Beethoven, or high-tech?

Actually, the concept of a "world" of music made occasional appearances before Burney and Herder. One of the high points in musical thought was Rousseau's dictionary of 1768, in which the musical world is illustrated by three notations—Chinese, Native Canadian, and European folk music—a harbinger of the dominant division of musics under the purview of comparative musicology before 1950 or so.

The end of the eighteenth century and the beginning of the nineteenth provide the earliest important reports on the musics of Asian cultures, most prominently the works of Amiot (1779) on Chinese music, of William Jones (1792) on the Indian raga system, and of Raphael Kiesewetter (1842) on Arabic music. Taken as a group, these examples (along with numerous less prominent others) show that European scholars were beginning to form a concept of music as a world of musics. These works, and some others like them, seem to have affected the authors of some nineteenth-century works that claim to be histories of music.

Philip Bohlman has discussed Herder in a number of publications (most recently 2002b, 2007) and lists him as an inventor—sometimes "the" inventor—of "world music." Herder deserves that title for several reasons: he paid attention to the music of the ordinary and rural people in addition to the art music of court and church; he considered and collected the folk music of diverse peoples in Europe—and added, late in life, some interest in non-Western music (Bohlman 2007, 4); and perhaps most important, he coined the term *Volkslied,* which labeled a genre that all peoples were thought to possess, the common core of a world music. Surely he had ideas of what the history of music, and of the folk music of the world's cultures, might have been, but in his day this subject was not one of the issues of scholarship. Suffice it to say that were he writing today, he, too, might have been of two minds. On the one hand, music had a single origin—he considered it coeval with speech, something inherent to humans ("hard-wired," one would say today), its character represented by what the world's folk musics more recently, perhaps in his time, had in common. On the other hand, each "Volk," each nation, had its own distinct folk music with its own long history. Although principally concerned with the words of songs, Herder was a competent and active musician, and his work pointed the way for a number of disciplines, including folklore, philology, literary scholarship, historiography, and even ethnomusicology. He speaks to us from another age, virtually another culture, but the musical issues he illuminates—universals versus cultural diversity, music as isolated art versus music as a mainstay of life—are in various ways still with us. Nonetheless, his importance to humanistic scholarship as a whole was so great that the two-page article about him in the 1974 edition of the *Encyclopedia Britannica* hardly mentions his interest in folk music and does not credit him as a seminal figure in the discipline of folklore.

AUGUST WILHELM AMBROS The first author who seriously confronted the issue of music and musics was August Wilhelm Ambros, the first volume of whose *Geschichte der Musik* (1862) is regarded by many scholars as a major landmark in the history of musicology. The first volume (five were planned) is devoted to non-Western music, the music of the ancient Near East, and the classical cultures of Greece and Italy. Ambros's discussion of the non-Western musics, based almost entirely on secondhand apprehension of theoretical sources along with a few bits of transcriptions (made without the use of recordings), does more than pay lip-service to a world-music concept. Ambros sees the world of music as comprising several areas that developed as a result of diffusion from culture centers—China, South Asia, and the Arabic world, to which he adds, by implication, the ancient Greek-Egyptian culture that led to Western music. Claiming that the ability of "musicking" is—using the modern term—innate in humans, he describes a series of situations (conflict, child-rearing, expression of joy or sorrow [3–4]) that as a group evoke the multiple-origin concept. Nevertheless, Ambros (xvi–xvii) suggests that the non-Western art musics should be seen as parts of his overall chronology because the musics of non-Western cultures should be acknowledged as ancient, perhaps antedating the origins of Western culture, although their development was truncated at a certain point, and they were overtaken by Western music, which continued to develop further. Without explicitly claiming to be writing about "world music," Ambros tries to establish it in both geographic and chronological frameworks.

CARL ENGEL   On a somewhat parallel track, the older of the two unrelated men named Carl Engel pursued a research program that followed Herder's as a precursor to twentieth-century ethnomusicology in its concern for the musics of the world's peoples. Engel (1818–82), who lived largely in England, pursued a number of interests in his career, including organology and piano music, but he is best remembered for his work on "national music." In his principal book on the subject (1864), he defines this as music "appertaining to a nation or tribe, whose individual emotions and passions it expresses, which distinguish it from the music of any other nation or tribe" (1864, 1). Rendering it as equivalent to *Volksmusik*, he nevertheless avoids issues that later came to dominate scholarly thinking about folk music, such as its presumed (and required) great age (as both style and repertory), its association with particular social classes, its rural provenance, and the question of authenticity; rather, he discusses a great deal of music that in the twentieth century would have been labeled as "vernacular"—functional folk songs, hymns, patriotic songs, and some European and a lot of non-European popular art music.

Engel's *Introduction to the Study of National Music* (1866) could not today be used as documentation of ethnographic or historical research, yet it is astonishingly broad and broad-minded. There are lots of notations, mainly from published sources, but many other transcriptions made by ear, and while the emphasis is on Europe (mainly England, Germany, and Central Europe), Engel tries to include music from many cultures, managing to present examples of and comments on music of Africa, the America of indigenous peoples, Persia, India, Central Asia, and China. Engel's principal purpose was to demonstrate that each culture has its own music, but following on the heels of that aim is an insistence that the world's musics have a lot in common with one another. He tells us that among nations and even continents there are significant parallels in performance practices of many kinds, in social functions, and even in specific tunes. He works hard to provide ways for comparing musics, and even when these turn out to be wrong-headed or of dubious relevance (e.g., a table indicating percentages of songs in major and minor in twenty-two European nations and ethnicities [1866, 174]), they show Engel as a uniquely forward-looking scholar. Arguably, this is the first general book about "world music."

It's worth mentioning, as virtually contemporary to Engel's, the work of Wilhelm Tappert (1890), whose small book *Wandernde Melodien* suggests that we look at the world not only as a group of musics but as a group of melodies, each of which has diffused throughout the world (well, throughout Europe) and maintained its integrity while taking up, in each venue, significant characteristics of local music.

GUIDO ADLER   If musicologists agree that they have a disciplinary "father," it is likely to be Guido Adler, whom I have described as the author of the most influential article laying out the field (1885) and principal editor of the first successful musicological journal. The field that was to become ethnomusicology, concerned with the musics of the world, makes only a cameo appearance in Adler's outline, but it is there, as "Musikologie— Untersuchung und Vergleichung zu ethnographischen Zwecken" (investigation and comparison for ethnographic purposes). The music of the world is there for more than just a speculative introduction to Western art music. In its first two volumes (1885, 1886), the journal, *Vierteljahrschrift für Musikwissenschaft* makes a stab at looking at the entire world, or at least the part of it to which musicologists have (had) access.

Forty years and many research projects later, at the age of almost seventy, Adler had moved away from a broad worldview, editing an influential compendium, *Handbuch der Musikgeschichte* (1924), that very clearly interprets "history of music" as the history of Western music. There is a brief chapter (ca. 30 pages, or 2.5% of the whole) by Robert Lach titled

"Die Musik der Natur- und orientalischen Kulturvölker," which looks at the history of world music as a sequence of increasingly complex scales, avoiding separation of nonliterate from Asian high cultures and beginning with several pages on origins. Evidently, it was Adler's view that there is *a* history of music; even the individual nations of Europe are not accorded separate histories until the modern era, beginning 1880. Folk music is mentioned occasionally, but the concept of folk song as a point of departure for art music, perhaps on a national basis, does not come to the fore. Adler's collection is characteristic of many larger histories of music published in the seventy years after the 1885 breakthrough.

SOURINDRO MOHUN TAGORE   The first prominent book that interprets the world of musics as a group of musics, each with its own history (though not neglecting interrelationships), is by a musicologist who worked outside the European scholarly canon, although he was significantly influenced by Carl Engel's work: the Bengali intellectual Sourindro Mohun Tagore. Tagore's *Universal History of Music* (1963; first published in Calcutta in 1896) is perhaps the earliest book in which some measure of equality is given to the treatment of the various continents. This is one of Tagore's last publications, following a long series of scholarly and hortatory works on Indian music and other subjects; much of his work is discussed in publications by Capwell (esp. 1987, 1991), who also describes his involvement in the creation of a national anthem appropriate to India as a constituent part of the British Empire. Active in many projects developing musical life in Bengal, Tagore organized his ambitious history of world music principally by discussing each of a multitude of nations, but he consistently emphasizes the ways in which music crosses national boundaries. Thus, he begins by pointing out that "the primitive tones of the human voice are much the same in all countries" but quickly moves to assert that "the Moors have exercised a perceptible influence upon the music of Spain" and "the well-known German 'Dessauer March' is of Italian origin" (Tagore 1963, 11).

Tagore's *Universal History,* based on fragmentary secondary and tertiary sources (except when dealing with Indian subjects), is valuable principally for its perspective; it tries to tell some important things about the music of every nation. Beginning with "The Savage Nations" (on tribal societies of the Americas and North Asia), it devotes some 100 pages to Asia (40 of them unsurprisingly on India—subdivided by regions—but several pages each on China, Siam, Japan, Korea, Tibet, Persia, etc.), around 45 pages to Africa, 115 to Europe, 35 to the Americas, and 25 to Oceania. In each case there is some account of older traditions currently still practiced and instruments, as well as a few assorted (and not very organized) historical issues. Often the matter of national anthems comes up, as also does the use of foreign musics (e.g., Italian music performed in Germany). Page 217 includes an account of opera in Germany, provides a few words about Mozart (and a list of six major works), and mentions minor figures such as Spohr and Gyrowetz. The main point is the inclusion of "chapterlets" on such obscure regions as Iceland, Borneo, Tyrol, and Dahomey. No doubt Tagore knew that his information was spotty and superficial, but he considered it important to make a gesture at showing that all nations had their music, that each deserved appropriate attention, and that the universe of music consisted of these separate, though interrelated, musics. It's a viewpoint that did not become prominent for several decades after Tagore's death in 1914.

An Indian successor to S. M. Tagore's universal history, almost a century later, is *Music of the Nations,* by Swami Prajnanananda (1973), who presents his book as a comparative study of the "musical systems of the civilised nations of the world." With chapters on India, Egypt, Greece, and Rome, on Arabic, Persian, Chinese, Japanese, Thai, Burmese, and Korean music, and on Russian and Western European musics, it cannot claim great authority. But it is worth mentioning as a modern attempt by a non-Western scholar to write about world music, and parallel to its Western counterparts, it does so from an Indian perspective, devoting its longest chapter to Indian music and providing a separate chapter on the influence of Indian music on the rest of the world. I don't know whether Swami Prajnanananda was inclined to irony, but it seems that he might be saying, "if you Europeans think I've provided an unbalanced, Indo-centric view of world music, this may tell you how we Indians are usually made to feel."

HUGO RIEMANN   In his long career as a musicologist and theorist, Hugo Riemann—already lauded in chapter 1—touched on an immense variety of musical subjects. Central in it was his *Handbuch der Musikgeschichte* (1904–13), a five-volume publication more or less contemporary to Tagore's, its first volume appearing in 1904. Enormously erudite and in control of the voluminous European literature on music, Riemann devotes the first volume of this work to ancient Greece, beginning with a thorough account of Greek and Roman sources. But he starts out with several caveats. Extolling the recent development of "musikalische Ethnographie" (1904, vi), perhaps the earliest use of this term, Riemann maintains that this is not history but observation of the present, from which, he warns, in a precursor to more recent thought, one must not extrapolate earlier stages of history.

He adds that while it has been customary to include Chinese, Egyptian, and Indian music as a prologue to the history of Western music, because these cultures were well advanced at the time of the flowering of ancient Greek culture, he feels they should not be seen as part of Western music history (1904, 1). Chinese music is too distant; Egyptian music, known only from depictions of instruments; and Indian music, a mix of materials of ancient provenance with influences from the beginning of the Islamic period in South Asia. Thus these and other non-Western cultures are only mentioned at various points in passing. Trying in a sophisticated way to separate history from other musical scholarship and recognizing that non-Western music is interesting not only for what it might tell about the West's earlier past, Riemann can be blamed only for little more than claiming inclusivity in his title, a fault that he shares with most scholars before and many long after his work.

Contexts for the Great Historical Compendia

Western scholars through most of the twentieth century, trying to look at the history of music comprehensively, have rarely done what Tagore tried to do—namely, write the history of all the world's cultures or nations. Mainly, if they touched on the music of "the world" at all, they did so to provide a context for understanding the history of Western art music. In the forefront of twentieth-century literature are several large compendia, a number of which covered the issue in essentially parallel fashion. Leaving aside some comprehensive histories of European music, such as the first edition of the *Oxford History of Music* (1901–5), the first serious attempt to assemble this kind of compendium may have been the ten-volume *Handbuch der Musikwissenschaft,* edited by Ernst Bücken (1927–31), which includes volumes on periods in European music history along with others devoted to overarching issues (e.g., performance practice) and narrower subjects (e.g., Lutheran church music). One volume comprises four parts, paginated separately (and possibly once available separately): "Instrumentenkunde" (the longest), "Musik der aussereuropäischen Natur- und Kulturvölker," a brief introduction to music of antiquity, and perhaps surprisingly, "Altslavische Volks- und Kirchenmusik," which seems to be included because its subject, like that of the non-Western section, is seen as exotica, even though the section discusses European cultures from Russia to Bulgaria and Serbia.

This four-part volume seems to have been intended as a supplement to the other nine. In Lachmann's thirty-three-page section on non-Western music, world music consists essentially of two categories, "primitive" and "Asian cultured" peoples and musics; each music group is presented as an essentially homogeneous corpus with stylistic and functional similarities among its constituents. Evidence for a particular point in the first part may be taken from African, Melanesian, and Native American cultures; for a point in the second, from Chinese, Javanese, and Indian cultures. It would be foolish to impute to Lachmann the attitude that all this music was just one big mix. But to him (as seen also in his book *Musik des Orients*) the similarities and relationships among the world's musics (Europe excepted) are the most important touchstones of insight. Peter Panoff's section on Slavic music is the only one in the entire set that has a part devoted explicitly to folk music. The understanding of popular music as a separate genre does not come into play at all.

A somewhat different approach was followed, a couple of decades later, by the *New Oxford History of Music* (1957–65), which departed substantially from its predecessor, *The Oxford History of Music,* a set that began with the establishment of polyphonic music in medieval Europe, thereby perhaps making a unique statement defining what music truly is. *The New Oxford* begins with a first volume (of ten) on "ancient and Oriental music," with a total of eight specialists providing chapters on "primitive" music (M. Schneider), the Asian high cultures (Bake, Farmer, and Picken), ancient Greece, and Jewish and Islamic traditions. The introduction, by Egon Wellesz, dwells on the essential difference between this volume and the others. It's surprising to read these rather uninsightful lines from the pen of the distinguished scholar of Byzantine music and student of Schoenberg: "In the East music has . . . still preserved its ritual, even its magic character. . . . To the Western musician conciseness of expression, clearly shaped form, and individuality are the highest criteria. . . . The Eastern musician likes to improvise on given patterns, he favors repetition, his music does not develop" (1:xviii). It seems that the editors of the *New Oxford* were more interested in fulfilling an obligation to appear modern than in providing a kind of world-music background for their concentration on Western art music. While much of the data on African, American Indian, and Asian musics in these chapters comes from recent sources, there is no attempt to show that these musical cultures are part of the modern, twentieth-century world of music.

Shortly after, and in some respects parallel to, the *New Oxford*, the *Histoire de la musique,* edited by Roland-Manuel, appeared as part of the series Encyclopedie de la Pléiade. The first of two volumes, published in 1960, includes in its 2000 pages a chapter on music in myth and ritual in non-Western (read "primitive") societies by M. Schneider (ca. 85 pp.), preceded by a 15-page chapter of speculative prehistory by C. Brailoiu. Chapters on Africa, Bali, China, Japan, India, and Vietnam occupy 200 pages; and after chapters on Egyptian, Mesopotamian, Jewish, and Greek music come three on music in "le monde Musulman" (Iran, the Arabic world, and Turkey, 165 pages). While the survey of non-Western musics occupies a small proportion of the total volume, it is really quite large, easily the equivalent of a well-sized volume. These chapters discuss the musics of their respective cultures holistically, looking at ancient as well as recent developments, including folk and art musics. In most cases one gets the feeling that ancient practices continued with only slight changes until Western musical culture intruded.

If these chapters provide a context, then the message of the Roland-Manuel collection may be, by both organization and tone, that in ancient times—perhaps the times of the ancient Greeks, putting it very generally—the various musics of the world were in a certain sense equal, but later on, the non-Western cultures stayed behind while Western music advanced. It does not present non-Western musics as manifestations of earlier stages of Western music.

Appearing in a new incarnation after fifty years, Bücken's *Handbuch,* now titled *Neues Handbuch der Musikwissenschaft* and edited by Carl Dahlhaus (1980–92), moved somewhat more closely to an even treatment of the world's cultures, devoting three of its twelve volumes to non-Western and European folk and popular musics, with a thirty-page chapter entitled "Jazz, Rock, und Popmusik." This is the first large compendium to include folk music within the concept of music history, and while "folk music" is separated from art music, its role in history and its historical components are given attention in a separate chapter. Lip-service, at the very least, is paid to popular music and, perhaps more significantly, to jazz, whose ambiguous place in the standard taxonomy has stood in the way of its inclusion in comprehensive accounts of music.

In contemplating the place of non-Western and folk music in large publications devoted principally to the history of art music, it seems appropriate to mention briefly encyclopedias, of which the most prominent, *The New Grove* (2001), comes closest to treating the world's cultures evenhandedly. It does so by providing survey articles on large world regions (e.g., Africa and the Middle East) and concepts (folk music) as well as an article on each of the world's nations. The same is basically true of the recent edition of *Die Musik in Geschichte und Gegenwart* (1994–2007). The presence of world music has increased in this genre through the last one hundred years, but the cleavage between Western art music and all the rest continues to be quite obvious.

The latest among the compendia approaching a history of world music, the *Garland Encyclopedia of World Music* (1999–2001), takes a more ethnographic than historical perspective. While earlier works emphasize history but provide a bit of ethnography (mainly for cultures in which source material is largely contemporary), the *Garland* has only a few chapters of specifically historical interest. In the volume on Europe (and to a small extent in others), the history of Western art music is given attention as simply one of many traditions.

All this suggests a very gradual move toward increasingly evenhanded treatment of the world's musics in works whose titles imply that this is what the reader should expect. At the same time, historical treatments of Western music—such as the six-volume *Oxford History of Western Music* by Richard Taruskin (2005), but going back to Paul Henry Lang's *Music in Western Civilization* (1941)—restrict themselves to Europe and increasingly avoid introductory lip-service to the great non-West.

The late twentieth century also saw a shift from the concept of music as a single unit with one history to multiple "histories." *Garland,* the second edition of the *New Grove,* and to some degree Dahlhaus's *Neues Handbuch* all move toward emphasis on the differences among the world's musics. It would have been a short hop from the recognition of the national and culture-specific histories to the idea that each culture also has its own musicology—that the world of musicology is really a world of many "musicologies." While this concept has been discussed (see, e.g., Qureshi in Nettl and Bohlman 1991) principally from a theoretical perspective, its application was attempted in a large compendium only once, in a project that was never completed. Under the leadership of Barry Brook, a project titled "Music in the Life of Man," later changed to "Music in Human Experience" was planned, with the support of UNESCO. Each of a dozen volumes was to include histories of regions and nations throughout the world, each written largely by scholars from that region. The usual distinction—historical treatment for Europe, ethnographic for all other regions—was to be replaced by an essentially historical perspective for all. This would have been a very distinctive sort of "history of world music."

Bridge to the "World Music" of Y2K

What connected these early historians with the authors of world-music textbooks in the late 20th century is, it seems to me, a group of comparativists, the most prominent of whom were Curt Sachs, Mieczyslaw Kolinski, and Alan Lomax, scholars whose work is also mentioned in chapter 5, in an essay that deals explicitly with comparative study.

The most important of this group was Curt Sachs, whose career could almost be described as a history of a world music. In a number of his publications, Sachs wanted to present the history of music (and dance) as a world event. His *Rise of Music in the Ancient World, East and West* (1943), which is part of the so-called Norton Series, in which each of the volumes is devoted to a period in Western music history, is largely about non-Western music; only some 75 of its 300 pages concern Greece and Rome. If one had eliminated this, one would have been left with a 175-page account of non-Western music, with a historical slant, rather idiosyncratically oriented (the music of "Islam" is presented largely as a preserver of ancient Greek traditions). That this wasn't done suggests that the editors and author considered non-Western music of interest only insofar as it could be shown relevant to the history of European music. Sachs ends with a short chapter entitled "Europe and the Road to Major and Minor." For him, the world of music today shows a number of historical strata, and Western music represents a tremendous leap forward that began in the Middle Ages. The concept of the present as a group of phenomena that represent historical strata goes back, in Sachs's work, to his *Geist und Werden der Musikinstrumente* (1929), in which the distribution of clusters of instruments throughout the world is interpreted, using the approaches of the *Kulturkreis* school of historical reconstruction, as twenty-three stages of development in the history of instruments.

Sachs wrote about the musics and particularly the instruments of many cultures, but his view of the history of world music mainly sides with a homogeneous beginning moving to a group of diverse branches, all of which ceased to develop at some point, with the exception of the Western, which for reasons of technology, social organization, and a certain kind of energy, kept moving forward.

It's a widespread view in the literature on music, one ethnomusicologists no longer accept. Actually, it seems that in his last book, *The Wellsprings of Music* (published posthumously in 1962), Sachs was beginning to take a different view, moving away from the concept of a single unified history of world music, beginning with the suggestion (based on the "logogenic" and "pathogenic" concepts he had previously used to describe the simplest musics) of two kinds of origin—the "tumbling strains," which suggest a genesis from emotional expression, and "one-step melodies," which suggest a development from speech. A series of stages in which many cultures participated—types of scales, polyphony, rhythmic complexity, professionalization of music—is followed by a brief critique of the concept of "progress" with respect to the European harmonic, dissonant, and technological models and suggests that the interaction of the world's musics may be the future.

In his *Rhythm and Tempo* (1953), Sachs ties the origins of musical rhythm to body movements and to the rhythm of speech, suggesting that in many tribal societies—and thus perhaps in early humanity—men and women sang and, he tells us in his *World History of Dance* (1937), also danced differently. These differences, originally markers of gender, became widespread categories in rhythmic typology, and thus Sachs might be saying that there are really two or perhaps more separate but gradually merging histories of rhythmic behavior.

In chapter 5, I comment on a number of the twentieth-century ethnomusicologists who have engaged in comparative study, but only a few undertook to look comparatively at all the world's musics. The person whose work led most directly to the issues surrounding the "world music" concept was Alan Lomax.

Mieczyslaw Kolinski, a pupil of Hornbostel who contributed to many facets of ethnomusicology, seems to me to have been something of a predecessor of Lomax. As a large number of extended articles (e.g., Kolinski 1959, 1961, 1962, 1965a, 1965b, 1973) show, he devoted much of his career to establishing systems for the comparative study of musical style traits. Like Sachs, he seems to want most fundamentally to know what the musical world is like—and often by implication, whether it is one or many. More specifically, he asks in separate publications about the nature of the world's scales, melodic contours, tempos, rhythmic structure, and consonance and dissonance. The implication throughout his work is that in music, stylistic characteristics range freely. He seems convinced that what's really important is the diversity, but he insists that there is one lens through which it can be perceived.

Alan Lomax was outstanding among the scholars who tried to contemplate all the world's music. While he did not attempt to narrate the history, his development of a technique for making comparative descriptions of musical styles and his theories of the determination of musical styles suggest a specific view of the ways music history works. He recognized that each of the world's societies had a music with which it principally identified (the "culture's favored song style") and that all were equally worthy of attention. In most of his work, he viewed these musics from a synchronic perspective. Chronology was not absent from his considerations;

for example, in his early delineation of folk-song styles (Lomax 1959), he viewed the soloistic and virtuosic music of the kingdoms and empires in his "Eurasian" musical area as developments from earlier, more participatory cultures (see Turino 2008 for discussion of this term), and he saw his "modern European" song styles as being more recent developments than the "old European" of the outskirts of Europe. But if Lomax is viewed as a historian of world music, it is mainly in his concern with determinants of musical style (Lomax 1962, 1968). Famously stating that "a culture's favored song style reflects and reinforces the kind of behavior essential to its main subsistence effort and to its central and controlling social institutions" (1968, 133), he saw the world of music not as a single unit but as a group of musics, the growth of each being determined by its unique social and economic history.

I think the concept and maybe even the term "world music" isn't such a new thing after all.

4

A Tradition of Self-Critique

For Beverly Diamond

In these paragraphs I wish to explore the suggestion that ethnomusicologists, in the relatively short history of their field, have regularly criticized the directions and basic assumptions of their discipline. It is surely not unique in this respect—all scholarship and all science is fundamentally about overturning received wisdom and accepted paradigms—but I suggest that self-criticism of ethnomusicology has more frequently than most turned on the nature of the discipline as a whole and on the character of musicology at large. To an extent, I further maintain, ethnomusicology has tried to function as a kind of corrective for certain attitudes and approaches of music research in general. In any event, ethnomusicologists, more perhaps than people in other disciplines, devote a lot of their energy to criticizing the course of their field. One might almost say that the practice of critiquing the discipline as a whole is part of their identity. It is a practice that goes back to the roots of the field around the turn of the twentieth century, and periods in which disciplinary self-critique were significant arose several times. Recently, at the beginning of the twenty-first century, a good many scholars have again begun to use a sharply evaluative lens in looking at what they and their colleagues have been doing.

In the Twenty-First Century

Let me begin by mentioning three critical trends that have been gathering steam in the first years of the twenty-first century, though they began a few years earlier, trends suggesting that major changes in the identity and basic character of ethnomusicology, or its place in the academy, may be in the offing.

During the spring and summer of 2006, the Society for Ethnomusicology's Internet discussion list hosted a debate that began with well-founded accusations of a particular insularity among American ethnomusicologists and led to the issue of scholarly hegemony as paralleling political hegemony. This discussion eventually moved to the issue of ethnomusicology as an international, or a universally applicable, or a nation- and culture-specific discipline. It is a debate that has its counterparts in some of the special-interest-group discussions at the society's annual meetings. To an underlying question of long standing in our field—whether data, facts, conclusions, and interpretations result from "objective" observations and universally recognized theory or in some ways rely on culture-specific or individual understandings—were added new issues, such as, "What kinds of persons should ethnomusicologists be? Should this be determined by your national or ethnic identity?" The notion that there are many ethnomusicologies—American, but also African American, Indian, Chinese, and so on—was aired, as was the contrary view that ethnomusicology requires a Western perspective. It was pointed out, for example, that in the second edition of *The New Grove*, no Indian or Chinese scholars specifically identified as ethnomusicologists were listed, whereas dozens of Europeans and North Americans were. This is both an accusation of neglect and an interpretation of different national attitudes toward the "e-word," for we know that many scholars from these two most populous nations don't like the term *ethnomusicology* and prefer to be known as "musicologists," even if their interests intersect with those of North American "ethnomusicologists." But the tone of the Internet discussion suggested that American ethnomusicologists weren't happy with their role and their image in the world of scholarship, and some ethnomusicologists elsewhere agreed with them. There was discussion of the insularity of all nationally defined groups of scholars, but the political and economic power of the United States gave the tendency of American scholars to isolate themselves from the rest of the world an especially undesirable aura. Everyone engaging in this discussion wished to increase the opportunity for crossing cultural and national academic boundaries.

The second trend involves determining whether we still need something called ethnomusicology. Early in the current century, Martin Greve (2002), known for his work on the musical culture of Germany's Turkish population, published an article subtitled "Vom notwendigen Verschwinden der 'Musikethnologie,'" (About the necessary disappearance of "ethnomusicology"), arguing that the kinds of research most academicians associated with ethnomusicology—the study of the musical and cultural "other" and fieldwork in a foreign environment—needed no longer (*could* no longer) be carried out and that whatever work can now usefully be done by ethnomusicologists should be subsumed in the larger discipline of musicology. Greve proposed that changes in the world of music over the previous twenty years—with respect to technology, communication, and politics—had undermined any justification of ethnomusicology as a separate field. In Germany, where academic positions in ethnomusicology have been declining in number, Greve's article (published next to an article criticizing the configuration of musicological training in Germany at large, by Adam, Heesch, and Rode-Breymann, "Über das Gefühl der Unzufriedenheit in der Disziplin" [2002; On the feeling of discontent in the discipline]) made a considerable splash, generating a debate about the continued usefulness of traditional ethnomusicology, with its configuration of methods centering on fieldwork and comparative study. It was all about getting rid of or holding on to disciplinary boundaries.

The third trend to develop around this time involves a different sort of erasure of boundaries. In the 1950s, scholars and teachers devoted a lot of energy to differentiating among art, folk, and popular music and other similar categories. Today, little attention is paid to these boundaries and to definitions of these terms, which are used far less in our literature than had been the case earlier, when North American and European scholars were eager to demonstrate that other musical cultures *did*—like their own—consist of various strata of music-making, that they all *did* have something like, or analogous to, the separate folk, classical, popular, or sacred and secular traditions. Now we're not sure that these distinctions work so well in any society, or at least we generally maintain that each society has its own configuration of musical strata. Indeed, the concept of the world of music as consisting of distinct and separable "musics," one of the paradigms of the second half of the twentieth century, has been under attack.

It is possible to argue that the world of music has changed more since 1990 or so than perhaps ever before, not so much in the creation of new sounds, styles, or genres as in the ways in which music is communicated and in the experience of musical perception. "Musics," if we can still use the term, are changing to be more like one another. Western harmony and Western instruments encroach onto traditions that were once dramatically distinct; at the same time, African and African-derived rhythmic structures and practices invade and often dominate, and timbres from India, the Middle East, and Indonesia change the ideals of sound. Concepts such as concerts and virtuosity play an increased role. Thus, musical diversity in the world has probably decreased—in ways similar to the drastic decrease in natural languages (see, e.g., Nettle and Romaine 2000)—to be replaced by an increasing number of "dialects" in music (like the number of dialects of the dominant languages, such as English, Spanish, Chinese, replacing those disappearing tongues). Perhaps ironically, however, in the face of all this homogenization, the normal musical experience of the typical individual throughout the world—surely of the world's urban dwellers—who has access to radio, the Internet, and all the other marvels of modern technology, has become more heterogeneous, more varied. To put it very simply, the world has become poorer musically, but individuals, excepting perhaps those in the most impoverished societies, may have typically become musically wealthier.

Recognizing this—implicitly rather than expressly—ethnomusicologists have begun to change their approaches, looking less at musical cultures in their entirety (as did Merriam in his *Ethnomusicology of the Flathead Indians* [1967]) and more at specific cases—events, genres, individuals, institutions, pieces (see, e.g., Meintjes 2003, about a South African recording studio; or Danielson 1997, a study of the great singer Umm Kulthum). And they seem to wonder whether this approach ought not to have been followed earlier on, and whether perhaps it would have tied them more closely to the traditional musicologists.

I have mentioned three groups of events suggesting that ethnomusicologists find themselves now, in 2007, in an era in which many of them are vigorously critiquing the identity and nature of their field. I will argue that this practice of self-critique has periodically characterized the history of our field, and my purpose in the following paragraphs is to make some forays into the history of this critical tradition. No doubt similar trends could be identified in other kinds of music scholarship, but I propose that ethnomusicologists have made more of a project of it. Perhaps it is true, as Alan Merriam said, that ethnomusicology has always been "caught up in a fascination with itself" (1964, 3).

Early Ethnomusicologists as Nay-Sayers

In important ways, the field of ethnomusicology has at times functioned as a critique of general musicology—or more specifically, historical musicology. A good deal of its literature is couched as response to the typical traditional academician's view of music, contradicting and correcting conventional wisdom and accepted knowledge. When I was a student in the late 1940s—I was one of only two or three in my institution studying what would later come to be known as ethnomusicology, interacting with a much larger group of music historians—I found myself constantly responding to generalizations about world music (or just plain "music") with contradictions such as "Yes, but in Central Africa they don't do this," or "It's quite different among the Arapaho." And when confronted with assertions about the specialness of Western music and its theory, I would say, "No, they have something equally complex in India." At that time, if someone had told me that ethnomusicologists were interested in universals, I would have countered by pointing to the specialness of each culture.

My gainsaying was not novel, however; more than a half-century earlier, the contradiction of conventional wisdom characterized some of the field's earliest publications. A. J. Ellis's epochal article "On the Musical Scales of Various Nations" (1885, 526–27) ends on a similar tone: "The final conclusion is that the Musical Scale is not one, not 'natural,' nor even founded necessarily on the laws of the constitution of musical sound . . . but very diverse, very artificial, and very capricious." A few years later, Carl Stumpf, too, tried to correct widely held assumptions. A remark in a review essay about the earliest publications on Native American and First Nations musics sounds interestingly up to date: "Die indianischen Leitern, wie wir sie bisher kennen, gehören also keineswegs einem 'archäischen' oder gar 'primitiven' Musikzustand an. . . . Die Beziehung zwischen den Tonauffassungen ganz andrer Art sein, ebenso die psychologische und die historische Enstehungsweise" (Stumpf 1892, 142). Stumpf is asserting that the Indian scales, as we know them at this point, do not belong to an archaic or primitive condition of life. To understand them, one must accept the existence of a great variety of understandings about pitch, and a variety of psychological and historical conceptions of their origin.

Twenty years later, the first article to speak to the special problems and methods of what was called comparative musicology (Hornbostel 1904–5) also distances itself from traditional musicology. Three of its points struck me as especially interesting. (1) Hornbostel maintains that comparison is the principal means of scholarly comprehension, and he clearly means neutral and not value-loaded intercultural comparison. This has been an abiding defense of comparative approaches in the face of severe criticism leveled at it since about 1950. (2) Comparative musicologists must broaden their perspective of the kinds of musical phenomena that should be examined, going far beyond "tones" to a great variety of sounds, including those that are intermediate between music and speech, music and noise. Hornbostel, by implication, attacks a narrow conceptualization of music. (3) Music is changing rapidly, and one must "save what can be saved, before airplanes are added to automobile and electric trains, and all of Africa is dominated by tarara-boomdeyay" (Hornbostel 1905, 97); here he emphasizes the importance of preservation as central to the field while recognizing the need to take change into account.

One would expect the new field of comparative musicology that became ethnomusicology to begin on a positive and optimistic note, but both Stumpf and Hornbostel sound a bit pessimistic. Their tone contrasts with that of Guido Adler's enormously influential earlier article laying out the discipline of musicology—centered on historical study of European music—in a positive and optimistic mood and seeing a process of consistent progress toward a clear goal: "Jeder Schritt, der zu dem Ziele [Lösung grosser wissenschaftlicher Aufgaben] führt, jede That, die uns ihm näher rückt bedeutet einen Fortschrifft menschlicher Erkenntnis" (1885, 20; Each step that moves us closer to our goals [solution of major scholarly problems] signifies progress in our understanding as human beings). In contrast to Ellis and Hornbostel, Adler wants to look forward and does not complain that his earlier colleagues had been on the wrong track.

If this tiny sampling of citations serves to suggest the diverging moods of the musicologies a century ago, then comparative musicology entered the academy with the task of providing a corrective to widely held beliefs. It continues sometimes in this function, looking critically at the hegemony and hierarchy assumed by some historians of European music, trying to broaden the perspective of educational institutions, hoping to institute a vision of music as a universal and as a world of musics. In doing this, however, ethnomusicologists have found themselves in a plethora of intellectual, social, political, and ethical problems that led to its tradition of self-criticism.

Thus, the period of rapid growth, the 1950s and early 1960s, included several events that seem to have had criticism of past practices as a major purpose. The 1962 meetings of the Society for Ethnomusicology (SEM) summarizing the state of the field and the 1963 symposium on transcription and analysis that, it was hoped, would get us over the uncertainties of these venerable techniques may illustrate this point (the proceedings of each conference were published the following year in *Ethnomusicology*). The SEM's critical mood was reflected early in its history by two landmark panels that dominated the 1958 annual meeting, formally titled "The Scope and Aims of Ethnomusicology" but in later publications referred to as "Whither Ethnomusicology?" A brief report by McAllester (1959) summarizing papers and discussion shows the two panels to have elicited wide-ranging discussions in which each speaker proposed what should be done in his or her area, implying broad criticism of past practices. These practices included excessive concentration on analysis (e.g., interval counting), neglect of cultures close to oneself, and failure to respect one's informants. The participants spoke past one another, however, and it is clear that there was then little agreement on where ethnomusicology should go. The most conclusive statement telling us to change direction came from Charles Seeger: ethnomusicologists should include Euro-American music and persuade music historians to study the histories of other cultures (McAllester 1959, 102).

Alan P. Merriam as Archcritic

After the founding of the SEM in 1955, the critical component of ethnomusicology was driven by a small number of intellectual leaders, perhaps most prominently Alan P. Merriam. Outstanding among his many contributions was his continued insistence that ethnomusicologists must decide who they are and what they should do, that what Merriam perceived to be an uncomfortable diversity should be replaced by a unity of direction. Throughout much of his career, he criticized the inability of people who called themselves ethnomusicologists to come together with an integrated statement of purpose, and a number of his writings emphasize this issue. His statements of unhappiness were always expressed with moderation and respect for divergent views, but he was nonetheless the paragon of the ethnomusicologist looking critically at his field.

Merriam's first significant publication on the subject, titled simply "Ethnomusicology: Discussion and Definition of the Field" (1960), was published shortly after he had completed a term as the first editor of both the SEM's newsletter and its journal, launching both publications. Noting that the literature of ethnomusicology was dominated by description and analysis of music, particularly melodic and pitch phenomena, as well as interest in taxonomy of musics and the origins of music, he hailed the broadening conceptualization of this field, praising what he saw as pioneering steps to include all (and not just non-Western) music and all aspects of musical life. Although his criticisms of earlier practices are gentle, Merriam clearly wanted this article to signify the turning of a corner. Insisting that emphasis on studying music as sound alone should be abandoned, he ends: "While the study of music as a structural form and as an historic phenomenon is of high, and basic importance, in my own view it holds this position primarily as it leads to the study of the broader questions of music in culture" (1960, 113).

"Music in culture" was the definitive characterization—a kind of coat-of-arms—of ethnomusicology in Merriam's most influential book, *The Anthropology of Music* (1964), but he continued to be perplexed by the multiplicity of definitions in use and not long before his death published a major critique of the subject (Merriam 1977). Citing, comparing, and classifying some forty definitions culled largely from American publications, Merriam argued that the proper way of defining a field is not simply to observe what its practitioners do but to formulate what it ought to be. He appears in this article to have given up the desire to unify, closing by saying, "I have no doubt that new definitions of ethnomusicology will continue to be proposed and that they, too, will reflect the growing maturity of the field and its practitioners" (1977, 198). Still, a tone of frustration appears in his discussion of definitions that stress "form" (i.e., the materials or peoples to be studied) against those focusing on "process" (i.e., the ways things are done, both by the world's peoples and by ethnomusicologists), which he clearly favors.

I think the field has indeed moved in Merriam's direction. Nevertheless, one may be bemused to find that the Society for Ethnomusicology avoids any specific definition, tending rather to dissimulate. In its mission statement, the SEM says it aims to "promote the research, study, and performance of music in all historical periods and cultural contexts." Its constitution says simply that the society exists "to promote research and study in the field of ethnomusicology." On its inside cover, the journal *Ethnomusicology* announces that it publishes articles in the field of ethnomusicology, "broadly defined." I'm astonished that a society with such a vague notion of what it includes can have been so successful—or perhaps the vagueness caused its success. The attitude of the International Council for Traditional Music (ICTM) is similar. When I was about to begin a three-year term as the editor of its yearbook, I asked ICTM president Klaus Wachsmann whether I should make an editorial statement of the publication's mission. "Oh no," he replied, "you could get into a lot of trouble telling people what they should or shouldn't include in 'ethnomusicology.'"

Relating to the World's Musicians

During the 1970s, it seems, North American ethnomusicologists were particularly concerned with a critical look backward and the need to change directions. A number of facets of this movement may be distinguished, but mostly it concerns issues that are fundamentally social or ethical, significantly involving the differences in power relations between Western and non-Western scholars, between scholars and their informants or consultants or teachers, and within the North American ethnomusicological community.

Allow me to present the prehistory of this development. Little thought seems to have been given to the complex problem of these relationships until 1955 or so, but it was not completely ignored. Already in the first substantive analytical article on Native American music, Carl Stumpf (1886) commented on the differences between one's own culture and another's in the perception and interpretation of music, doing so when speaking of Nutsiluska, his principal informant in the band of Bella Coola people who were touring Germany, presenting songs and dances. In his case, the relationships were opposite to those subject to criticism later, for he claims (426) that he could appreciate Nutsiluska's songs (he didn't claim to "understand"; his words were "hineinfinden" ["enter into"] and "ohne Unbehagen hören" ["listen to without discomfort"]), but he insists that Nutsiluska would not have apprehended Bach's "St. John Passion." Never mind Stumpf's perhaps unjustified claim for himself and his condescending and surely wrongheaded view of his Bella Coola associate; he does broach the idea that there is no universal aesthetic standard.

Only gradually did ethnomusicologists come to embrace the (now laughably obvious) idea that one should find out how the members of a host society think about and analyze their music. How strange this concept may have seemed at an earlier time is illustrated by the obscure placement of one of the first articles on the subject, "Music in the Thinking of the American Indian," by George Herzog (1938), which in a few pages touches on the fundamental concept of music in a number of Native American traditions, making points that later researchers would have made the subject of extended discourse. This article seems to me to be enormously important in the history of our field, and yet neither Herzog himself nor the world of ethnomusicologists (then or now) seems to have accorded it much respect. I have always been astonished that these concepts did not play a major role in Herzog's better-known and larger works on the same musical cultures and that this article—which appeared in the most obscure of publications—was not quickly reprinted in a major journal. Clearly these issues were seen in 1938 as quite secondary.

It took some decades before we began to think that perhaps we couldn't understand someone else's music at all, and longer yet for this critique to be joined by a related question: what are the social and political implications of doing research "on" people best designated as "the other?"

The first of these two connected developments may best be dated to the 1960s and associated with anthropology's development of "the new ethnography," which emphasized the importance of discerning a society's own perception and appraisal of its culture, produced the concept of the "emic/etic" contrast, and ultimately cast doubt on the possibility of positivistic objectivity. Through the 1990s, this view pervaded the fields that participated in postmodernism, and in ethnomusicology its earliest statement may be Merriam's discussion of "folk" and "analytical" evaluations in ethnography (1964, 209–10).

The coalescing of these issues has to do with the Western academic society's recognition of the need to face issues of intercultural (and intracultural) power relations. The development of the emic/etic interface in the 1970s may be the starting point, but beyond that, it seems fair to claim that during this decade more than any other, the papers read at meetings of the SEM and the special panels looked at the past quite reproachfully. An uncommon number of paper titles begin "Toward a . . .," suggesting the need for and proposing new methods and approaches.

Thus, in 1970 the SEM established the "Committee on New Directions," whose charge was to study and make recommendations for the improvement of all these relationships. Although it didn't accomplish much, it marked the beginning of a permanent component of the organization eventually collected under the label "ethics." This component was represented by a succession of various committees, study sessions, and policy discussions, and such considerations now characterize the field, much in contrast to other societies for the study of music—the American Musicological Society, International Musicological Society, Society for Music Theory, and Society for American Music—in which these matters are more typically left to individual discretion.

During the 1970s and 1980s, one of the most prominent critical voices was that of John Blacking. Throughout his career, Blacking questioned many concepts of conventional wisdom: tradition, change, musicality, and nature and nurture in music. He did this in a number of important publications whose very titles suggest that we ought to turn a corner: "Some Problems of Theory and Method in the Study of Musical Change" (1979), "Towards a Theory of Musical Competence" (1971), and "Challenging the Myth of Ethnic Music" (1989); the rhetoric of his most influential book, *How Musical Is Man?* is full of normative statements such as this: "we must be able to describe exactly what happens to any piece of music. . . . we shall never be able to do so until . . ." (1973, 89). Reading Blacking over the years, I always had the feeling that, despite his polite respect for earlier publications, he believed the field had taken a lot of wrong turns and needed to be redirected.

Among the influential publications of this period central to the tradition of critique, one of the most vehement is K. A. Gourlay's "Towards a Reassessment of the Ethnomusicologist's Role in Research" (1978), which argues for the researcher's active political and social involvement to liberate and save music (and not just by archiving it) and its people(s) and against the possibility of pure objectivity. Gourlay ends with a bleak picture of what may happen if we don't change our ways:

> When the oil runs out, coal reserves are exhausted, and solar energy discovered to be pie-in-the-sky, the seas polluted with atomic waste and the lands so overpopulated that there is no room for crops, the Karimojong [of Uganda] may yet have the last laugh, as they trudge around the periphery of their land in search of water, driving their cattle before them, and entertaining themselves with a new song to celebrate the mounds of useless motor-cars, the unplayable tapes of their own music rotting in the archives of the West, and people who have recovered the use of their legs but have forgotten how to sing. (32)

What Are We Doing There?

The most significant area of ethnomusicological self-criticism of the late twentieth century may be nicknamed "What are we doing there?" The entire course of intercultural study, the validity of participant-observer fieldwork, the intellectual and political implications of cross-cultural study, and the translatability of cultures—all these were and continue to be called into question. One thrust of this field of consideration concerns what has broadly been called "ethics" and includes the rapid growth of self-reflection and self-awareness of scholar within environment. According to Slobin (1992a, 329), publications that speak to the issue of ethics were rare or absent before 1970, and a brief statement by Barbara Krader in *The New Grove* (1980) was the first mention of it in a standard reference work.

A second strand signals the rise of—or renewed attention to— "ethnomusicology at home," however "home" may be defined, a kind of concern once considered the closest thing to "armchair ethnomusicology" and thus relegated to a kind of second-class status supposedly requiring less effort, knowledge, commitment, and perhaps courage.

By the late twentieth century, then, a good many voices were raised to support the claim that the central ideas of the previous hundred years had been misguided and that in important respects ethnomusicology on the American and Western European model had moved in the wrong direction. Among the most influential authors speaking to this issue has been Kofi Agawu. An example of misdirection, Agawu claims (see Agawu 1995, 2003), is the unified concept of "African music" as held by mainstream ethnomusicologists, which he portrays as an invention of Western scholars sitting in their armchairs, with no correspondence to African or objective reality.

The dissatisfaction many of the world's scholars felt with the standard intercultural approach was driven home to me at a 1988 conference attended by American and (then) Soviet scholars. The Soviet scholars did not appreciate the Americans' desire to do fieldwork all over the world; they viewed this as a kind of scholarly colonialism that took unfair advantage of musicians and local scholars and were convinced that it resulted in inadequate scholarship. Instead, they promulgated the practice of doing research in our own nations, regions, or communities, where, since we are scholars, we would still be seen as "outsiders."

The last two decades have seen a considerable increase in the proportion of papers and publications dealing with music at "home," taking account of the increased diversity of the "home ground" and the population of scholars and including topics related to ethnic, national, generational, and economic minorities. This increase shows the effectiveness of this most recent line of criticism. At the same time, there is a tendency for ethnic and other communities to try to restrict the amount of observation by rank outsiders. Thus, "What are you doing here?" is the question behind the increased disinclination of Native American communities in the United

States to tolerate fieldwork by outsiders. The concept of the "field" has been thoroughly reconfigured. And there's the newly established area of applied ethnomusicology, with its purpose of using ethnomusicological knowledge to benefit people and communities other than those of the scholars and their students.

"What are we doing here?" applies as well to the growing understanding that the position of the observer and the identity of the participant are essential considerations in fieldwork and interpretation. Most significantly, the constantly expanding literature of gender studies in ethnomusicology is perhaps the largest body of writing in which ethnomusicologists critique their past, but here of course we have lots in common with many disciplines. The total thrust of works such as, for example, Moisala and Diamond's *Music and Gender* (2000), seems to me that we should all start over, with a different perspective, different methods, and new forms of interpretation—which is not at all an unreasonable directive, were it possible to undo the past, and surely appropriate for the future. This thrust is, of course, part of the strong movement of gender studies in academia worldwide, but in ethnomusicology one should also see it as part of the field's unique tradition of self-critique.

The Monkey on Our Back

I've mentioned the word *comparative* several times already, but it stands at the center of what I think was the most significant change in attitude during the twentieth century. The issue of comparison has been a kind of monkey on our disciplinary back for over a century, and its history is broached in chapter 5. It is a story with many twists and turns, but briefly, whereas the value of intercultural but also intracultural comparative study has gone up and down through the history of our field, the term *comparative* suffered a sudden decline after 1950, for reasons that only partly relate to actually carrying out comparisons.

The term *vergleichende Musikwissenschaft* may have first been uttered in print by Adler (1885, 14), who used it in his text as if everyone knew what he meant, even though his outline of musicology employs a synonym, *Musikologie* ("musicology"?); he probably chose that term, with its *—ology* suffix, to emphasize the subject's scientific nature: the study of the world's musics "for examination and comparison for ethnographic purposes." *Vergleichende Musikwissenschaft* was not perhaps a happy choice of term, but in its time it was clearly understood to suggest multicultural scope. The term was used, though not widely; surveying the literature before 1950 I find it in a few titles of articles by Hornbostel, the title of a journal, and of a compendium of studies. It did not overwhelm the early-twentieth-century scholarly reader in the way the term *ethnomusicology* appeared in many titles and in virtually every piece of ethnomusicological writing for some years after 1955. There's an odd discrepancy: the terminological change from *comparative musicology* to *ethnomusicology* was supposed to accompany a major paradigm shift, from comparison of musics to the study of music in culture, from musicological to anthropological concerns. Before 1950, however, when the field was called "comparative musicology," there really wasn't a lot of explicitly comparative study to which the term could explicitly refer, certainly not intercultural, though there were a few publications involving Kulturkreis geographic distributions, some on musical areas, and a number on tune relationships. In contrast, research on music in culture was common enough—old-fashioned by later standards, but hardly absent. But the name change to *ethnomusicology* was presented in 1953, in the first SEM newsletter, and embraced almost immediately in the Anglophone world and elsewhere. It was even announced in synthetic works by such authors as Curt Sachs (1959, 4; 1962, 15). The change in name, though, did not accompany any brave statements about changes in direction, and it soon became clear that two major proponents of what was called ethnomusicology, Alan P. Merriam and Mantle Hood, had totally different ideas of what the word meant. Nevertheless, I think the change in terms functioned as an important critique about the positioning of ethnomusicology among disciplines.

The point is that while comparative study, as illustrated by many works of Mieczyslaw Kolinski and Alan Lomax, did not cease in the 1960s and 1970s, continuing to occupy about the same proportion of research as it did before 1950, it received less attention and respect. But why is that so? There seemed to be lots of good reasons to be wary of comparative study as the defining strand of this discipline. "Is our music interesting only so it can be compared to other musics?" was a common question of musicians from Africa and Asia. Or comparative study was denigrated because it ultimately sought to uncover universals, which doesn't work anyway; because it was simply directed to useless speculation about history and prehistory; or because we can't carry out comparison until we know properly what we are comparing, a criticism often voiced by Mantle Hood. Further, it would be pointed out that each musical system is so complex that it can be understood only on its own terms. We can do statistical comparison on repertories and styles, in the manner of Sachs, and Kolinski, and Lomax, but comparative study is harder when we try to carry it out on ideas about music and music in human behavior. We compare structures but aren't able to compare meanings. All these claims have been voiced as objections to comparison. The point is that about 1950, various notions coalesced to create a movement that worked hard, and with some success, to move away from the concept of ethnomusicology as the field of intercultural comparison.

The effort after 1955 was not single-minded. After all, Kolinsky and Lomax published their most significant works later. In addition, some people were of two minds on the subject. In his last work, published posthumously in 1982, Merriam, who had once denigrated comparative study as being concerned only with history, included an article titled "Objections to Comparison," an energetic rejoinder to anticomparativists. Nevertheless, the field moved in other directions, and in the 1980s and 1990s comparative study became a kind of bywater to the dominant trend in ethnomusicology, which was to carry out detailed, thick ethnography with essentially culture-specific interpretation.

Quite interestingly, the years after 2000 seem to have produced the beginnings of a contrary movement, as some ethnomusicologists have criticized the avoidance and discouragement of comparative study and recommend its revival, albeit in more sophisticated forms. As examples, let me mention an article by Martin Clayton (2003), and works by Mervyn McLean (2006) and Albrecht Schneider (2006). Particularly notable, further, is a long essay by Victor Grauer (2006) that envisions a successor to cantometrics, with the hope of uncovering a kind of world prehistory of music back to its origins. An ambitious group of endeavors. As a group— with some others—they constitute the kind of disciplinary critique that seems to characterize the history of ethnomusicology every few years.

Conclusion

Merriam thought that what we needed was a unified methodology and a body of theory we all espoused. At the end of his life, he gave up on this. But he had established the threefold model of music, although he did not propose that it should be the discipline's coat-of-arms, and aspects of it remained, at least in the sense that a single question could subsume the purposes of the discipline. Recent versions of this approach—that we ought to reduce the fundamental purpose of this field to a single question—are best illustrated by articles by Timothy Rice (1987, 2003), who, drawing on a critique of Merriam's model and others associated with it, produced what he considered to be a statement of the field's fundamental question, a kind of umbrella for all research, under which individual projects would occupy small spots. Rice asked his basic question for the field of ethnomusicology in 1987: "How do people historically construct, socially maintain, and individually create and experience music?" Later, in 2003, he reformulated but continued a three-dimensional model. He abandoned the static model of cultures that he considered (2003, 151) characteristic of ethnomusicology in Merriam's time and emphasized their dynamic nature, looking to ethnographies that "trace the movement of subjects in location, metaphorical understanding, and time, and the differing experiences that such movements entail" (174). In both cases, the purpose was to turn the field around.

My contention that ethnomusicology has far surpassed other fields of music research in its tendency toward changes of direction wrought by self-criticism—criticism of the practices and procedures of the discipline going far beyond correction of details and culture-specific findings—is certainly impressionistic and not based on any hard data. Yet the historical record indicates that comparative musicologists and ethnomusicologists have changed their ways frequently and dramatically over the last century, changed perhaps, if we compare today's practices with those of 1905, beyond recognition. They parallel changes in technology both in musical culture and in research techniques; in the world's politics, economics, and social organization; in societies' conceptions of music; and more. These changes clearly also result from the fact that we, as scholars, interact not only with written and recorded and filmed data but also, much more importantly, with human beings.

And so, many of our publications—more than those of our colleagues in the humanities—are not principally about field data or analysis; instead, they are about how we as a profession go about our work, and much of this concern appears, as well, in the culture-, repertory-, and musician-specific studies. Around and shortly after 2000 CE, however, we see an unusually large body of critique, while at the same time the world of music changes more rapidly than ever before. Some propose that we have been concerned with the wrong things all along. Many ethnomusicologists have become uncomfortable with the "e word" and wonder whether it properly explains what they do and what it may suggest to others.

Revisiting Comparison,
Comparative Study, and
Comparative Musicology

· ·

This is a meditation about the concept of comparison in ethnomusicology and its history. I wish to contemplate some of the central literature defining comparative study, briefly sketch the history of some of this endeavor's major landmarks, and also—since some conclusions come from observation of oral rhetoric and discourse—bring in a personal perspective. Some important surveys of this history have been published recently, particularly by Albrecht Schneider (2006), Mervyn McLean (2006), Victor Grauer (2006), and a bit earlier, Martin Clayton (2003). My comments cover much the same ground, although—particularly compared to Schneider's essay—less comprehensively, and thus they present little that can be claimed as new data or information. I am grateful to Albrecht Schneider for inviting me to write on this subject so as to contribute to the dialogue about essential aspects of the history and future of ethnomusicology that has in effect been initiated by these publications. Professor Schneider has also made significant recommendations regarding the content of the ensuing paragraphs.

Let me begin with three observations, which I will then expand.

First, the term *comparative musicology* and its non-English equivalents, principally *vergleichende Musikwissenschaft* and *musicologie comparée*, existed without much controversy for about half a century. Then, after 1950, they were abandoned rather suddenly and rapidly, replaced by *ethnomusicology*, *ethnographie musicale*, and *Musikethnologie* (along with some synonyms), terms that have never been defined unanimously or with precision.

Second, in music research, the concept of comparison has over the last fifty years come to have a questionable and even unsavory reputation; nevertheless, a large proportion of the most significant research depends on comparison of one sort or another for its identity and effectiveness. Some of the concepts of greatest currency in recent scholarship—e.g., "world music," universals, evolution of music, diasporas—require, for their development, some kind of comparative approach.

Third, comparative studies in music are subject to difficulties and problems that require fine-tuning of method and careful insight into the relationship of cultures, cultural domains, and musical elements. Despite these difficulties, certain important aspects of music lend themselves particularly and perhaps uniquely well to inter- and intracultural comparison.

Schneider's view, and to a degree those of McLean and Grauer as well, places comparative study at the center of early research on non-Western and folk music, seeing it as a methodology that generally declined over the course of the twentieth century but is now encouraged by a kind of revival; my interpretation differs slightly. I am inclined to accord comparative study itself a position of modest prominence throughout this history but suggest that its prestige and the perception of its position at the center (or the outskirts) of the discipline have had a more oscillating history.

From Adler's "Musikologie"

In my days as a student, around 1950, my principal teacher, George Herzog, who was considered by many the leading scholar of non-Western music in North America and the vicar, if you will, of Hornbostel in the New World, talked unabashedly about "comparative musicology." In 1950, and again in 1955, Jaap Kunst (1950, 1955) was still using the term, though with caveats. As late as 1957, Marius Schneider (1957, 1–2) headed the first section of his survey of "primitive music" "Comparative Musicology." But of course the term goes back to the beginning of the late nineteenth century. Eventually the term was used to refer to syntheses or compendia of non-Western music, but it is interesting to see that the first lengthy survey, in the first volume of August Wilhelm Ambros's monumental music history (1862), which is full of comparative statements, does not use the term *comparative musicology*. Indeed, Jonathan Stock (2007) makes a good case for designating Alexander John Ellis (1885) as the first comparative musicologist, although to my knowledge he did not use the term.

I am unable to ascertain when the term was first used, but Guido Adler employs it in 1885, the year that Ellis published his comparative work, in the article where he famously lays out the field of musicology, with its two main branches—historical and systematic—and mentions as part of the latter something he calls "Musikologie." In the tabular outline (1885, 17), it is defined thus: "Musikologie (Untersuchung und Vergleichung zu ethnographischen Zwecken)," which brings up several questions. *Untersuchung*, best glossed as "investigation," is general enough, but what is to be investigated? *Vergleichung*, "comparison," is again vague, as its basis might be the world's cultures, one culture, one composer's oeuvre, and so on, but the purpose, "zu ethnographischen Zwecken," acknowledges the presence of a variety of cultures in the world and hints at an interest in some kind of relationship between music and other domains of culture. The concept of "ethnographie," in that period ordinarily defined as the description of culture without the theoretical underpinnings that might have required use of the phrase "ethnologische Zwecke," is also significant.

In his text commenting on the outline, Adler goes further. Although the outline puts "Musikologie" into the systematic branch, the text (14) gives it a status of a complementary subject ("Nebengebiet dieses systematischen Teils"), foreshadowing the tripartite scheme of musicology now widely used. The text (14) also includes, as a synonym for *Musikologie,* the term *vergleichende Musikwissenschaft*, whose task it is, says Adler, to compare the world's musics and to classify them. Why the word *Musikologie* is used at all is not clear, but my impression is that this formulation (i.e., use of the suffix *-logie*) may have given the concept a bit of a scientific aura, an attitude one later finds in Robert Lach's contemplation of the field (Lach 1924, 1925). In any event, Adler, whose interest in Western art musics was significantly aesthetic, perhaps saw the world's other musics as of interest mainly to sciencelike contemplation—at least for the time being.

I doubt Adler believed that classifying was all the musicological profession should do with non-Western music. Rather, I suspect that he saw this as a first step. Confronted with a vast body of hitherto unknown material, the first thing one might do (or maybe the first thing a proper Germanic scholar might do) would be to impose some kind of order, to classify and group. Adler depicts the goal as "vergleichen und nach der Verschiedenheit ihrer Beschaffenheit zu gruppieren" (1885, 14; to compare and group according to their distinct characteristics). The fact that he described "vergleichende Musikwissenchaft" as a new and "dankenswert" ("promising" may be the closest gloss) field, a field with lots of potential, suggests that he expected much more to be done than simple comparison and classification. And the repeated use of the term *ethnographische Zwecke* suggests that he saw the results of this field to have an important role in ethnography, ethnology, anthropology.

It's important to remember two other aspects of this article's context. First, this was a brave statement by a young scholar, a man who wanted to push ahead and probably saw this outline as the first of various future attempts. Born in 1855, Adler was only twenty-eight or twenty-nine years old when he wrote this article (though he never revised it over his fifty-five-year career). And his forward-looking conception of "vergleichende Musikwissenschaft" had to be based on a tiny body of research and literature.

The term *vergleichende Musikwissenschaft,* then, evidently sneaked unheralded into the terminology of the newly established discipline of musicology in 1885. It took twenty years for it to experience a kind of formal introduction. It occurs, interestingly, in an anthropological journal where the technical advance of sound recording is set forth (Hornbostel and Abraham 1904), but its first significant appearance in a musicological context occurred in 1904–5 when Hornbostel, in an article originally delivered as a lecture for the Vienna chapter of the International Music Society, began by saying, "Einem jungen Spezialgebiet einer Wissenschaft fällt die Aufgabe zu, seine Daseinsberechtigung zu erweisen" (1904–5, 85; A new specialty within a discipline has the task of justifying its existence [my translation]). Hornbostel then turned to a defense of comparison, pointing out, given its significance in epistemology, the need to start by comparing the new with the known, and from this, thorough analysis of the individual manifestation may follow. Extolling the successes of comparative linguistics and comparative anatomy, he proceeded to suggest that musicology entered the comparative realm rather slowly because it lacked technology for acquiring reliable data, a situation that, however, was being mitigated by the recent development of the phonograph, which would now become an indispensable tool. The article goes on to discuss in detail aspects of transcription, interval measurement, and analysis, but in the end it does not go into the matter of comparison very much.

Conceptually, the field then remained on a kind of plateau, a period of about fifty years during which the expression *comparative musicology* was widely used but not widely examined. An occasional series, *Sammelbände für vergleichende Musikwissenschaft,* appeared in the 1920s, and the journal *Zeitschrift für vergleichende Musikwissenschaft* was published from 1933 to 1935. An important contrary example is the previously mentioned monograph by Robert Lach (1924), which introduces the field to an academic public but emphasizes the potential of comparative musicology for an understanding of the evolution of music, in a manner related to the methodology of parallel disciplines such as comparative linguistics and comparative anatomy, and, as he states more emphatically a year later (Lach 1925), to art history. In important ways, Lach reestablishes the cooperative relationship of comparative musicology and historical musicology, rather in contrast to the attitude of other scholars, for whom the two musical disciplines constitute opposite poles of a continuum. Lach's work, and a more clearly introductory book by Curt Sachs (1959) first published in 1930, also had the function of encouraging wider acceptance of the term.

But while some clearly comparative work was carried out under its rubric, the term *vergleichende Musikwissenschaft* denoted, it seems to me, two additional things: first, obviously, the study of non-Western music and of Western music outside the scope of Western art music, and second, an attitude that somehow, one could discuss all the world's musics under a single umbrella. In most respects, comparison was an informal discourse resulting from a desire to give broad characterizations for surveying the world's musics and to falsify widely held generalizations about human music. Responding, for example, to beliefs that pentatonicism characterizes only certain cultures, comparativists might have been inclined to reply, "No, pentatonic scales of various kinds are found in all corners of the world," or in reply to assertions that all cultures have musical instruments, "No, the people of such-and-such a place seem not to have any." But the literature on non-Western and folk music from 1900 to 1950 does not include much in the way of comparative statements. The "comparative musicologists" didn't do all that much outright comparing. They did, I think, believe that insights could be gained from comparison, that the term *comparative* suggested that one could look at all the world's musics from the perspective of one lens, and that comparison could lead to a new understanding of history.

Comparative Musicology and Comparative Method

In some of the literature (e.g., Lach 1924; see also McLean 2006, 310–17; A. Schneider 2006), there is the implication that comparative musicology requires a rather rigorous comparative method, somewhat like that of comparative linguistics (see Anttila 1972) or perhaps the (otherwise named) historical-geographic method of folklore (see Nettl 2005, 323–24), or in a more general way, that of comparative literature. Each of these fields developed a method of intercultural or interlingual comparison leading to a class of conclusions. Comparative study, as the terminology usually suggests, was thought to be the centerpiece of these disciplines. But in comparative musicology, no single comparative method was developed. While the concept of comparison may have perforce undergirded a contemplation of the world's musics, the great majority of published research studies before 1950 did not actually engage in comparison.

Nevertheless, a proper interpretation of disciplinary history leads us to several bodies of work—projects, they might be named—in which a technique of comparison is fundamental. Let me mention three examples.

The first technique is to find a way of describing musical style that facilitates the comparison of styles. Many of the studies of individual repertories by Stumpf (1886, 1911), Hornbostel (e.g., 1906), and the collaboration of Abraham and Hornbostel (e.g., 1906) try to establish a method of stylistic description that would make comparison possible and convenient. Thus, what has sometimes been called the "Hornbostel paradigm"—focusing on scalar structures and pitch relations and giving attention to singing style and tone color—seems to have been developed in part for establishing an approach to a description of music that might facilitate a comparative method. The purpose of enabling comparison was not emphasized (however, see Lach 1924 as a contrastive example), but perhaps these early scholars simply took it for granted that a single, broadly applicable approach would be essential at least for the early development of this discipline. Hornbostel's approach was taught, though only occasionally followed, by George Herzog, and it is in a sense the basis for schemes of comparative description that were developed, after 1950, by Kolinski and for the cantometrics projects of Alan Lomax during the 1960s and 1970s. There were other attempts to provide templates, including but hardly limited to the statistical approach promulgated by Merriam (Freeman and Merriam 1956) and a broadly applicable approach to analysis suggested by Herndon (1974). A natural accompaniment to these schemes for comparing musical styles are the numerous schemes for describing and comparing instruments, the best-known of which is that of Hornbostel and Sachs (1914). Some classification schemes for instruments found in a variety of cultures are themselves subjected to comparative study by Kartomi (1990).

The second technique that stresses comparison involves reconstructing history through the geographic distribution of style traits and instruments. The study of geographic distribution of music, important in music studies from 1900 or so and into the 1970s, has naturally required comparison. Much of this research makes use of comparison as an informal way of imparting information, but more specifically, several approaches were used for a wide body of data, or in divergent world areas or musical domains, justifying the term *comparative method*. Most prominent of these in the first half of the twentieth century was the so-called Kulturkreis approach, whose results were analyzed in detail by Albrecht Schneider (1976) and shown to have had far-reaching scholarly consequences. To list just a few of the influential studies following this approach, I will mention Curt Sachs's study of instrument distributions and the resulting chronology (1929); Marius Schneider's summary world history of polyphonic styles (1934), based substantially on geographic distributions; and the relationship of pentatonicism and matriarchal/matrilineal social structures in the work of Werner Danckert (see A. Schneider 1979; Danckert 1939). Although hardly as rigorous as the methodology of comparative linguistics, the attempts to present relationship clusters as historical strata can be considered a comparative method, though one whose general usefulness has not been established.

The musical studies that borrow their approaches from the development of the "culture-area" concept were more informally conceived and had limited ambition (see Nettl 1954a, 1965; Merriam 1964, 295–96; McLean 1979; Collaer 1958, 1960), placing more emphasis on taxonomy and less on historical reconstruction. Classifying the typical musical styles of Native American tribes or nations and grouping them requires comparisons of style traits—scales, rhythmic types, forms, sound ideals—and determining the degree of homogeneity and diversity within a repertory requires some kind of systematic comparison (see also Lomax 1968). Musical style has turned out to lend itself to comparison of this sort better than many other domains of culture do. Music as an aspect of culture—what Merriam called "behavior" and "concept"—are less easily quantified and have lent themselves less well to a comparative grid. The notion of musical areas belongs mainly to the period between 1935 and 1960. Although the construction of culture areas (by scholars such as A. Kroeber [1947], Wissler [1917], and Driver [1961]) rested on the assumption that those areas would have relevance to the reconstruction of history, with the use of guiding tools such as the rather vague concept of "culture climax" (intensity of concentration for a cluster of characteristics), musical areas have not been widely used for speculating about history.

The third and last technique I'll mention that implicitly stresses comparison is to reconstruct history through geographic distributions of units of musical content (rather than considerations of style). By "content" I mean identifiable works—usually compositions, but conceivably other units, such as themes or subdivisions (e.g., lines)—that can be identified even when some of their style traits change. This may refer, for example, to pieces that retain their identities through change of scale or mode in folk-song variants (for theoretical discussion, see, e.g., Bayard 1950; Salmen 1954; Jardanyi 1962), transformation of themes, arrangements, reorchestrations, and even divergent interpretations in performance. The concept of "musical content" in ethnomusicology has largely been used in comparing folk-song variants. Indeed, the concepts of variant and version, of tune family and tune type, have depended on the comparative study of units of musical content that are—or might arguably be—in some sense related. The distinction between stylistic similarity and genetic relationship has played a major role here.

One of the earliest examples of the study of "content" distribution is Wilhelm Tappert's (1890) suggestion that European tunes wander through the international art- and folk-music repertories, but it remained a major genre of research in European and Euro-American folk music into the middle of the twentieth century. A great many scholars have participated in this genre of study; besides those listed previously, Béla Bartók (1931), Walter Wiora (1953), and Bertrand H. Bronson (1959) should be mentioned. Each of these scholars was involved in distinctive national approaches to the issue. Fundamental to the study of tune relationships is the development of classification systems, which grew from the need to classify melodies in the burgeoning collecting movements that began before 1900 but whose formal beginning goes back to an exchange between Oswald Koller (1902–3) and Ilmari Krohn (1902–3). The classification of folk tunes declined after 1960 or so, although it continued to have a presence, especially in Eastern Europe (see Stockmann and Steszewski 1973), but it also influenced the establishment of tune classification in other domains of music, such as hymn tunes (Temperley 1998). Reconstructing the history of melodies by comparing presumed variants continued, though with diminished interest, into the late twentieth century (see, e.g., Cowdery 1990; Hungarian Academy of Sciences 1992).

While my interest here lies largely in the pursuit of intercultural comparative study, it's important to point out that comparative work of many sorts within a musical culture or repertory has never been abandoned, although in some respects, like its intercultural analogue, it has encountered conceptual as well as political difficulties. Some of the methodological problems—measuring degrees of difference and similarity, for example—emerge at all levels. Lists of studies making large-scale comparisons would occupy pages, and they would include work as diverse as comparisons of classification systems in Indian music (see, e.g., Powers 1970); comprehensive mapmaking projects, such as the musical atlas of western Rajasthan (Neuman, Chaudhuri, and Kothari 2006); and comparisons of performances in one mode by one musician (Nettl and Riddle 1974).

Arguments about Terminology

The bodies of literature just mentioned make significant use of comparison in various ways. The degree to which they are explicitly "comparative" might be questioned, but they typically do not consider the issue, provide no rigorous comparative method, and in the end probably do not constitute a large proportion of the studies on non-Western and folk music. Looking, for example, at the large body of literature on Native American music from before 1950, we see only a few publications (importantly including Roberts 1936) that engage specifically in intercultural comparisons, and only one (Herzog 1936a) presents itself as having a principally comparative purpose, doing so with its title, "A Comparison of Pueblo and Pima Musical Styles." Jaap Kunst (1955, 9) was surely correct in pointing out that "comparative musicology" directly engages in comparison no more than do other fields.

Kunst is said to have introduced the term *ethno-musicology* (with a hyphen) in 1950, but I seem to recall conversations showing that some American scholars (Melville Herskovits, Richard Waterman, Alan Merriam), using as models words such as *ethnolinguistics, ethnohistory,* and *ethnobotany,* developed the term independently and had begun using it informally at the same time. For Kunst, subject content—all music outside the scope of Western art and popular music—served as the defining element; for the Americans, it was the association of music with other domains of culture. It is striking, however, that the term *comparative musicology* and its German and French equivalents, enjoying a relatively calm existence for a half-century, were—as I previously suggested—rather suddenly abandoned and replaced. Soon after 1950, one saw the old term only occasionally, and *ethnomusicology,* sometimes rendered as *Musikethnologie* or *musikalische Völkerkunde* (see Bose 1953; Reinhard 1968; Olsen 1974), took over and began to appear frequently throughout the literature. There seemed at the time to be little resistance, and the change is sometimes mentioned with little explanation. When the Society for Ethnomusicology was founded, in the early 1950s, no one questioned the term (though the hyphen was briefly an issue of debate). Indeed, the notion of comparative study, growing in a number of social disciplines (see Sarana 1975; Warwick and Osherson 1973), played a decreasing role in statements about the principal questions of ethnomusicology (see, e.g., Rice 1987). Egger (1984) shared Rice's attitude; in an analysis of ethnomusicology (defined as the study of non-Western and of European folk music) in its relationship to other disciplines and fields, he devotes only one page (59) to a discussion of comparison, treating it almost as a minor area of activity.

Actually, a conscious shifting of gears becomes evident soon after 1950. Thus, Curt Sachs, in the 1959 revised edition of his 1930 survey, *Vergleichende Musikwissenschaft: Musik der Fremdkulturen,* points out the shift: "[der] alte name [dieser Wissenschaft], vergleichende Musikwissenschaft, führt irre und ist allgemein aufgegeben worden . . . sie ist Musikgeschichte geworden. . . . In den Ländern englischer Sprache ist der offizielle Name Ethnomusicology und in Frankreich, Ethnomusicologie oder ethnographie musicale" (1959, 5; The old name, comparative musicology, is misleading and has been generally given up . . ., has become part of music history. . . . In the English-speaking nations, the official name is *ethnomusicology* and in France, *ethnomusicologie* or *ethnographie musicale*). In his last book, *The Wellsprings of Music,* Sachs also introduced the new term, though with some trepidation. He admits that *comparative* is misleading, but "with or without hyphen, the word [*ethnomusicology*] is somewhat unwieldy and its meaning obscure to people who have not even a clear idea of musicology without a prefix. The musikalische Völkerkunde of the Germans and the ethnographie musicale of the French seems to put an exaggerated stress on the ethnological part of the aggregate" (Sachs 1962, 15).

Interestingly, this issue of terminology and the ambivalence regarding terms appears already in the previously mentioned first book devoted principally to theory and methodology of our field, by Robert Lach (1924). He asks (is he one of the "blind men" defining the elephant?) why the term *vergleichende Musikwissenschaft* should be used for a study of the world's traditional musics when this field does not engage in comparative work more than other humanistic fields do. Contemplating Adler's *Musikologie,* he finds it etymologically indefensible. *Musikalische Folklore* is too explicitly devoted to European folk music, and *musikalische Ethnographie* is unsatisfactory because it implies study of one individual culture at a time. Thus, he defends *vergleichende Musikwissenschaft*, which suggests to him, given certain caveats, the concept of all traditions from the perspective of a world of music (distinct musics?), a definition congruent with some—or at least parts of—modern definitions of ethnomusicology.

For Lach, the relationship of comparative musicology to natural sciences is primary; rather than consider the individual phenomena of music simply in their historical and cultural setting, comparative musicology contemplates them in the much broader framework of scientifically observable events, as part of a structure of a natural process of evolution (Lach 1924, 8, 12).

In any event, the arguments about the validity of the term *comparative musicology* and the role of a comparative approach to the world of music, seen as a recent phenomenon by some, have actually been around for a long time. So, while the "comparative musicologists," even including Lach, seemed to agree widely on their scholarly mission, the scholars who called themselves ethnomusicologists have had difficulty agreeing on definitions of their field (see Merriam 1977).

Objections to Comparison: Responding to McLean

One would think that this change of terminology, from *comparative musicology* to *ethnomusicology*, would accompany a significant change in scholarly activity. It is possible to make a case for seeing this as a major shift, and indeed, Mervyn McLean (2006, 314–16), in collating the history of the field, sees a general avoidance of comparative study as characteristic of the second half of the twentieth century. He thinks that the change in terms may actually have stimulated a kind of flight from comparative study but suggests several more seriously conceived reasons for what he considers an unjustified abandonment. He cites Mantle Hood, who in several publications and many lectures criticized researchers for making intercultural comparisons before they thoroughly understood the cultures, musics, works, systems, and so on to be compared. Other reasons McLean gives include the association of the concept of comparison with early and eventually abandoned conclusions of comparative study, particularly the Kulturkreis school; the complexity of music, which has both structure and meaning, each of which may be interpreted differently by cultural insiders and outsiders; and simply the difficulty of comparative study.

One of the issues that has confronted comparative studies is the difficulty of measuring degrees of similarity and difference in music itself, and even more, in musical behavior and conceptualization. Musics that sound similar to some may appear thoroughly different to others, and although both Hornbostel's analytical paradigm and Lomax's cantometrics method try to overcome the problems, lots of questionable conclusions have been drawn (see, e.g., Barbeau 1934, 1962).

I largely agree with McLean, and it seems easy enough to sweep away Hood's criticisms of comparison. It makes sense to say that, faced with an apple and an orange, one should not compare them before having examined each, though one could learn something important just from noting differences in color and acidity and thickness of skin, and perhaps geographic provenance, and from similarities in shape and size—without insisting on the most thoroughgoing possible chemical and biological examination. We can learn something significant, for example, from the recognition that typical structures of geographically distant Native American musics, such as the standard public ceremonial songs of Blackfoot of the Northern Plains, the peyote songs of the Oklahoma Kiowa, and the Californian majority of songs of the Yahi (i.e., the songs of Ishi), share an important feature—they are binary but use asymmetrical (sometimes called "incomplete") repetition—and this is significant even absent an accounting for other aspects of style and laying aside (for the time being) the interpretations that singers in any of these cultures might attach to the various form types. Thus (*pace* Hood [1963b, 233] and Blacking [1972, 108]), one need not know "everything" about a music before making comparisons, and one doesn't have constantly to invoke the difference between structure and meaning. McLean's last reason, the difficulty of comparative study, appears to suggest the importance of sloth in determining research design. Surely each ethnomusicologist has moments of laziness, some more than others, yet most research thrives on the difficulty of the task, so here I am not convinced.

McLean suggested, also, that comparative study was abandoned because its early manifestations—the work of the Kulturkreis school (he mentions Marius Schneider and Curt Sachs) in particular—came to be discredited, producing "an irrational distaste for the whole idea of comparison" (McLean 2006, 315). Fundamentally in agreement with this interpretation, I wish to offer some additional comments. After World War II, it seems to me, three questions were important in the general discourse of ethnomusicology in the English-speaking world: (1) Is comparative study valid? (2) Does it have political ramifications? (3) Should it be the centerpiece of this discipline? These questions lead to further considerations.

On the third question: if we undertake to engage in comparative studies, does this necessarily mean that they should be the identifying marker of the discipline? Some non-Western musicians—from Japanese to Indian to African to Native American—have over the years quizzed me along several tracks relevant to this question. Did the term *comparative musicology* suggest that we—Europeans and North Americans—studied their music only to compare it to ours or to compare non-Western musics to one another? What could possibly be the purpose of such comparison, if not to prove which music is "better," to glorify one at the expense of others, or to determine what stage a music occupies in a world history of music? Such questions clearly hit their mark. As late as 1957, Marius Schneider, in a subsection titled "Comparative Musicology," maintains that although the available material on tribal music is "of recent origin," he wishes to "bring into historical order the medley of primitive, transitional, and advanced cultures which still exist side by side" (1957, 1–2). According to Schneider, comparative musicology—the discipline—had as its primary aim "the comparative study of all the characteristics, normal and otherwise, of non-European art" (1).

But I also remember frequently hearing people ask just what was so interesting about the music of the Arapaho, or the Basongye, that a person should devote years to their study. I and my colleagues at the time, unable to be convincing about the intrinsic complexity of even numerically limited musical systems, often took recourse to the reconstruction of history, or the functionality of the music, or the understanding of the musical world and its universals, all of them dependent on large-scale intercultural comparison.

National and Disciplinary Politics

Let me expand further on McLean's thoughts. Although in general comparative study with historical agenda occupied scholars before 1950 only to a limited extent, some began to see it as the central marker and activity. After World War II, when scholars from English-speaking nations (plus some Dutch and Scandinavians) began to play a major role in the study of non-Western and folk music, the centrality of comparative study came to be disreputable for several reasons not directly connected with the concept of comparison. Broadly speaking, all have political foundations involving oppositions and developments that followed and to some degree resulted—often quite indirectly—from World War II: the defeat of the governments of the main German-speaking nations; the pressure to decolonize much of Asia, Africa, Oceania, and in some respects, parts of the Americas; the dominance of American- and British-derived styles of anthropological thought; and the growth of American music education.

The concept of "comparative musicology," with its ties to Kulturkreis theory, folk-music classification, and the Hornbostel paradigm, was seen in the militarily and also academically victorious nations as essentially German or Germanophone and thus associated—unjustly in most cases—with the racist theories of the Nazi movement (never mind that a number of the scholars associated with these positions were themselves victims of Nazi ideology). To many younger American and British scholars of the 1950s, it was important to get away from the old, the "German," the speculative, and certainly from anything that had racist implications. Thus, while the founders of the Society for Ethnomusicology expressed respect for Hornbostel and Stumpf, for folk-song scholars such as Bartók, and even sometimes for the stands of the Kulturkreis school (see Merriam 1964, 289), they and their colleagues wished to move in other directions, distancing themselves from the Germans and Austrians. The notion that musical style elements might be genetically (i.e., racially) determined, promulgated by some ethnomusicologists (see, e.g., Bose 1952), was abandoned for half a century for ideological as well as scientific reasons (see Födermayr 1971).

This attitude went hand-in-hand with newly conceived ideas about the relationship between scholars (from Western, "developed" nations) and the people whose music they studied. (For an early statement of the position, see Gourlay 1978.) This issue deserves lengthy historical treatment, but let me say only that with the early manifestations of globalization in communication, musicians and scholars coming from, say, India, Japan, or Africa saw no reason that their music should be limited to a subfield of the "real" musicology or that their music should be worth noting only in the context of intercultural comparison. The same kind of problem soon arose with the development of the concept of "ethnomusicology" and the occasional use of the term *ethnomusic* to denote music of the non-Western and Western "other."

One of the most important innovations in post-1950 ethnomusicology was the development of training systems that included the study of performance. A development most associated with Mantle Hood (1960; 1971, 230–45) and his successes at UCLA, and secondarily with David McAllester and Robert E. Brown at Wesleyan University, it was substantially aided by certain other conditions of its time. The interest of Western composers—especially Americans such as Colin McPhee, Lou Harrison, Henry Cowell, and Roy Harris—in Asian music and in such devices as the Orff gamelan led American and other Western music-education systems to an increased involvement with non-Western music. The centrality of hands-on approaches to music teaching in American universities, and American music educators' increased interest in giving students firsthand performing experience, tended to privilege Asian art-music systems—particularly the gamelan traditions—and focus attention on the uniqueness of these systems. Quite appropriately, as funds for extended fieldwork by ethnomusicologists and their graduate students became more widely available, scholars began to specialize more. Recognizing the complexity of even small musical cultures, and devoting themselves to individual societies and repertories, they put comparison on the back burner.

The comparative study of folk music, although often totally devoid of national issues, seems also to have suffered for political reasons, being seen by some as an expression of no longer valid nationalism and even irredentism and by others as an expression of radical political causes (Bohlman 1996, 2002a). Nevertheless, the concepts initiated by folk-music researchers— tune types and families, for examples—continued into the later twentieth century (see, e.g., List 1979a; Hungarian Academy of Sciences 1992).

Finally, there is the somewhat ambiguous role of anthropology. The decreasing interest in comparative study in the dominant anthropological schools—the disciples of Franz Boas, A. H. Radcliffe-Brown, B. Malinowski, and Claude Lévi-Strauss—significantly influenced musical studies. This was importantly true for Melville J. Herskovits (1945), who tried to measure similarities and differences in various cultural domains in a study of several African-derived New World cultures. Many anthropologists did still engage in comparative study (see O. Lewis 1956), but these researches decreased in significance as anthropology switched its emphasis from quantitative to qualitative methods and increasingly focused on reflexivity and interpretive discourse. One should not overstate the case, however. The occasional forays into comparative methodology in ethnomusicology—for example, those of Kolinski and Lomax—received, it seems to me, greater interest from anthropologists than from music-oriented scholars. Further, the central figure in anthropological ethnomusicology after 1950, Alan Merriam, tended to encourage comparison (McLean 2006, 315) and once admitted to me, in the context of criticizing "comparative musicology" as interested only in history, that we in ethnomusicology (including himself) seem to spend most of our time making comparisons.

The most vocal opponent of comparative study, as pointed out previously here and by McLean (2006, 315), was Mantle Hood, who considered it a major obstacle to progress, on some occasions criticizing such faults as "a premature concern with the comparison of different musics [that] has resulted in an accumulation of broad generalities and oversimplifications" (Hood 1963b, 233; see also Hood 1971, 343). Nevertheless, Hood too acknowledged the usefulness of comparative study—once the individual cultures being compared are sufficiently well understood—for solving certain problems and answering particular questions (1971, 342–44). Merriam, usually presented as intellectually opposed to Hood's approaches, does not look at comparison all that differently, having in the 1960s proposed a method and purpose of comparison different from that of the pre-1950 period and insisting "that the approach must be cautious, that like things must be compared, and that the comparison must have bearing upon a particular problem and be an integrated part of the research design" (1964, 53). During the period when comparison (as a concept) seemed to be particularly unpopular, Merriam (1982)—in what was probably his last work, published posthumously—wrote a lengthy article defending it against arguments proposed by Hood and Blacking.

But if the term *vergleichende Musikwissenschaft* seems to have been used most in connection with so-called tribal societies, its most prominent use in French appeared in the title of a work by Alain Daniélou (1959). His *Traité de musicologie comparée*, which was published in a series devoted to science and engineering, is actually a comparison of the tone systems of Chinese, Indian, ancient Greek, and European scales and theoretical systems, following a discussion of music universals that serves as a jumping-off point. Interestingly, Daniélou (1973, 34–46) on various occasions objected to the term *ethnomusicology* as degrading to complex art musics such as India's. Quite likely, the title of his comparative study is intended as specific to his project and not as a designation of the discipline in which he was working.

Opposition or Synthesis? The End of the Twentieth Century

For reasons already suggested, it has been widely believed that ethnomusicology started out "comparative" and after 1950 abandoned this approach and that various schools of American ethnomusicology claimed superiority over others by avoiding comparative study. In fact, however, I maintain that the studies of non-Western and folk music before 1950 were not, as Kunst also pointed out, "especially" comparative and that after 1950, comparative study continued to play a major role. The change in terminology, away from *vergleichende*, resulted from changes in political relationships among nations and parts of the world and in the nationality of the principal population of the field.

Further, scholars widely perceive a developing opposition in ethnomusicology between the anthropologists, who consider comparative study essential though sometimes dangerous, and the musicians, who consider musical systems unique and comparison dangerous and in the end impossible. Another strand of conventional wisdom has been to present the history of ethnomusicology as moving away from comparison. I suggest, however, that while this conventional reading of history reflects the dominant rhetoric, in actual practice the attitudes toward comparison have been fairly consistent, and comparative study has played a significant if not dominant role throughout the century.

Interestingly, publications that support and encourage comparative study continually appeared after 1965. The term *comparative musicology* is gone, but there is plenty of comparative method. An important survey of what had been done appeared among the many works of Walter Wiora (e.g., 1975), who, significantly, distinguishes between the terms *vergleichende Musikforschung* ("comparative music research"), by which he means individual research projects in which comparison plays a role, and *vergleichende Musikwissenschaft* ("comparative musicology"), which he takes to be the (unsatisfactory and obsolete) designation of a discipline. Wiora (1975, 7) criticizes the substitution of *Musikethnologie* for *vergleichende Musikwissenschaft* (i.e., *ethnomusicology* for *comparative musicology*) but does not propose a better term. He then proceeds to survey several dozen studies, largely published after 1950 and many from the years just before his book, that are in fact comparative. The developments in the world of music during the era of globalization have also given rise to comparative studies, such as Slobin's identification of "micromusics" (Slobin 1992b). Clearly, comparative study has not been abandoned; it has only ceased to be the diagnostic feature of ethnomusicology, and in some respects its existence has been "under the radar."

Perhaps most did cease to regard comparative study as the centerpiece of the discipline, but that was not true of Alan Lomax. His cantometrics project has to be the best-known interculturally oriented comparative project after 1960 or so, and there is no doubt (though perhaps he did not say so in print) that Lomax considered this work central to our field. Though seemingly abandoned for a time, it has recently—since Lomax's death—been revived, though also revised, by Victor Grauer. In a lengthy essay, Grauer (2006) argued that a more sophisticated approach to cantometrics—both the analytical method and the assessment of the relationship between music and culture—can provide answers to the most fundamental questions about music: its origins, its worldwide history, and its role in society. Grauer seemed to be proposing a paradigm shift, a return to comparative study as central to ethnomusicology.

Grauer's approach connects not only to cantometrics, with its interest in large musical areas of differing homogeneity, but also to the interest in universals that produced a number of publications in the 1970s (e.g., Blacking 1977; Harrison 1977; Wachsmann 1971; see Nettl 2005, 42–49). In the pre-1950 period in ethnomusicology, comparative study emphasized the diversity of the world's musics, and the dominant discourse reflected a desire to deny that they all had anything in common. It was the continuing interest in comparative study after 1950 that moved the search for universals to a position of greater prominence, to the extent that many scholars felt motivated to weigh in on the issue from one perspective or another.

This thread continued into the early twenty-first century, together with an increased interest, particularly in the English-speaking world, in systematic musicology, including cognitive studies, psychology and biology of music, and what has come to be known as "evolutionary musicology" (see, e.g., Wallin, Merker, and Brown 2000). Here a renewed interest in the origins of music has brought ethnomusicologists into a relationship to scientists reminiscent of Hornbostel's and Stumpf's use of the methods of psychologists and physicists and of Lach's interest in evolution. Comparative study has come to be broadened, seeking, for example, universals in human music to provide a base for comparison with forms of animal communication.

The need for a return to comparative study, but with a higher degree of sophistication, has been emphasized in an essay by Martin Clayton (2003), who suggests that comparison of one dimension of musical sound or structure (or of musical culture) must be made against a moving and diverse template, a kind of moving target. For example, to compare the melodic structures of two cultures, one must attend to the differences between the ways those cultures conceive of music—their theories of music. Clayton proposes to "address the relationship among sound, as an integral aspect of human interaction; the experience of producing, perceiving, and responding to that sound; and the processes by which people imagine that sound to possess structure or to convey meaning" (2003, 66).

This is surely what many of Clayton's predecessors had in mind. Their difficulty, illustrated constantly in Lomax's work, arises from the (relative) ease of dividing musical sound into elements that appear to be easily quantified or characterized (e.g., the number of pitches in a scale or phrases in a stanza) or classified (iterative, progressive, and reverting forms) compared to the problems of drawing such lines among the ways societies conceive of music. Thus, dividing the world into pentatonic and heptatonic cultures appears to be easier than separating cultures based on their ways of conceiving the creation of songs. Easier, to be sure, but perhaps also misleading, and possibly not capable of leading to worthwhile conclusions. A problem with comparative study has been our inability to find satisfactory ways of comparing, with equal degrees of confidence, all aspects of musical culture and sound. Albrecht Schneider (2006) therefore proposes a renewed association of ethnomusicology and systematic musicology, scientifically based comparative studies of musical structure (see also A. Schneider 2001).

How then to outline the history of comparative study in music research? Historians of Western art music have "always" engaged in a lot of comparison, but it has involved limited fields—a variety of versions of one work, the wandering of a motif through the works of one composer, the relationship of a composer's folk-derived style to the rural folk repertory he had heard, the similarities and differences between schools of opera as developed in different Italian cities, the question of periodization. Only in a few specialized studies (e.g., Becking 1928, whose classification of composers by rhythmic character into groupings headed by Mozart and Beethoven foreshadows cantometrics) did music historians attempt the kinds of things typical of ethnomusicological comparisons.

But the discourse in the world of Western art music—the response of audiences and the relationships among musics—is unremittingly comparative. Discussion of composers, works, and performances almost always takes place within a context that invites comparison (other Baroque composers, other concertos by Mozart, other interpretations of the Waldstein I've heard, other recordings of "Death and the Maiden," and "when I last heard her play this . . ."). Comparison in terms of quality, and merciless ranking. Small wonder, perhaps, that Indian, Chinese, and Native American musicians who are acquainted with Western conversational habits think that "comparing" means deciding which is better.

In ethnomusicology, responsible comparative study has never been judgmental, and one wonders why this issue should have become such a bone of contention. That comparative study may be difficult and requires careful methodology, that one must avoid drawing unwarranted conclusions, that one must be aware of the contexts in which the elements selected for comparison exist—these things one readily stipulates. Beyond this, the reason for the controversy surrounding the value of comparison has been largely an issue of terminology.

The history of comparative study has been two-pronged. As a practice, it has always been with us, subject in its individual projects to sometimes justified and sometimes unreasonable criticism. We have not been able to get on without it. In a kind of parallel history, the term *comparative* and the concept have had their ups and downs. Before 1950, the term was used often with insufficient justification, for comparison (we were reminded of this by Kunst, Sachs, Merriam, and others) did not play a special role. After about 1950, it began, sometimes justly and often not, to be associated with various undesirable qualities—racism and "culturism"; prematurity; superficiality; neglect of contexts; the understanding that in comparative study, some data will have to come from sources other than the investigator's own fieldwork; or unwillingness to recognize that each culture was worthy of study on its own. Even those studies that were clearly inter- or intraculturally comparative—to say nothing of the field as a whole—withdrew from the comparative terminology. More recently, and particularly in the twenty-first century, we may have become ready to admit that much of what we have always done has had a basis in comparison. Comparative study is again becoming respectable among a variety of recognized methodologies of the ethnomusicological arsenal.

II

In the Academy

6

Ethno among the Ologies

A slightly revised keynote lecture given in early June 2003, this essay has an exceptionally personal basis. The occasion was a conference celebrating the fiftieth anniversary of the graduate program in folklore at Indiana University and dedicated to Warren Roberts, its first Ph.D. recipient in folklore. The initial reference is to the Indiana University commencement on June 15, 1953, fifty years before the present lecture was delivered. It's the first of several occasions on which I used the lions-and-cheetahs metaphor.

Lions and Cheetahs?

It was just fifty years ago about a week from today (on June 15, according to my diploma) that Warren Roberts walked up to the podium in the old football stadium behind the Field House and received his degree from President Herman B Wells, his name called out by Graduate Dean Ralph Cleland. Actually, as the letter *n* precedes the letter *r*, I was just six or eight degree recipients ahead of him and thus some sixty seconds academically his senior. Warren Roberts was a good friend, and we took several classes together, principally with Stith Thompson, and in the early 1950s, my wife and I probably socialized more with folklorists than with anyone else. But I have to tell you where I'm coming from in this talk.

I was the first student here to undertake specialization and dissertation work in ethnomusicology—the name had been invented but wasn't yet very current, and we called it "comparative musicology"; my principal teacher, Dr. George Herzog, a professor of anthropology, used to call it, in a slightly gingerly tone, "the comparative field." In my last years of study, I actually took more work with anthropology professors than with anyone else. And my dissertation work, on the distribution of musical styles in Native American music, was most clearly inspired by Stith Thompson's comparative studies of North American Indian tales (Thompson 1929, 1953), by Carl Voegelin's classification of languages (C. Voegelin 1945; C. Voegelin and F. Voegelin 1977; and especially C. Voegelin and Wheeler-Voegelin 1944), and by Harold Driver's culture-area studies (based on Kroeber; see Driver and Massey 1957; Driver 1961). The people in the School of Music thought me something of an eccentric, maybe even an "apostate." But my degree was in music, and there was never any doubt in my mind that I was a kind of musicologist—one who should know something about anthropology and folklore and linguistics, but certainly a kind of musicologist. And the subject of my talk reflects this—should I call it ambivalence? Or ambiguity? Or ambidexterity? Or in some ways, maybe ambition—of ethnomusicology in its history in the United States.

When I wrote the title of this talk, I was perhaps unconsciously remembering a *Nova* TV program called "Cheetah among the Lions," depicting a rather sad situation in a valley where a tiny group of cheetahs were constantly being pursued and persecuted by a larger group of more powerful lions, with the few cheetahs who survived doing so only on their wits and their exceptional speed. The zoologist-narrator suggested that the lions were afraid that allowing the cheetahs to multiply would cut dangerously into the available food and water resources. A strange and unsympathetic association, I admit, but perhaps not totally inappropriate at certain times in our history (see Nettl 2005, 446–51). Moreover, the Music Department was not populated solely by "lions." Above all, those working in general or, if you will, historical musicology often accepted the ideas and concepts of ethnomusicologists and welcomed them as colleagues. When I was a graduate student here in the School of Music, in the early 1950s, the musicologists readily accepted me as one of them, and we made common cause against all the other music students, who looked down on us as mere scholars, as people who, once we graduated, would get in the way of playing and singing. But looking for a teaching job was another story. At teachers' agencies—that was the standard way of identifying music-department jobs in those days—advisers shook their heads sadly about such an outlandish field with an unpronounceable name. And when a job came along—for myself and for some colleagues—the musicologists sometimes worried. Do we really need someone to teach *only* courses on non-Western and folk traditions? If one spoke of the need for a second ethnomusicologist to balance the five music historians, one heard "The ethnos are taking over." Indeed, there was a time when the lions-and-cheetahs metaphor applied.

True maybe of the 1950s, the main period of my remarks. But not true in earlier times, and no longer true now, either. The predecessors of ethnomusicology before and shortly after 1900 seemed to be central to the developing musicology. The first two volumes—1885 and 1886—of the *Vierteljahrschrift für Musikwissenschaft,* the first journal claiming to represent musicology, contain twenty-three articles, and of these as many as five could be considered old-time ethnomusicology. Anthropology was involved early on, too, with figures such as Alice Fletcher, a bona-fide anthropologist, while others had nonmusical disciplinary associations as well—Carl Stumpf (psychology), A. J. Ellis (mathematics and physics), Otto Abraham (medicine), and even Erich von Hornbostel (psychology, anthropology) (for short biographies, see McLean 2006). But in the end, they all saw themselves as contributing principally to the field of music. Later, in the 1930s, when the predecessor of the American Musicological Society, the New York Musicological Society, was formed, some of its principal actors were theorists, such as Joseph Yasser and Joseph Schillinger; composers, such as Henry Cowell; librarians, such as Harold Spivacke and (then) Oliver Strunk; ethnomusicologists, such as George Herzog and Helen Roberts; and only a couple of traditional historians, such as Otto Kinkeldey, along with the great generalist Charles Seeger (Crawford 1984). How American musicology changed from a field in which various types of musicology were more or less evenly represented to one in which historians of Western art music were numerically dominant has to do with the immense diaspora of European humanistic scholars fleeing Nazism and Fascism, the Holocaust, and war (Brinkmann and Wolff 1999).

American folkloristics also changed about that time. It gradually consolidated into a coherent discipline from what had been a group of scholars—many of them principally collectors of antiquities—working in English and German departments but publishing a journal that made contributions mainly to anthropology, a group that, for leadership, looked to a group of Europeans who were more than anything else antiquarians theorizing and conjecturing about prehistory.

Back to musicology, though: while folklore was consolidating, in mid-century, musicology seems to me to have become more scattered. By the early 1950s, music historians had generally grown ambivalent at the idea that students of non-Western musics (to say nothing of theorists, acousticians, or psychologists) could meaningfully contribute to their general enterprise. Ethnomusicologists responded in several ways. One was to establish first the *Ethnomusicology Newsletter* and then the Society for Ethnomusicology (SEM)—which initially lived under the protective wing of the American Anthropological Association. Their second response was to develop a school, if you will, of ethnomusicology that looked at the music of non-Western, largely Asian, cultures from the perspective they perceived as that of historians of Western art music and music departments in general. This was the school developed in the first instance by the programs at UCLA and secondarily at Wesleyan, Michigan, and Seattle, and it had two principal characteristics. One was the privileging of art or classical traditions, with an interest in showing that they excelled by standards similar to those used by historians of European traditions. And since music historians were always expected to exhibit a minimum of competence performing Western music, the second was the heavy promotion of teaching non-Western traditions through performance by Americans.

Through the 1960s and 1970s, speaking now very broadly, two somewhat contrastive approaches vied for attention, Alan Merriam heading one and Mantle Hood leading the other, and if you were a student you could become an anthropological or a musical ethnomusicologist—or have a foot in both camps, if, for example, you chose to come to Illinois. But these two approaches had too much to give to each other to remain separate, and by the 1980s, I think, a kind of mainstream was established in practice but even more in training; the typical student got involved in performance, at school and in the field, and also read a great deal of anthropology. By now, I guess, even though there are misgivings about the authenticity of gamelans and mbira ensembles at American and European schools, as well as concerns about the usefulness of critical theory and worries about reflexivity, the validity of the culture concept, and what have you, a kind of mainstream type of ethnomusicologist developed. I used to worry—in the 1980s—that when members of the SEM got together, there was hardly anything that you could reasonably expect all of them to know or know about. Now I think there's a shared core of knowledge and commitment.

Of course, the activities of the typical ethnomusicologist changed enormously. I can hardly enumerate the ways. Let me try a couple. Preserving the world's music through field recording used to be a central activity; now we're just as much interested in the recordings, whether tapes, LPs, CDs, or videos, produced by these same cultures for their own use. The central technique used to be transcription. We still teach transcription and expect our students to have that expertise, but few spend much time doing note-by-note transcription in Western notation, and we have a larger arsenal of techniques. When I was a student, music historians were engaged in interpreting meaning, intent, significance of composers, works, genres, and so on; ethnomusicologists saw themselves as more scientific, establishing incontrovertible facts. More recently, the historians have become the positivists—excepting the few "new musicologists" whom I'll mention later—and we in ethno, along with our anthropological models, became the interpreters. At one time, *synchronic* and *diachronic* were the distinctive labels; now, we ethnos are just as much concerned with history as are those other historians. Long ago, we eschewed popular music and music that exhibited cultural mixes as inauthentic; now we're mainly interested in how musics and musical cultures affect each other.

What's It Doing in Music Departments?

At the 2001 meeting of the SEM, there were two panels titled "What is ethnomusicology doing in music departments?" I didn't get to hear them, but they were evidently very interesting. But when I described the title to friends in my school of music, and some others, they asked, "Why should this question come up? Where else should ethnomusicologists be?" By implication, these questions suggest that they have become established and now we need them. Most programs in musicology at major American universities now consist of the two branches, historical and ethno, interacting and sometimes competing, but always allied in relationship to other musical and outside disciplines.

In most of these programs, the faculty stands in a ratio of maybe two ethnos to three or four historians. A far cry from my own beginnings at Illinois, in 1964, when I was the only ethno among six historians and was nevertheless asked whether I would teach "only" ethnomusicology courses.

So the cheetahs have managed to survive—maybe by being more flexible and adaptive, and more imaginative, than the majestic but stodgy lions.

A survey of teaching positions and assignments suggests, very roughly, that maybe 80 percent of people who call themselves ethnomusicologists associate themselves principally with the musical disciplines, and only some 20 percent, with anthropology or folklore. But if you were to survey the publications that provide intellectual leadership, and the intellectual leaders themselves, you would find the proportion of anthropologically leaning scholars to be vastly greater. Moreover, the leaders who come from musical disciplines tend to have strong backgrounds in anthropology, too. So why have ethnomusicologists had so much influence on the field of music and not nearly as much on anthropology?

There are many reasons, no doubt, but let me mention a small study I carried out some years ago (see also chapter 8, "The Music of Anthropology," in this collection) to see how anthropologists—not those who specialized in ethnomusicology, the Merriams, Blackings, Watermans (Richard and Chris), McAllesters, Felds, and Frisbies, but garden-variety social anthropologists—have dealt with music in presenting the whole of culture in textbooks. I surveyed some twenty texts from the 1970s and 1980s. Most totally omit music; if there is coverage of music, it's brief, far less than is devoted to visual art and the verbal arts. And while discussions of art are likely to deal with Japan, India, and Native Americans, material about music is usually illustrated with examples from European symphonic music and American jazz. Social anthropologists who profess to love music exhibited similar attitudes. Oscar Lewis (1942), who did his dissertation fieldwork with the Blackfoot people and thus gave me helpful advice for my own work, was an excellent amateur singer of opera. He was naturally interested in and sympathetic to Blackfoot culture, but he couldn't see how I could stand Blackfoot music. Lévi-Strauss was immensely knowledgeable about Western music, yet in his thorough analyses of South American Indian mythology, he never goes into the obvious fact that many of these myths, when performed, included a lot of singing—which is perhaps more striking given that his best-known book, *The Raw and the Cooked* (1969), is organized by references to Western musical forms and, dedicated to music, gives a notated quotation from the French composer Jacques Chabrier.

The point is that in Western academic culture, musicians have made it known that others can't really understand and talk about music, while people in other fields stay away, saying, when opportunities for comment arise, "I'm no musician." It has to do with deeply held attitudes toward music in Western culture.

Those Good Old Days

Nonetheless, ever since 1885, when Adler published the first explicit definition of the field, musicologists have always claimed to include the kinds of things that ethnomusicologists do—study the world's musics from a comparative and relativistic perspective, study music in or as culture, and include all the different kinds of music in a society under their purview. Never mind that many musicologists in their own work and in their teaching don't always adhere to these criteria. And so ethnomusicology has affected the field of music more than it has anthropology and other social sciences. I have a feeling, for example, that at Indiana University, ethnomusicologists have a lot more influence on their colleagues in anthropology—and unquestionably on folklorists—than is the case at most other places, and I look back at my days as a student seeing a pleasant kind of togetherness in the basement of Rawles Hall and the folklore library in the old Main Library on Indiana Avenue, when the likes of Warren Roberts, Bruce Buckley, Dov Noy, Hal Hickerson, Jack Mickey, Howard Kaufmann, Dell Hymes, and myself would sit around and chew the fat, sometimes continuing to late-evening bull sessions. But it's actually a situation that didn't get transported elsewhere, and I look back to it with a lot of nostalgia, and with gratitude, and I think it was in those times that the particular configuration of studies that make up the Indiana University approach to ethnomusicology got started. I can't help digressing a bit, because one of the most vivid memories of my days as a graduate student here are of social events at Stith and Louise Thompson's house, on Ballantine Road. There's a bit of description and a photo in Dr. Thompson's memoirs, published only recently (1996), but I remember some of the songs. Stith always began with "Mary Hamilton" or "The Four Marys," and Warren Roberts would continue with "The Titanic" or "Acres of Clams." Dov Noy sang something from the Israeli storehouse of songs, and Bruce Buckley usually started with "Sam Bass"—who, as you know, "was born in Indiana, which was his native home; at the age of seventeen young Sam began to roam" and ended up in Texas, and you know that can be a bad end. Bacil Kirtley usually abstained, and I tried to help with a peyote song I had learned from an Arapaho singer who had visited IU. I was always moved by the fact that Stith Thompson, this great scholar who was supposed to keep his head in the motif index, could sing some songs; he gave me a new view of the world-class academician. Indeed, Dr. Thompson kept surprising me; in 1957, when my family and I were living in Kiel, Germany, the Thompsons appeared, invited by Kurt Ranke, a major figure in German folkloristics, and Stith proceeded to give a lecture in pretty flawless German. I gotta tell you, in 1953, I was happy to receive, as did Warren Roberts, a degree from the hand of Dean Ralph Cleland, the distinguished botanist, but I rather wished that Dr. Thompson hadn't just retired from deaning (he had been dean of the Graduate School for several years) a year earlier and had been present to give us our diplomas himself.

The events that really put Indiana University on the world map of folklore and ethnomusicology were two conferences: the third conference of the International Folk Music Council (IFMC) and the Mid-Century Conference on Folklore, held one after the other from July 14 to August 4, 1950. Sixty-five registered scholars attended the folklore conference. Its four sessions, which consisted largely of discussion panels that have been transcribed in a volume, *Four Symposia on Folklore* (Thompson 1952), were devoted to collecting, archiving, disseminating, and studying folklore. Scholars of verbal art and music interacted under the benign leadership of Thompson, whom the Europeans present obviously respected enormously (in an era when Europeans didn't so easily respect American scholarship). Some of the big wheels present included Otto Andersson, from Turku, Finland; Walter Anderson, from Kiel, Germany; Ake Campbell and Sigurd Erixon, from Sweden; Reidar Christianson, from Oslo; Albert Lord, from Harvard; and lots more.

But the music scholars who came to both the folklore and the IFMC conferences were possibly an even more distinguished crowd. It was during the folklore conference that I met many of the authors on whose publications I was later to depend. In 1950, having just graduated with my B.A. and only recently taken "Folk and Primitive Music" with Dr. Herzog—the only course on music he regularly gave—I didn't realize just how significant this event would be. Herzog was the local arrangements chair, rather a "round" job inimical to his square-peg personality. My task was to be his gofer and to help Dr. Thompson, too, and like a good part of the academic community of Bloomington, I was terribly excited. So excited, indeed, that I came down, at age twenty, with a case of measles that kept me at home for the middle ten days.

But I did hear a lot of the IFMC sessions and met Charles Seeger, Richard Waterman, Gertrude Kurath, Bertrand Bronson, Samuel Bayard, Marius Barbeau, Alan Lomax, and Barbara Krader, all people with whom I have often interacted ever since or whose publications I have used over and over. By the time the IFMC (then renamed the International Council for Traditional Music [ICTM]) met in Slovakia in 1997, I was the only one present who remembered the earlier event and could relate (Nettl 1998) to a group photograph of many of those individuals published in volume 3 of the IFMC's journal, which appeared in 1951. I marvel, today, at the youngish look of figures then in their thirties and forties, almost all of them now departed (Charles Seeger, Bertrand Bronson, Samuel Bayard, George Herzog, and Albert Lord), and at the middle-aged look of people now in the realm of legend (Maud Karpeles, Walter Anderson, Otto Andersson, Stith Thompson, and Marius Barbeau). All scholars on whose shoulders we now work.

After those meetings, everyone in folklore and ethnomusicology thought of Bloomington as one of the disciplinary capitals. And at that point I determined to stay on in Bloomington for graduate study. Anyway, at the end of the summer, Wanda came back from two months of being an art counselor at a girls' camp in Massachusetts, and I was ready to resume kibitzing in the Art Department's pottery studio.

Lions and Lambs

Excuse this digression, but I had better get back to the topic I left, examining in some detail the history of the relationship between musicology and anthropology in American academia and their differing emphases. No complaints: at my institution, the University of Illinois, down the road, I've been treated just wonderfully by my colleagues in anthropology, and so have the rest of the folks who teach ethnomusicology. I go to all their parties and am entitled even to attend department meetings. But very few graduate students in garden-variety social anthropology—not counting a few who specialize in ethnomusicology—take even a course or two in ethnomusicology. Conversely, virtually all graduate students in musicology take courses in ethnomusicology, though it's not a requirement. It seems that by now, in many institutions, one can't be a "complete musicologist" without knowing something about ethnomusicology, while anthropologists are glad to have ethnomusicology available but feel they can personally live without it. Of course, the music-department people think of ethnomusicology as an anthropologically oriented field; to them, one of the benefits of ethnomusicology is that it brings anthropological perspectives into their lives.

And so I come back to my contention that ethnomusicology has significantly affected musicology and music. I've spoken so far mostly in terms of education, of relationships in university and college departments, but the world of pure scholarship—I never thought I'd find myself using that term—participates, too. Of course, music historians think of ethnomusicology as a "smaller," younger brother, though the label of youth is not particularly justified, considering that both areas use 1885 as a kind of starting date. Ethnomusicologists think of the interests of most music historians as arcane, dealing with a corner of music that's definitely admirable but of interest to a small minority. And the people who are called systematic musicologists—those working in the psychology of music, psychoacoustics, cognitive studies, and the like—see themselves as the quintessential music scholars who are concerned with the most fundamental questions of all. (A lot they know!)

But things have tended to come together, and rather than lions chasing cheetahs, the metaphor changes to the lion and the lamb lying down together, though I'm not sure who should be the lamb. Take, for example, the recent compendium entitled *Rethinking Music,* edited by Nicholas Cook and Mark Everist (1999), the most important attempt in the 1990s to assess the state of music scholarship. This book looks carefully at musicology—music research—to assess the past and chart new directions. Six of the twenty-four essays are by out-and-out ethnomusicologists; about eight, by scholars well known as historians; and the rest, by theorists, semioticians, and students of popular culture. This compendium reflects developments in other major research tools. The revered *Grove's Dictionary of Music and Musicians* (*New Grove* 2001), its editions from the nineteenth century through 1954 a haven for true believers in the exclusivity of the Western art-music canon, was enormously enlarged in 1980, including for the first time long and authoritative articles on the musics of the world's cultures and on vernacular traditions. In 2001 the next edition appeared, enlarged from twenty to twenty-nine volumes, half of the enlargement devoted to longer and more thorough coverage of musics outside the canon. The same is true of the new edition of the German MGG (*Musik in Geschichte und Gegenwart* 1994–2007).

Giving space to ethnomusicology is fine. But is there really a substantive rapprochement? How is anthropological perspective brought to the humanistic historians? Are the two fields doing things that are more alike than they used to be? Let me mention two areas that suggest an affirmative answer:

First, the "new musicology" began challenging the more traditional musicology during the 1980s. Related to so-called postmodern movements in other humanistic fields, it began to move into new areas, busting the traditional canons of great music; incorporating gender studies, gay and lesbian studies, critical theory, cultural criticism, and many other kinds of interpretation, some very insightful (see, e.g., McClary 1991; Solie 1993;

and a number of essays in Cook and Everist 1999); and pursuing some others totally off the wall. Maybe most important, the movement foregrounded the notion that music can be understood fully only if one takes into account the culture from which it comes and in which it does its work, the culture that affects and constructs it. Where did the new musicologists get these ideas? Well, such notions have never been quite absent among historians, and not many have told me that reading ethnomusicology was what brought them to these interests. But the "new musicology" bears many relationships to the "old" ethnomusicology, and while some historians haven't liked to hear me say, "But we've always known or believed that," this turn of events provides lots of common ground, common areas of interest. One of the dramatic moments in this rapprochement occurred at a 1993 meeting of the AMS (see *JAMS* 48 [1995]). Its plenary panel titled "Music Anthropologies and Music Histories," consisting of two ethnomusicologists, two historians, and a theorist—but you couldn't tell them apart—was attended by hundreds, and the papers (about Renaissance perceptions of ancient Mexico, Western ideas of African rhythm, jazz, eighteenth-century opera, and Indian music scholarship) were all subjected to postmodern interpretation. There's no doubt that the emergence of the new, postmodern musicology has drawn music historians and ethnomusicologists together.

The second movement concerns a smaller number of scholars, but I feel that it's equally significant in cementing the interaction of musicology and ethno. It's what we sometimes call "ethnomusicology at home," and it concerns—as the term suggests—the ethnomusicological study of our own backyard. It's the kind of thing folklorists have always done, but my own earliest experience of it occurred when I began to teach at Wayne State University, where Thelma James was teaching folklore by assigning her students to collect folkloristic artifacts from their families in ethnic Detroit. Ethnomusicologists, however, have long promulgated the idea that the study of non-Western and folk traditions—excuse me for using such old-fashioned terms—calls for methods different from those required for the study of Western art music. When I tried asking questions I had asked of Native Americans, about things such as their taxonomy of music, in the environment of Detroit, I found some interesting things but didn't get much attention. By the 1980s, though, ethnomusicologists were more ready, and I think that the first important study of Western art-music culture by an ethnomusicologist was Henry Kingsbury's dissertation, begun under Alan Merriam, dealing with a music conservatory in the eastern United States (see Kinsgbury 1988). I tried my hand at this (Nettl

1995), attempting to interpret Western art-music culture as a tug-of-war between the values of Mozart and those of Beethoven (the values as we interpreted them, for these composers were probably very different from the pictures we conventionally have); from this I came to do an interpretive ethnographic study of midwestern university schools of music, mainly Indiana University and the University of Illinois. Kay Shelemay (2001b) worked with the early music movement in Boston, and students at Illinois did ethnography in local musical institutions, including their university's (Livingston et al. 1999). In various other ways, "ethnomusicology at home" made rapprochements with historians of Western music who themselves began to interpret what they found in ways related to the ethnographies of ethnomusicologists. And of course they all were also influenced and inspired by the directions of folkloristics, especially as a field focusing on the analysis of performance.

The Principal Questions: Past and Future

Well, I must turn to my final subject. It's clear to you that I think ethnomusicology belongs foremost to musicology; musicology now can't live without it. But it also belongs to other fields—anthropology and folklore and maybe even psychology and cognitive studies. My satisfaction in being in ethno arises from the fact of all these relationships. I feel we've arrived and that we are on a plateau wondering (collectively; I'm not sure any one person has these thoughts) what to do next. What is the future of ethnomusicology?

Except for playing some quarter-limit poker, I'm not a gambling man, and so I don't want to predict. Nor do I wish to tell my colleagues what they should be doing. But let me approach the issue from this angle: What are the questions I would like to see answered? What were the questions we were asking in 1950? Have they been answered? Let me try three. But first, I guess I have to point out that while ethnomusicologists have always had questions, these were rarely articulated for the field as a whole. In the late 1980s, Tim Rice formulated a model for ethnomusicology on the basis of a single complex question: "How do people historically construct, socially maintain, and individually create and experience music?" (Rice 1987, 473).

I think Rice did a good job putting most of the ethnomusicological eggs in one basket, encompassing most what we all do. In my early years, however, I perceived three questions on the surface: (1) What causes different cultures to have differently sounding music? Or, what determines a culture's principal musical style? (2) To what end do the world's peoples use music? What does music do for them? (3) How do the world's musics transmit themselves, maintaining continuity and also undergoing change?

I first entertained these questions when I was a student, or they were the ones that my teacher, George Herzog, articulated by asking questions such as, Why does that American Indian music sound as it does, and why is African music so different? What kinds of songs do these people have, how do they name them, and what does that mean? And how do they learn the songs? Do they have to sing them exactly as they learned them? How do they come about?

Well, later these questions became more generalized and they might be stated more elegantly. But by the 1980s, when I was looking around the literature for progress to report in my book *The Study of Ethnomusicology* (2005), they were still around: What are the cultural and aesthetic determinants of musical style and structure? What are the relationships of music to human and supernatural beings? How does music move through time, from its origins to the establishment and transmission of styles, repertories, and individual works? We were still mainly concerned about the nature of musical sound, the relationship of music to society and culture, and the sweep of history in the broadest sense.

I don't think we've answered these questions, but a variety of scholars have provided some major theories that speak to them—Alan Merriam, Alan Lomax, Steven Feld, and John Blacking come to mind. I tried (Nettl 2005) to identify central questions, perhaps to no one's satisfaction. Interestingly, each of these issues relates ethnomusicology to another field— historical musicology, sociocultural anthropology, folkloristics, and education. But I feel that ethnomusicologists might do well to look at these questions broadly again, in the light of the kinds of things the musical world has experienced over the last half-century.

Moreover, there are questions we did not ask fifty years ago and that stand at the forefront in ethnomusicology today, and I think they are the ones to which the field will increasingly turn. Again, just a quick sample:

The first question in fact comprises several concerning ethnomusicologists' relationships to their objects of study. What are our obligations to the people, the musicians, whose music we have studied? What is our role in the protection and use of intellectual property? (When I was a student, the question of performers' or informants' rights played a very small role; we dealt with artifacts far more than people.) What are the roles of cultural insiders and outsiders, and can we make such a distinction? In the 1950s, this last issue was not widely recognized; we began to pay more attention to it in the 1970s, yet even now we have failed to grapple successfully with the issue of participant-observation, the question of who speaks for a culture, and the definition of culture—is it what people in a society agree on or what people in a society argue about?

A second question involves the relationship of ethnomusicology to the technologized world. I'm an old-timer and thus quite ignorant of this area, so let me just say that ethnomusicological study of recording, distribution, globalization, and the role of the Internet are essential for giving us an understanding of today's musical culture. Many younger scholars have bitten off parts of this new puzzle, but obviously we're just at the beginning. As a basis, though, let me point out that on the one hand, distinctions among musical cultures seem to be receding—are we coming to Lomax's feared "cultural grayout"?—and musical variegation is maybe declining. On the other hand, the typical individual in the world has access to a vastly greater variety of music than was the case fifty years ago.

The third question returns me to the beginning of my considerations. What is the role of ethnomusicology in education? In the 1950s, the few of us beginning to teach were an academic luxury. When I told colleagues that our branch of musicology was asking the most fundamental questions, I got curious stares. Now, ethnomusicologists provide courses that fulfill world-music requirements for music-education students and general-education requirements in foreign cultures, and their offerings have become an essential part of any musicology curriculum. But thorough integration hasn't yet occurred, and we should address ourselves to the task of influencing our neighboring disciplines and fields further. We should persuade anthropologists that they can easily learn to deal with music as a major aspect of culture and that they must include it because, as Paul Bohannan (1963, 48) famously said, it "has been proved one of the most diagnostic traits of any culture." We should go further in persuading our music-history colleagues that approaches developed in ethnomusicology might be crucial in interpreting historical and recent events and in issues such as the relation of performer and audience, the history of performance practice, and the reception of music. We should persuade psychologists and biologists interested, for example, in the origins of music and the relationship of animal sounds and human music that knowing something of the immense variety of the world's human musics, and the fact that each society has its own, unique configuration of the concept of music, would add to the sophistication of their theories. We could even persuade our old-time folklorist colleagues that they should take tunes into greater account in their study of the verbal texts. There's more, but let me stop enumerating.

As the cheetahs of the academic valley surrounded by the musicological lions—and probably the tigers and foxes of anthropology, the leopards of folklore, and the elephants of the sciences—we've survived and thrived, made our place. The lions have been unexpectedly kind, and we cheetahs might be in danger of joining them as kings of the valley. It's a comforting feeling. But we in ethnomusicology need to remain cheetahs, to maintain our intellectual swiftness and our disciplinary flexibility, learning from musicology, folklore, anthropology, and other disciplines so that we may continue claiming to deal with music's most fundamental problems.

7
· · · · · · · · · · · · · ·

On the Concept of Evolution
in the History of Ethnomusicology
· ·

Introduction

Let me present some major questions in ethnomusicology:
how did music come about in the first place, and what links
a society and its particular brand of culture to a particular
kind of music? This question is also related to a recent body
of literature that, broadly speaking, involves the relationship
of music to human evolution. This area of study has largely
been the purview of scientists and scholars in the fields of
biology, psychology, animal communication, and to
a degree, linguistics, and much of its efforts have
concerned the origins of music. Landmarks among
these studies include the collection edited by Wallin,
Merker, and Brown (2000) and Steven Mithen's *Sing-*
ing Neanderthals (2005), which relates the origins of

music to a variety of human social and biological functions. These works are among the leading publications in what is beginning to be a coherent subfield of musicology, "evolutionary musicology." Interestingly, the area of study is of interest at least as much to people working outside musicology (and ethnomusicology) as to those within it. The main purpose of the following paragraphs is to briefly survey how the concept of evolution has functioned in the history of ethnomusicology.

Evolutionary musicology may be a new term, but the concept of evolution has played a considerable role in the history of ethnomusicology. When I say "concept," however, I don't necessarily mean evolution as biologists understand it or even the more colloquial sense of "a series of related changes in a certain direction," either in nature or culture, in a universe of phenomena or a single phenomenon. But whether they are talking about the development of music as part of human evolution as understood by biologists or about what they perceive as some kind of directional change, ethnomusicologists have tended to use the Darwinian concept—or what they think it is, correctly or not—as a point of reference.

There are several areas of ethnomusicology that have been particularly affected by the concept of evolution. I'll try to comment on three (with the caveat that my understanding of biological evolution is primitive at best but in the hope that some findings of ethnomusicology may be helpful in this context today): (1) the concept of the origin of music and the related issue of musical universals; (2) the reconstruction of history, or better said, the conjectural history, of music as a whole and of individual musics and the formulation of laws according to which music changes; and (3) the ways in which musical systems change in certain details to survive in essence. To determine how these issues relate to evolution, we need to answer further questions. Evolutionary biologists may wish to know whether music as a general phenomenon is an adaptation, analogous to having hair or eyes. Humanists may ask whether, even if music is not a biological adaptation, the concept of Darwinian evolution, based on reproductive fitness, might be helpful in interpreting the history of music or musics—that is, whether music is analogous to a species or whether the development of different musics is analogous to speciation, and if so, what this may mean. And we all should ask whether the development of different musics by different societies represents the adaptive development of a more general trait, as in hair type.

Origins

Biologists and ethnomusicologists have most immediately joined on the issue of music's origins, as seen in the 1997 conference in Fiesole on the origins of music (sponsored by the Institute for Biomusicology, Östersund, Sweden) and the ensuing, previously mentioned collection edited by Nils Wallin, Bjorn Merker, and Steven Brown (2000). Clearly, biologists and other scientists have in recent times shed important light on why and, to some extent, how music may have originated, but the origins of music played an important role in the early decades of ethnomusicology as well. Two of the earliest synthetic works—Richard Wallaschek's *Anfänge der Musik* (a translation of Wallaschek 1893, which was titled *Primitive Music*) and Carl Stumpf's *Anfänge der Tonkunst* (1911)—use the concept in the titles, not because these books concern how music came into being, but because they deal with the musics of tribal societies and thus were thought to represent the earliest extant human music. Or maybe because they felt that writing about tribal music could be justified only by associating "primitive" forms with the contemporary musical culture as an illumination of its origins. Although later conventional musicologists such as Curt Sachs (1940) and Siegfried Nadel (1930) continued to theorize about the origins of music, they typically did not refer to Darwin's ideas in any detail, and after about 1950, except for a handful of people who made half-hearted attempts, ethnomusicologists considered it a dead issue for many years.

Interestingly, in the period after 1965, a few scholars, including Alan Lomax (1968) and John Blacking (e.g., 1977), moved back to this issue. Blacking did so through his interest in the biology of music making and, as it were, the origins of music in the individual; Lomax, in the development of music in the individual culture unit, looking at each music (or a "society's favored song style") as if it were something like a biological adaptation. To the extent that ethnomusicology, defined most easily as the study of the world's music from a comparative perspective and of music as a component of culture, could shed light on the origins of music, it did so by using comparative study to identify musical universals and to explain what music accomplishes for humans—or the purpose for which they developed music. (I'm not sure to what extent one can speak here of an opposition between intentions consciously carried out and genetic mutations that give rise to behavior.)

In looking at the history of ethnomusicology, I have tried to distinguish four issues that might be discussed: the need for music, premusical kinds of behavior, a kind of moment of invention, and the earliest music. Generally, a human need for music was approached through the study of the uses and functions of music that all cultures have held in common, with emphasis on small, isolated societies. Premusical kinds of behavior were theorized as a form of communication that preceded the development of language and possessed certain characteristics of music—for example, length, stress, and pitch distinctions. The earliest music was considered to be something like the music of certain tribal peoples, which was seen as exceedingly simple or as containing only a few of those components that play a major role in Western urban music. The moment of invention? That's always been a mystery, but then, the moment of invention by musical creators from Native Americans to Beethoven has always been a mystery.

This all may make some sense, although it is admittedly speculative, but looking at what we know and don't know about the world's extant musical cultures may motivate us to be skeptical. First, why did humans or prehumans create music? Ever since Hornbostel's (1904–5) article on the problems of comparative musicology, four primary purposes have been repeatedly listed—to increase opportunities for mating, associated with Darwinian theory; to add structure to culture through elevated speech, associated with Spencer and then Wagner; to aid in performing rhythmic labor, associated with Carl Buecher; and to communicate at a distance, associated with Carl Stumpf (summarized in Sachs 1943, 19–20). The ethnomusicological canon then also included later work by Siegfried Nadel (1930), who suggested that music was invented as a way of communicating with the supernatural—but mechanically, that might be in the "elevated-speech" category. More recently, Jeffrey Miller (in Wallin, Merker, and Brown 2000, 329–60) suggested a refinement within the Darwinian tradition, viewing music as an adaptive mechanism for sexual selection, the organism demonstrating fitness as a mate by exhibiting energy, creativity, and flexibility, qualities that would help ensure survival. A recent conference on the evolution of music and language in Reading suggested various other factors for the development of music, including its role in maternal behavior, its ability to stimulate behavior that is both individual and social, and its role in expressing group superiority. Attendees also heard the conclusion that music is not a part of natural selection and that "some of the things that make life most worth living are not biological adaptations."

Some ethnomusicologists, I among them, may find the "fitness-to-mate" theory attractive, but we don't have much information in our arsenal of world-music information that would support it. But let me say a word about universals, the music concept, and other species.

What was the earliest human music like? The typical approach of eth-nomusicologists and others has been the identification of so-called universals. I say "so-called" because the term means various things—it may refer to something that is present in every musical utterance, or found in all cultures (though identifying what is a culture has its own problems), or found in the great majority of cultures—anthropologists call these statistical universals. Our disciplinary ancestors, Wallaschek, Stumpf, and Hornbostel, were interested in the discovery that what they considered to be the world's simplest musics, which includes music of small, isolated societies, as well as certain children's songs in many societies, had important features in common: a small number of tones and note values; pitches separated by intervals roughly of a major second or minor third; forms consisting of repetition and perhaps variation of short bits of music; and the primacy of vocal music. These kinds of singing were considered to be cultural universals and thus perhaps representative of the world's earliest music. One tried to establish a "primitive" layer of music, a strategy that can still be identified in a kind of archeological approach to the study of music repertories. At the same time, musical characteristics or traits such as the two-tone and three-tone scale were abstracted and associated with the earliest human music in more complex contexts. (See also an imaginatively defined predecessor of all these, the "Hmmmm" suggested in Mithen 2005).

But the identification of musical universals faces a problem: the criteria used to identify them have typically been taken from the musical discourse of Western academic music culture. There are ways in which these musics, which seem so similar to us, are actually not so alike. Singing styles may differ greatly, as they do, for example, when measured by Alan Lomax's dimensions of vocal width, nasality, tremulo, embellishment, and rasp. Intonational and rhythmic variation may seem to us academicians like random differences, but they may in fact bear musical significance (see Lomax 1968). Thus, a practitioner of cantometrics trying to isolate all musics featuring a high level of nasality would end up with a collection of data including some simple and some complex musics.

I want to add a word of caution to the widespread belief—I confess to having once been a believer—that the cultures with this very simple style must represent musical behavior of early humans because obviously they haven't been able to develop music beyond a level of simplicity. There is now some evidence that the musical repertory with only simple songs may often have resulted from the colonialism of the last several centuries, under which certain tribal societies became so impoverished and isolated that they abandoned much of their cultures' complexity and left themselves with only their simplest components. This area of study hasn't been widely developed and remains to be pursued.

But just as our evaluation of musical simplicity is rooted in the Western academic canon of music, in which complexity is an inordinate aesthetic value, the way we look at the world's musics typically results from a holistic notion of music as encompassing a vast number of sounds and ideas about sound. We, American and European academicians, belong to a culture where everything from George Antheil's airplane motor to John Cage's four minutes and thirty-three seconds of silence is accepted as music. We say that all cultures have music, but really, we mean that all cultures have something that sounds like what we conceive to be music. We also colloquially transfer this to other species; birds sing (we say), as do whales, but dogs and cats usually don't. Now, it is widely known that most of the world's languages don't have a traditional word for "music," and the various things they do that sound to us like music may be widely different categories in their cognitive maps. Persian musicians think of instrumental, metric, composed music as quite a different thing from vocal, nonmetric, improvised chant or song. Steven Feld (1982) found that Kaluli culture and language distinguish a variety of sounds—speech, poetry, singing, and weeping, all associated with various kinds of birdsong. The point is that if we were to look at the origins of music starting with the perspective of another society or culture, we might find ourselves drawing different conclusions.

For example, we might speculate that music had not one single origin but several; that different motivations or even adaptations might have led to different kinds of sound that only Europeans—maybe erroneously—subsume under one concept. As imaginary examples, certain kinds of singing solo performance might have come about as a result of the fitness-to-mate adaptation; group singing, from the need to support the advantage of group action and cooperation; instrumental music, from the advantage of long-distance communication; variation on a theme, from the usefulness of identifying distant individuals; and dance music and lullabies, in other ways yet. It's a tempting thing to imagine, but I don't have a theory and am only trying to point out that our idea of music as one "thing," a thing that came into existence once, in one way, may be too narrow for reasonable contemplation. In thinking of cultural universals as a guide to the earliest music, we should bear in mind that cultural diversity in the music concept may lead us to see diverse origins for the kinds of things we now unite under the concept of music. It's interesting, by the way, to see that Curt Sachs, in his last work, *The Wellsprings of Music* (1962), came close to this conclusion.

Finally, on ethnomusicology and the origins of music: ethnomusicologists are omnivorous. They'll write papers about anything that anyone says is music, and so of the various kinds of musicologists, ethnomusicologists are most likely to welcome contributions on communications by birds, whales, and gibbons. I have read quite interesting work on these forms of communication in other species and the tendency of some to distinguish different kinds of communication that we might see as analogous to speech and singing. But from an ethnomusicological perspective, I'm not sure how they are relevant, except by analogy, to the human picture in which we don't even have a cross-culturally valid concept of music or a reliable accounting of universals. Indeed, universals of various sorts have been around for a hundred years of ethnomusicology, but we have gradually come to have less faith in them, and our faith in our ability to discover what led to the development of music has not increased.

I think we're probably safest to consider the origins of music as a series of separate events, derived from a variety of social needs and processes, united only by their use of sound distinguished from ordinary speech. Perhaps they came together, many millennia later, as "music" only in some select societies, such as the modern European, with its tendency to bifurcate (e.g., "music" versus "speech"). Had another of the world's societies become culturally dominant, we might conceivably be talking not about "music" but about a variety of sound types, each of which had an independent origin.

History

The history of music is probably a tiny blip in the study of biological evolution. Once music was developed, the question of whether there is "a" history of human music or "a" typical culture-specific music history is probably trivial from a biological perspective. But the concept of musical development has played an important role in musicology, and its practitioners have seen themselves influenced—though perhaps erroneously— by biological evolution. Most important here is the belief in an inevitable order of events. The major synthetic works about world music by scholars already mentioned—Stumpf (1911) and Sachs (1962), Marius Schneider (1934, 1957), Hornbostel in his 1905 article introducing "comparative musicology," Walter Wiora (1956, 1965) in his proposition of four stages in world music, and, indeed, many historians of Western music before the 1960s—suggest that all musics pass through certain stages, moving from two- and three-tone melodies to pentatonicism and then diatonicism; from monophony to heterophony and then to polyphony and homophony, attaching this sequence to the development of Western art music from the Middle Ages and suggesting that the world's musics differ because we have found them at different stages of evolution, much as it was popularly believed that different animal species represent different rungs on the same ladder. Musicologists have long abandoned this notion, but traces of it often persist, as, for example, in the concept that certain numerically simple musics are representative of the "Stone Age" and the assumptions that go with recent speculations about origins. In fact, this notion of an inevitable order rests on a misunderstanding of evolutionary theory; nonetheless, it drew much of its presumed credibility from its association with science.

The discovery of a generally applicable order of events depended on speculation about relative simplicity and complexity of musical phenomena as well as their geographic distribution, widespread but isolated pockets indicating age. I won't rehearse the various critiques of this notion, but I do want to mention two competing approaches. One, associated with the so-called Kulturkreis school of ethnology (its history interpreted in A. Schneider 1976 and summarized in Nettl 2005, 320–38), saw the world as a group of gradually superimposed areas of diffusion, each representing an era whose remnants can be discovered in leftovers of contemporary distribution. A major musicological work emanating from this strand of thought is Marius Schneider's *Geschichte der Mehrstimmigkeit* (1934), which posits four universally applicable stages on the basis of both relative complexity and geography, plus four areas/stages in European cultivated polyphony. The other approach, associated with the concept of culture area as developed by Franz Boas and Alfred Kroeber, suggests that each culture area has its own unique history, resulting from adaptation to its environment, but that within each, there are features of a certain typical history—for example, the existence of a culture center in which the area's traits are developed to greatest intensity and diminution of its character on the borders. All this in some way relates to the idea that ontogeny recapitulates phylogeny, which has played a role in ethnomusicology, although those terms haven't been widely used. Human musical development, particularly the musical utterances of young children, provided a template for a world history of music. Beginning with Heinz Werner some ninety years ago, many of us have been fascinated by the idea that the stages suggested for a world history of music can be discovered in individuals' musical development, but we are frustrated by the absence of intercultural and thus perhaps universally valid studies.

Finally, ethnomusicological literature over a hundred years has tried to grapple with a fundamental question: is it more fruitful to look at the world of music as having a single, more or less monolithic, history or as having a group of separate histories? And if the latter, does this lend strength to the argument for multiple origins of music?

These remarks suggest that ethnomusicologists have been greatly influenced not so much by theories of biological evolution as by their (mis) conceptions of biological evolution. One of the striking characteristics of this literature is its treatment of music as a kind of biological organism. We know that musical creation, performance, and reception are decisions made by humans, as individuals and as social groups. Nevertheless, musicological literature often speaks of music as if it had a life of its own, obeying certain internally valid laws. Here we think we are following biology, in which the course of events is underpinned fundamentally by random mutations, whose cultural analogue is a kind of trial-and-error process.

Adaptation

Ethnomusicologists have shown a strong interest in the origins of music and can provide critiques of theories developed in other disciplines. They have a strong interest in the history of the world's musics and have approached their studies in part with influence from their conception of biological theories. A third relationship is found in studies of the ways in which musics compete for survival in situations of intensive culture contact and change.

Since 1965 ethnomusicologists have been centrally interested in studying how the world's musics have changed under the influence of Western and Western-derived musical culture and the musical culture of modernized technology, from wax cylinders to the Internet. Although this research has most frequently focused on the often deceptive Western/non-Western dyad, the general issue involves the strategies people have used to permit their music to survive in an environment where other musics—more powerful technologically and symbolically—have competed for cultural resources such as audience and performers. Ethnomusicologists realize that humans developed these mechanisms to keep their music, but again, it has sometimes been useful to look at musics as if they had lives of their own.

I can't summarize this by now vast literature. It's important, however, to realize that ethnomusicologists have considered music to be a concept broader than that of our everyday discourse, including what many might call its cultural context. In the 1960s, Alan Merriam (1964, 1967) provided a model that is still helpful, a view of music as consisting of ideas, behavior, and sound, each of these affecting and affected by the other; when one component changes, the others do as well.

Let me mention some of the things included in this framework of thought. The basic assumption has to be that for humans as groups or societies, cultural survival is secondary to physical survival but nevertheless essential; societies may be forced or motivated to change their culture to survive, but all sorts of reasons can influence a group's decision whether to change, maintain, or abandon their cultural forms. Many Native American peoples have given up traditional religions and become Christian, but they moved older religious traditions into a category of practices maintained for tribal identity. They may have kept up much of their traditional music yet also acquired what they call "white" music, giving it, too, a place in their lives. But when it comes to matters of subsistence, for instance, older traditions have been completely abandoned. The maintenance of traditional music in such a case can be seen as a mechanism for the survival of the culture.

Ethnomusicologists have been interested in the specific ways in which societies have changed their music in order to preserve it. In some societies, for example, the musical system adapted to Western musical practices, and elements such as Western-derived harmony and increased emphasis on composition over improvisation gained ascendancy; this mechanism one might call Westernization because traditional music survived by acquiring musical traits central to Western music.

Elsewhere, in what we may call modernization, traditional musical sounds were maintained at the expense of placing them in Western-derived social contexts. Consider the following examples. On the one hand, musicians in the South Indian classical traditions seem to have placed their music into a modernized cultural context, changing ideas about music. Specifically, they put it into a modern concertlike context and abandoned the seasonal and hourly requirements governing raga selection to permit a festival-like concentration of performances in late December, performances that otherwise present the music tradition essentially uninfluenced by Western musical sounds. On the other hand, the Iranian classical tradition was maintained through the twentieth century by adopting harmony, privileging composition over improvisation, and introducing Western notation and larger ensembles imitating Western chamber and orchestral groupings. Similarly, Australian Aboriginal peoples adapted the didgeridoo, once restricted to a limited area of northern Australia and used only as a drone instrument with singing, to various uses compatible with Western ideas about music. It was taken up by tribes elsewhere and eventually used in virtuosic solo performances, in ways somewhat consonant with the Western notion of music as quintessentially instrumental with emphasis on virtuosity. Eventually it became emblematic of Aboriginal culture, prominent enough to become one of a small number of symbols ensuring the existence of that culture in the presence of fundamental changes in daily life. Indeed, it ultimately came to symbolize not only Aboriginal culture but Australianness as a whole. (These illustrations and similar ones are discussed in more detail in Nettl 1985.)

Conclusion

In a number of ways, then, the concept of evolution has played an important role in the history of ethnomusicology. Ethnomusicologists have interpreted the concept, ultimately derived from Darwin, in various ways, some no doubt unfaithful to proper evolutionary theory. On the one hand, the study of the world's musical systems and of music as part of human culture might well provide relevant critique to theories of the origins of music, even though most ethnomusicologists have given up this idea. On the other hand, in their attempts to construct ideas about the long-term history of the world's musics, and in their interpretation of the ways in which intercultural contact has affected—and failed to affect—the state of music, their efforts have depended substantially on ideas that came from biology and from what they thought evolution must be about.

8

The Music of Anthropology

Ethnomusicology has always struggled to find its proper disciplinary base. I estimate 80 percent of ethnomusicologists come from a professional background in music and regard themselves principally as members of one of the musical disciplines. The other fifth largely consider themselves to be anthropologists, and while they are a minority, they have been responsible for most of the field's intellectual leadership.

But let me approach my subject from another side. For some fifty years, I have known two kinds of anthropologists. Those of the first kind call themselves ethnomusicologists, and they include major figures such Alan Merriam; my teacher, George Herzog; David McAllester; Steven Feld; Richard Waterman and his son, Illinois's Chris Waterman; John Blacking; Daniel Neuman; Charlotte Frisbie;

Anthony Seeger; Regula Qureshi; and many other distinguished scholars. They are practitioners of the anthropology of music. The other group of anthropologists consists of . . . well, of all the rest. They accept and support the Merriams and Herzogs because they regard music as one of the constituent domains of culture, and—I'm making rapid leaps—they see their profession as involved with all of culture, with the interrelationships among all domains, including music. Alan Merriam, titling his most influential book *The Anthropology of Music* (1964), tries to persuade his readers that ethnomusicology belongs to the discipline of anthropology.

So I have asked myself this from time to time: if there is an anthropology of music, is there also a "music of anthropology"? Or a "music *in* anthropology"? In other words, what position does music have in anthropology at large, in those publications that present or deal with the field of anthropology as a whole or human culture at large or that holistically address the whole field of anthropology or deal with culture as a whole? I want to suggest some reasons for my conclusions, but I must warn you that I based those conclusions on a relatively modest sample of the literature, that I have a lot more about history than about the most recent past, and that what I have for you is work in progress.

Here is the plan. I will provide some historical background by touching briefly on the role of music in German, American, and British anthropology in the first several decades of the twentieth century; I will then look briefly at three distinguished anthropologists who saw themselves also as musicians of one sort or another and survey first a few prominent American textbooks and then a few general books directed to the professional. Finally, I hope to show how anthropologists' attitudes toward music can be interpreted as illustrating general Western attitudes toward music. Some of what I'll say may seem critical or professionally self-serving, but my intention is to be analytical, not critical. I have no agenda for proposing change but hope to shed some light on a small corner of the nature and history of our discipline(s).

Three National Schools

In the late nineteenth century and the early twentieth, the anthropologists who foregrounded music in their publications fell into two groups. One was the German *Kulturkreis* school—the leaders were Wilhelm Schmidt, Fritz Graebner, Leo Frobenius, Bernhard Ankermann (see Lowie 1937)— with later offshoots reaching as far as the United States, particularly in the work of Clyde Kluckhohn. These scholars were substantially influenced by the pioneers of ethnomusicology, Erich von Hornbostel and Curt Sachs, and music, especially musical artifacts, played a role in their determination of historical strata (see A. Schneider 1976). Sachs conducted a major Kulturkreis-like study of the world's musical instruments, ending up with twenty-three strata; his ensuing book (Sachs 1929) is considered a major contribution to German diffusionist literature. The possibility of dividing music into sectors, traits, or dimensions attracted German diffusionists to music (aside from the fact that German intellectuals around 1900 thought of music itself as a quintessentially German field). So, according to Schneider, the Kulturkreis anthropologists considered their ethnomusicological colleagues an indispensable part of their team.

The majority of scholars in the second group, less exotic to us today, were American, and most of them were, directly or indirectly, students of Franz Boas, who as a teacher encouraged ethnomusicology but also stimulated an interest in music among his students generally (Boas 1927). Prominent among the latter was Melville Herskovits, who did so much to establish African studies in American cultural anthropology (see, e.g., Herskovits 1941; Herskovits and Herskovits 1936). His obituary by Alan Merriam (1963a) describes his strong involvement with Western music in his student days. He was even a spear-carrying extra at the Metropolitan Opera. His studies of West African and Afro-Brazilian cultures and of Suriname include much on musical culture and style, and his most influential book, *The Myth of the Negro Past* (1941), provides a pioneering discussion of the relationships between African American and African musics; Herskovits also made comparisons between various Africa-derived cultures in the New World.

Among other associates of Boas, Robert H. Lowie included important discussions of music. In his ethnography of the Crow (Lowie 1935), he brings up songs and what people said about them, and he gives a separate account of music as a domain of culture. In his many works on the Blackfoot, published mainly before 1912, Clark Wissler (Wissler 1912; Wissler and Duvall 1909), not directly a student of Boas but significantly influenced by him, has much to say about songs, their uses in ritual and social life, their words, and even Blackfoot ideas about music. Edward Sapir (1910) dealt with language-music relationships in "Song Recitative in Paiute Mythology." In *Growing Up in New Guinea*, Margaret Mead (1930) gives an interesting appraisal of cultural expectations of music and an account of Manus views of musical talent and the way music is learned. A short but quite insightful ethnography of music—the kinds of things an ethnomusicologist would like to know—appears in *Coming of Age in Samoa* (Mead 1928). These prominent works before 1940, moreover, are not isolated examples.

In contrast to these two groups, a third group of scholars usually referred to as the British school of social anthropology seem to have been less involved—in their professional work—with music. It is harder to find mention of music in their ethnographies. Even so, Bronislaw Malinowski, whose ethnographic work on the Trobriand Islanders has always been regarded as exemplary because of its comprehensive detail, did pay attention. His interest in and preference for Western classical music is made clear in his posthumous *Diary* (1967). In *The Sexual Life of Savages* (1929), however, he mentions Trobriand music, instruments, and songs at various points, appearing to regard this music as a proper part of the cultural system and comparing it to Western music at least by implication when, for example, he points out that Trobriander women are impressed by men with good singing voices.

Radcliffe-Brown, on the other hand, seems to have nothing on the subject. And some of the successors to these scholars—let me give some random examples: John Beattie in *Other Cultures* (1964), John Middleton in *Black Africa Today* (1970)—also stayed away from music. Raymond Firth had a lot to say about music in Tikopia, mainly in unpublished field notes used by Herndon and McLeod (1980), and in a late work on songs, with ethnomusicologist Mervyn McLean (Firth 1990), but curiously not in another work of opportune subject matter, his influential book *Symbols, Public and Private* (1973).

Schools of anthropologists differed not only according to their roughly national provenance but also over time. Before I look at the chronology, however, let me mention three major figures in anthropology who seem to have had a particular relationship to music.

They Knew and Loved (Western) Music

In my experience of them, American and Western European university professors in all fields oscillate between cultural relativism and ethnocentrism, but among those domains of culture that are importantly aesthetic—I mean religion, arts, and style of dress or cuisine rather than social structure, distribution of labor, or agriculture, though I know this is a questionable distinction—they tend to be particularly ethnocentric about music, fashion, and food. They will gladly have African sculptures in their living rooms, but they shy away from trying the recipes in *The Anthropologist's Cookbook* (Kuper 1977). They read *The Tale of Genji* but don't want to hear gagaku. Overstated perhaps, but I could give you lots of supporting anecdotes. Furthermore, although Western intellectuals love music, they often claim that it's difficult to understand, and they draw a sharp line between "musicians" and others. Why? That's another lecture. But possibly three very brief case studies may shed light.

The work of Claude Lévi-Strauss, whose interest in music is well known and documented, serves as an exemplar of the Western intellectual's ambivalence. Take his highly influential book *The Raw and the Cooked* (1969). It's dedicated "To Music," with a notated quotation from Emmanuel Chabrier, and its chapters—which are largely about myths of South American Indians—bear the titles of musical forms and genres: "The Fugue of the Five Senses," "The Good Manners Sonata," "The Opossum's Cantata." The introduction contains a substantial discussion of the homology of music and myth, but the conception of music in this work appears to be exclusively Western. Lévi-Strauss regards music in a sense as a cultural universal, as he also demonstrates the universality of myth, but one is left with the suggestion that to him, the character of this "universal" music is simply the style of classical music of nineteenth- and twentieth-century Europe. At the same time, his detailed and insightful discussion of South and North American myths has virtually nothing about the fact that the performances of these myths as narratives often include singing. And yet, Lévi-Strauss, clearly a person whose knowledge of Western music matches that of the professional, believed that understanding music is essential to understanding culture, writing:

> But that music is a language by whose means messages are elaborated, that such messages can be understood by the many but sent out only by the few, and that it alone among all the languages unites the contradictory character of being at once intelligible and untranslatable—these facts make the creator of music a being like the gods and make music itself the supreme mystery of human knowledge. All other branches of knowledge stumble into it, it holds the key to their progress. (1969, 26)

Lévi-Strauss's holistic view of culture seems to brush aside the problems of music as something that cannot be interculturally defined. He seems to see music, somewhat like myth, as a single human system, not, as is common among ethnomusicologists, as a group of discrete systems somewhat like languages. His sensitivity to Western music thus informs his analysis of culture. Conversely, his understanding of myth has informed the analysis of music by such ethnomusicologists as Steven Feld (1982) and Pandora Hopkins (1977).

I've had an interesting time trying to figure out the role of music in the career of Siegfried Nadel, too. Actually, he had two careers, and they have little to do with each other. I confess that at one time I thought he was two people. Beginning as a student in Vienna, he worked in music, musicology, and psychology and in particular was a student of the then prominent ethnomusicologist Robert Lach. When I was a music student in the late 1940s, I was especially impressed by three works: a small book about xylophones in Africa, Asia, and Oceania (Nadel 1931), completely in the line of Kulturkreis scholarship; a speculative book about dualism in the history of Western music; and the most intelligent article on origins of music I know, published in the American music journal *Musical Quarterly* (1930).

Much later I ran into *A Black Byzantium* (1942) and *The Foundations of Social Anthropology* (1951), by S. Nadel. It didn't occur to me that this could be the Siegfried Nadel of the marimbas. The radical change from Kulturkreis museum work to British-style social anthropology, and the absence of any indication that the author had specialized knowledge of music, made me wonder for years. True, *A Black Byzantium* has some remarks on drummers and rhythmic patterns, but *Foundations,* which ranges widely through cultural domains, mentions music only in passing. It may be that Nadel wanted anthropologists to realize that specialized knowledge was needed for working in certain cultural domains. For example, he suggests that only musicians can understand music, saying, "No anthropologist would dream of claiming that, merely through being an anthropologist, he could also study primitive music." The same should be true of economics, he goes on to say. Clearly, also, he sees music and other arts as somehow less related to the heart of culture than are domains involving social structure and economy. "There is no link between group organization and homophony or polyphony in music. . . . The style in art, then, exists in its own right, entailing and presupposing no determinate social relationships" (1951, 88). I disagree, and Nadel today might well change his position after having read more recent ethnomusicological literature. I'm amazed, however, to find this fundamental change in his attitude. And reading Morris Freilich's (1968) long article on Nadel in the *International Encyclopedia of the Social Sciences,* I was mildly amused to see a passing reference to his experience as an opera conductor but nothing on his ethnomusicological writings.

For my third musician-anthropologist I have to select Oscar Lewis, a colleague, until his untimely death, at the University of Illinois. He participated directly in the Western classical music tradition but avoided music in his anthropological work. A lifelong excellent amateur singer of opera and voice student in our school of music, and a cantor in synagogues, Lewis had a comprehensive knowledge of Western art music. Nonetheless, virtually no mention of music appears in his many works resulting from his field research in Latin America, in India, and earlier, among the Blackfoot. He does, however, make interesting remarks in the article he titled "Manly-Hearted Women among the Northern Piegan" (O. Lewis 1941; he particularly mentions Ruth Lewis's collaboration on this article).

Being a pioneer in Blackfoot research, Oscar Lewis was helpful to me as I was getting ready to do some work in Montana. He had great sympathy for the study of music as culture in an ethnomusicological sense, but he could not understand why I might want to analyze the songs of the Blackfoot, or for that matter, how I could even stand to hear them for a sustained period. I believe that Professor Lewis's attitude toward the cultures he studied was in all respects as analytical and relativistic as one may expect of an anthropologist. Only when it came to music did he move toward ethnocentrism.

So we see Lévi-Strauss and Lewis heavily into Western music but leaving out the consideration of music in their general ethnographic work, and Nadel, with his powerful background in ethnomusicology, deciding that in its details, music really was not integral to culture.

Into the World of Texts and Introductions

I'm not sure whether textbooks accurately reflect anthropologists' overall view of their field, but if we want to see how they wish to present their discipline to the world, showing what it consists of and how it works, that's one place to look. A related genre might be general works directed to the profession as a whole. To give a historical perspective, showing how anthropology presented the cultural domain of music, I have here a small sample, going back to the 1930s, that is neither scientifically selected nor really up to date, ending as it does in the early 1980s.

Textbooks by some of the old masters sometimes mention music. *General Anthropology*, edited by Boas (and not published until 1938), has an essay by Boas, "Literature, Music, and Dance," whose section on music deals mostly with the relationship of music to language, particularly mentioning tone languages, though he also touches on musical-tone systems, rhythm, and instruments. Kroeber's *Anthropology* (1948; originally published in 1923), a book Harold Driver used when I took "Intro to Anthro," has no section specifically devoted to music but mentions it several times, once in connection with a study of Jamaicans in which children of whites, blacks, and "browns" were evaluated comparatively for general intelligence and musical aptitude. Like Boas, Kroeber mentions music-language relations but makes no attempt to present music itself as a domain of culture. In contrast, visual art is heavily represented. Among other old-master texts, I'll mention the one by Ralph Linton (1936), who got into music a bit, and the one by Leslie White (1949), who didn't.

The numerous American texts written after 1950 do devote an occasional page, but in contrast, visual art usually gets a good bit of space. Interestingly, my superficial survey suggests a decline in the music of anthropology into the 1970s, after which music began to pick up again.

Let me list some examples. Marvin Harris's widely used *Culture, Man, Nature* (1971) originally had not a word about music. The fourth edition, which came out in 1985 under the gentler title *Culture, People, Nature,* has some eight pages explicitly on the arts, including about 150 words on music, with material largely based on Alan Lomax's (1968) work relating culture types to musical styles and types. Hoebel and Front's *Cultural and Social Anthropology* (1976) provides eighteen pages on visual art but nothing on music. Philip Bock's *Modern Cultural Anthropology* (1969) has three pages suggesting that music matters to anthropologists only as an expression of cultural values, and Bock refers to McAllester's *Enemy Way Music* (1954) and Lomax's work. An interesting commentary on anthropologists' attitudes appears in one sentence from Bock: "A folklore tradition can be related to its cultural context more easily than can most of the other arts. Music . . . is particularly difficult to deal with." After I had read that sentence, I met Professor Bock and found, unexpectedly, that he is a fine amateur musician and member of an Albuquerque group that performs early music, a man heavily into Western music.

In looking at some of the texts, I get the feeling that anthropologists suspect that much can be learned about culture from its musical domain but that there is something dangerous, as Nadel intimated, about a non-musician's trying to talk about music. Paul Bohannan's *Social Anthropology* (1963) has only eight lines on music, but significantly, one of them says, "Music in non-Western tradition has been seriously neglected by all but a handful of anthropologists, in spite of the fact that it has been proved [he said this in 1963!] to be one of the most diagnostic traits of any culture" (48).

Roger Pearsons's *Introduction to Anthropology* (1974) has a bit on music, more on art. William Haviland (1974; rev. ed., 1981) says more, discussing elements of musical sound and instruments and suggesting the usefulness of looking at functions of music. The fourth edition of Carol and Melvin

Ember's text (Ember and Ember 1985) has five pages on music, mainly on material by Lomax. Conrad Phillip Kottak (1974) has quite a bit on art, and about one percent of the book is on music. And so it goes.

There are a few oddities in the history of textbooks. Felix Keesing's *Cultural Anthropology: The Science of Custom* (1958) has several pages on music, deals with instruments, and includes several paragraphs discussing how music can be used to illustrate relativism, along with a list of some ethnomusicologists. Its successor, *New Perspectives in Cultural Anthropology,* by Roger and Felix Keesing (but mostly by Roger—see Keesing and Keesing 1971), explicitly dropped the musical materials, announcing a decision to deemphasize material culture, historical linguistics, folklore, and art in favor of social structure and organization. Volume 2 of Barnouw's *Introduction to Anthropology* (1971) speaks briefly about the universality of music and extends the music concept to other primates, pointing out that chimpanzees drum with their hands and therefore, Barnouw hopefully assumes, love music.

Anthropology may be concerned mainly with cultural diversity, but the textbooks sometimes approach musical diversity in a gingerly way. Beals and Hoijer's (1965) text offers three pages, mostly on Western music. Collins's *Anthropology: Culture, Society, and Evolution* (1975) has no discussion of music but uses it to symbolize the concept of culture; the chapter on that subject is headed by two photographs, one of an African ceremony, presumably with musical content, and the other of a symphony orchestra.

I think I've said enough to give a sense of music's place in this literature. I have no statistics, but let me try to generalize about texts since 1950. More than half the texts from 1950 or so to 1980 have a bit about music, usually two to four pages. Their discussions of music focus on Western forms more often than do their discussions of other cultural domains. Command of the literature of ethnomusicology in anthropological annals seems usually limited to Lomax, McAllester, and (I'm bemused to find) an ancient and thoroughly obsolete book by myself; the writers fail to capitalize on obvious opportunities in, for example, work by the distinguished ethnomusicological anthropologists Richard Waterman, Alan Merriam, and John Blacking. Music gets far less space than visual art. There is certainly no attempt to give a picture of the world of music. Generally, however, while music declined in coverage before about 1975, the late 1970s and 1980s saw a bit of increase. For instance, the fourth edition of Sarna Nanda's *Cultural Anthropology* (1994) has ten pages on art and only four on music, but these four present an organized if brief survey of music on several continents.

Still, I get the feeling that most textbook authors are frightened of dealing with music. They're not just scaredy-cats, I assure you; it's an attitude foisted on the lay public by the academic music profession. Thus, in texts organized as readers, where ethnomusicologists can contribute directly, there is greater enthusiasm. I'll mention only the readers by Peter Hammond (1975), with a chapter by Norman Whitten; Alan Dundes (1968), with one by Merriam; and Goldschmiedt (1977), with one by Lomax.

Dipping into the Professional Literature

Allow me also to make a brief foray into the writings in sociocultural anthropology that are evidently directed to the profession, the things anthropologists write for one another—not those that present their specialized research projects and findings, but the ones that discuss their views of the discipline as a whole. Trying to sample this vast literature, I wonder whether I have a tiger by the tail. I'll try excursions to my own library shelves.

First, to the prehistory. E. B. Tylor's book *Anthropology* (1881), written before ethnomusicology was even in its infancy, has six pages on music, mostly Western to be sure, but there's a bit on the music of the ancients and of "rude tribes." But a half-century later, when ethnomusicologists were reading papers at anthropology meetings, there had been little progress. H. G. Barnett's insightful book *Innovation: The Basis of Cultural Change* (1953) mentions music only in a short, interesting passage that makes the reader wonder why the line of argument wasn't carried further, for the author obviously realized the usefulness of music and its quantifiability for identification of innovation and various kinds of change. The several works of Edward T. Hall (e.g., 1961 and 1983), which incidentally are read widely by ethnomusicologists and which in some cases almost cry out for illustration from musical behavior, have a few spots where music is mentioned, and Hall provides interesting food for thought, for example, in remarks about the relationship between musical rhythm and the perception of time. But except for a sentence about Japanese music and two about Navajo songs, he usually limits his remarks to Western classical music. In Julian Steward's many works, for example, *Theory of Culture Change* (1955), I've found no mention of music at all. Even where it might have seemed virtually obligatory, he remains silent on the subject. For example, volume 5 of Steward's *Handbook of South American Indians* (1949) is devoted to the comparative ethnology of the area and includes the section "Esthetic and Recreational Activities," which runs to some 150 pages, yet it contains not a word about music, though there is, by contrast, a large section on visual art by Kroeber and pages on games and gambling, stimulants and narcotics, religion and shamanism—all closely associated with music. But was the information there?

Jules Henry's *Culture against Man* (1963), Leslie White's *Evolution of Culture* (1959), and Robert Redfield's *Primitive World and Its Transformations* (1953) have nothing. The same is true of later works of a general sort by Richard Adams and Clifford Geertz and most recent works dealing with the culture concept and ethnography.

So discussion of music gradually decreased in these influential general works about the field, but the trend occurred in histories of anthropology, too. The earliest one I know, Lowie's *History of Ethnological Theory* (1937), had a couple of pages on music and predicted, "Comparative musicology, hampered by inferior techniques until quite recent times, rose to a new plane with phonographic recording, and is promising to bear effectively on some of the central problems of ethnology" (255–56). But the more recent major histories by Marvin Harris (1968), George Stocking (1968), and Leaf (1979) have no music, reflecting the declining attention to music found in the history of textbooks.

While conducting fieldwork the earliest anthropologists tended to make recordings of music, assuming that these would be studied by musicologists who needed not or could not do fieldwork. As a matter of course, it seems, field researchers would make recordings and then occasionally include in their publications a chapter on music and transcriptions of songs by a specialist. Several of Hornbostel's and Herzog's works appeared as such appendices. But the notion of music as a field worthy of brief mention that might be best left to the professional did not find an analogue in other arts or other domains.

Fifty or more years later, the whole business of field recording music has changed so much that there's nothing to compare to those early days. Still, whereas general works on the field were saying less and less about music, the tradition of Lowie, Wissler, Herskovits, of paying attention to music in general ethnographies of individual societies, continued to have its representatives. I'll mention a handful of examples. Professor Norman Whitten's works, such as *Sacha Runa* (1976), on peoples of Ecuador, say a lot about the interrelationships of music, symbols, and power. Colin Turnbull's (1961) studies of Central African Pygmies depict a society much concerned with song and music. Milton Singer's (1972) work on South India uses cultural performances as an analytical concept and tells about devotional singing groups and dance concerts in Madras. Ellen Basso's (1985) study of myth and ritual in a South American Indian culture looks at musical performance as central to the understanding of culture. Gene Weltfish's book *The Lost Universe,* published in 1965 but based mostly on earlier research, has a good deal on music. But these important works are nevertheless exceptions.

Let me make a couple of additional points that may round out the picture. First, the periodicals that gave ethnomusicological publishing its start in the United States were anthropological. The early works by ethnomusicologists, whether trained in anthropology or music, were prevailingly published in the old *Journal of American Folklore,* which in its first decades was definitely an anthropological periodical, and *American Anthropologist.* It's fair to say that through the 1950s, perhaps two-thirds of the significant articles on ethnomusicology appeared in these and related journals. In Europe there was less of this, but the journal *Anthropos* also tended to play such a role. But I want to stop throwing bibliography at you.

And despite the tendency for anthropologists to stay away from music— it may seem paradoxical—the first two institutions in the United States at which one could seriously study ethnomusicology were departments of anthropology, at Indiana University and Northwestern, where George Herzog and Richard Waterman, respectively, had begun to teach in the late 1940s.

One of the Most Diagnostic Traits; or, Like the Barking of Dogs?

Among the domains of culture, music has received a unique treatment in social anthropology. It has played a small and for a time even declining role, and while other domains were usually illustrated with data from African, Asian, and Native North American cultures, anthropologists more often drew on Western forms when discussing music.

Let me suggest three or four areas to search for an explanation. First, the decline of musical inclusion coincides with the development of ethnomusicology in the United States as a distinct field with a substantial population, a field whose leadership came substantially from anthropologists. It may not be surprising that ethnomusicological submissions to anthropology journals decreased as ethnomusicologists began to have their own journals— and that anthropologists may have said to themselves, "Well and good. We gave ethnomusicologists a start by letting them publish in our journals, but now they are standing on their own feet and can live independently." This may explain why ethnomusicology departed from the general journals, but not how music gradually departed from the rest of culture in the general works on theory and ethnography and in textbooks.

Second, ethnomusicologists had failed to provide a great deal of important data by the time the literature I am surveying was published—and to a large extent, they still haven't provided it. There are large areas of the world for which there is no reliable literature to draw on. For example, the *Handbook of Middle American Indians,* some twenty volumes, has one forty-page chapter on "drama, dance, and music" by the distinguished dance scholar Gertrude Kurath. Most of it is about drama and dance. I thought they should have done better but then realized that there is just very little known (except to the Indian people, who may not want to write books) about this music. If ethnomusicologists did some of their jobs better, one might expect the results of their research to be included more often.

Third, and a bit more fundamental, Western society's conception of music seems to give it a role that removes it from the rest of culture. There is an ambivalence that has caused music to be both desired and feared, the musician to be simultaneously wanted and avoided. Music is a field where the ordinary rules of society need not apply. The piano virtuoso is a kind of magician who does the incomprehensibly difficult. The musician gets away with behavior not generally tolerated, perhaps as a person with unconventional dress, hair style, sexual mores, or language. Musicians are often foreigners or members of minorities. Music becomes something to fear or something that one should not take seriously and is permitted to trivialize.

Possibly for the same reason, musicians especially in the academic world, have distanced themselves, saying, in effect, "You can't talk about music if you are not a professional"—which means being able to read music, analyze forms, and even play. Ultimately of remote origin, this set of attitudes has produced a major division between the rhetoric of musicians and of laypersons. Nonmusicians avoid talking about music analytically for fear of criticism, a fear that, say, nonartists or non–story writers feel far less when talking about visual art or literature. American anthropology students readily take courses in the anthropological study of art and literature; when it comes to music, many have been likely to decline, saying, "I'm not a musician." Anthropologists in North America and Western Europe, like others in their culture, have bought into this exclusion of music and the exclusiveness of musicians.

And fourth, I've already alluded to the tendency of members of Western society (and maybe others as well) to be more ethnocentric about music than about other artistic domains. Maybe not Western society alone. The historian of the Middle East Bernard Lewis wrote: "The music of an alien culture, it would seem, is more difficult to penetrate than its art. Western interest in the arts of Asia and Africa is far greater than in the music of these continents. Similarly, Muslims appreciated and even reproduced Western art long before they were able to listen to Western music" (B. Lewis 1982, 262). Only a handful of the thousands who would visit an exhibit of Middle Eastern art can be found at a concert of Persian or Arabic music. Concerts of Indian, Korean, and Persian music in the United States have prevailingly Indian, Korean, and Iranian audiences. Those Americans who do listen to non-Western music are usually musicians in Western society.

I've heard the following critical reactions to non-Western music by educated members of my society: "Is this really music?" "You can't mean you enjoy this." "Do these people know what they are doing?" "This is interesting because it is obviously ancient." "I know this is supposed to be the music of a great culture, but I just can't stand listening to it." "One doesn't have to know much to compose this music." "No wonder it's so weird; it isn't even notated." And to me: "Do you also do research on normal music?"

Members of certain non-Western societies have similar ideas about their music's cultural specificity. They similarly cannot understand why an American might wish to study or even love Indian, Chinese, and Plains Indian music. I dragged a Japanese colleague here at the University of Illinois, an expert on both Western and Japanese music, to an Indian concert. After five minutes he whispered to me, "What can one possibly get out of listening to such music?" Middle Easterners could be as intolerant as Europeans. A medieval Arab in northern Germany said, "I have never heard worse singing than that of the people of Schleswig. It is a humming that comes out of their throats, like the barking of dogs, but more beastlike" (in B. Lewis 1982, 262).

For whatever reason, there seems to be a special relationship between a society and the special musical language of its culture. There's a lot one might say or speculate concerning this suggestion, but I want to say only that I think that the use (or lack of use) of music by anthropologists who are not themselves ethnomusicologists results in part from this relationship.

The field of music has had a curious relationship to—or role in—anthropology. All along, it has had greater significance in North American anthropology than in German or British schools. In its early days in America, anthropologists were inclined to include music in their presentation of individual cultures (at least by including transcriptions of music prepared by their ethnomusicological colleagues). They were sometimes inclined to write a bit about music in their general presentations of the field of anthropology and to acknowledge its significance in presentations of culture at large. During the second half of the twentieth century, possibly intimidated by the growth of ethnomusicology, the willingness of American anthropologists to deal with music in general works gradually declined, something that is difficult to square with the increased role of anthropological perspectives in the leadership of the ethnomusicological profession. During the very end of the twentieth century, music began to reappear, very tentatively, in the literature of general anthropology.

The present situation, and even more, the history, may astonish the reader acquainted with the history of ethnomusicology. My purpose has not been to find fault with what is, after all, a characteristic of modern Western culture. If indeed fault there is, it perhaps lies most with those of us in ethnomusicology who have not found ways to persuade our anthropological colleagues that a layperson can, without inordinate effort, learn to talk competently if not expertly about music and who have not sufficiently underscored that music, in Bohannan's words, "has been proved one of the most diagnostic traits of any culture."

III

· · · · · · · · · · · · · ·

Celebrating Our
Principal Organizations

The IFMC/ICTM and the Development of Ethnomusicology in the United States

This chapter and the next, constituting a pair, have important parallels and also exhibit contrasts. Both were invited keynote papers presented at meetings of the International Council for Traditional Music (ICTM) in locations that were once under Warsaw Pact hegemony. They were read at the fortieth and fiftieth anniversaries of the ICTM—chapter 9 in what was then East Berlin, and chapter 10 in Nitra, Slovakia—after the breakup of the "communist empire." Taking rather different perspectives, the two papers nevertheless refer to some of the same events in the early history of the ICTM. I beg the reader's indulgence from some overlaps.

Introduction

At least as far back as the incorporation of the Royal Society of London for Improving Natural Knowledge in 1662, it has been understood that association, discussion, exchange of information, and debate among scholars and scientists are essential to the development of scholarship and research. The very existence of the Royal Society contributed to the development of science, particularly in Britain during the seventeenth and eighteenth centuries, and much was accomplished as a result of the associations therein formed. Similarly, the establishment of the Internationale Musikgesellschaft in 1899 provided musicology an international forum and fostered the development of general European rather than simply national approaches. In the United States, the establishment of the American Folklore Society, a bit over one hundred years ago (i.e., 1888), brought together literary artists and scholars, musicians, and anthropologists in a way that made possible the peculiarly interdisciplinary configuration of American folkloristics.

The development of ethnomusicology in teaching and research had much to do with the establishment and character of the societies whose purpose was (and is) the support of this then new field. In the United States, the ICTM has had a significant but rather special place. In this chapter I would like to trace its role, show its relationship to the Society for Ethnomusicology, and try to view what has happened via the character of American education and culture.

The Bloomington Conference of 1950

In his recent book about musicology, *Contemplating Music*, Joseph Kerman (1985, 159) notes the "magnetic force that ethnomusicology exerts upon Americans" as a result of the peculiar and energetic mix of musical cultures, classes, and political, social, and religious backgrounds in the United States. Indeed, Americans have had a history of both scholarly and institutional support for pre-ethnomusicological research since the late nineteenth century. And yet, I feel that the 1950 conference of the International Folk Music Council (IFMC) in Bloomington, Indiana, bore special significance. I had the good fortune of attending much of it in the capacity of a newly graduated college student. This grand event has been substantially recorded in volume 3 of the IFMC's journal, where the papers were published in abstract, and in the excellent descriptive report by Professor Evelyn Wells (1951). A look at the contents of volume 3 tells us about the scope and direction of those meetings. The papers are largely about European folk music, and many are descriptive and ethnographic. It is interesting to see the large number of prominent names: Saygun, Barbeau, Bayard, Lord, Herzog, Jackson, Karpeles, Kurath, Seeger, Waterman. All in all, it was not a meeting focusing on methodology and theory. Still, there are methodological landmarks: one of Bronson's earliest attempts to do statistical comparative study, an early essay in musical ethnography of Negro churches in Chicago by Waterman, and Charles Seeger's first presentation of his melograph—curiously, "presented" but not read at the meeting, though published in the proceedings.

The character of the conference can be assessed even better in another publication emanating from a conference that immediately followed the IFMC meeting and was thus attended by most of the same people: the "Mid-Century Conference on Folklore." This conference was for all intents and purposes a continuation of the IFMC meeting, and the book *Four Symposia on Folklore,* edited by the host of the conference, Stith Thompson (1952), faithfully records the discussions, including lengthy position statements, laying bare the purposes and attitudes of the scholars present. It tells us a lot about the issues of the time.

The four symposia deal with collecting, archiving, making available, and studying folklore. The issues include the question of authenticity, especially the degree to which urban and modernized forms are to be accepted for study; the need to make "complete" collections; the study of the history of forms and units in folk literature; and the existence of the "folk" as a distinct unit. Finding ways to preserve dying traditions and thus reacquaint people with their past was a chief aim of these symposia. Besides folk-music scholars, those present included some of the most illustrious figures in folklorics from the first half of the century, such as Walter Anderson and Otto Andersson.

Faithful though they may be to the discussions and papers at the IFMC conference, the accounts published in the council's journal don't quite give the flavor of the meeting. If you'll allow me to reminisce, the scene I perhaps remember best occurred during a presentation by Marius Barbeau in which he sang examples of American Indian music. As he was singing, I was surprised by a figure suddenly rising in the back of the room but quickly realized that it was Gertrude Kurath, moved to dance by Barbeau's melody, improvising her art. The next day, Mrs. Kurath herself was ready to read a paper, but she seemed to be absent and the audience was perplexed. Just as the chairman was about to give up, we began to hear the approach of someone singing an Iroquois song, and a dancing and singing

Gertrude soon entered, sat down, and delivered her paper. There were many such moments, at which love of the material and the art, participation in folk culture, and scholarship seemed to be closely interwoven.

Scholars accustomed to traditional academic conferences might have been mildly scandalized by such goings-on, but at this meeting, no one seemed to have serious trouble reconciling these elements. After all, even the revered Stith Thompson was known to sing Child ballads at his grad-student parties. Walter Anderson, the paradigmatic scholar of the historical-geographic method, was an accomplished raconteur. And still, I have the feeling that one of the major divisions in American ethnomusicology, as it was to manifest itself later, relates to the scenes I've just described. One group of scholars—mainly those with an interest in the discipline of folklore and those who came from the world of practicing musicianship—seemed to move between intellectual and artistic modes as readily as do historians of European art music who are also accomplished organists, cellists, or choral conductors. Another group, including some who came mainly from anthropology, might indeed love and even play music—but typically not the music they studied. These scholars might well take the musician-folklorist-scholars to be involved in frivolous folderol. Such rather stiff-backed critics, however, were later to provide much of the intellectual leadership of American ethnomusicology and were among the principal founders of the Society for Ethnomusicology. Not many of them came to Bloomington in 1950.

American Paradigms: Herzog and Seeger

So the 1950 meeting illuminates one kind of division among American scholars, but there are also others worthy of our attention today. Like American culture generally, ethnomusicology has long experienced a kind of dualism between a dependence on European models and forebears and the desire to act and innovate independently. In our field, the two sides of the American character were foreshadowed by such figures as the European-trained Theodore Baker and the essentially autodidact Frances Densmore. But for more characteristic paradigms, we should look briefly at the work of George Herzog and Charles Seeger (for bibliography, see Krader 1956 [for Herzog]; Seeger 1977, 345–63). Seeger, much the senior, had a long, distinguished career as a conductor and scholar. Herzog has frequently been named as the person who brought European-style comparative musicology to North America, but significantly, his ability to compromise and strike a balance among several European and American traditions created a generally acceptable and ultimately highly influential approach. Not that the blending of views is an American specialty, but something like it was necessary for the establishment of a uniquely American culture. In the same way, I think that Herzog's blending of viewpoints helped to create one side of the distinctively American-style ethnomusicology.

In Herzog's methodology, three approaches stand out. He began his studies at the Royal Conservatory in Budapest, and although I have not been able to ascertain that he studied directly under Béla Bartók and Zoltán Kodály, he regarded Bartók's approach to folk-music research as canonical, a methodology to be emulated in other areas of the world, and he used aspects of it in his later research in American Indian music. He proceeded to study in Berlin, with Hornbostel, working for a time as his assistant and becoming his disciple.

I don't know why Herzog left Europe without completing his doctoral studies, but he emigrated in 1925 and took up the study of anthropology at Columbia University under Franz Boas, whose approach to that field was similarly many-sided and syncretic. The point is that he was able, from all these European-based strands of methodology, to fashion an approach that was the most comprehensive to date in its view of musical culture. His mature studies on American Indian music thus combined the elements of his background and served as models for the holistic approach to music that came to be widely used in ethnomusicology in North America.

Whereas Herzog was a synthesizer and compromiser, Seeger was a loner (in his intellectual work) and an iconoclast. The two had similar concerns in the 1930s, shared certain political views, and also worked on the establishments of organizations, helping to re-create in America the defunct Gesellschaft zur Erforschung der Musik des Orients (renamed Gesellschaft für vergleichende Musikwissenschaft in 1934), establishing in its place the short-lived American Society for Comparative Musicology. But while Herzog marshaled various viewpoints to bear on a single goal, Seeger looked successively at different goals, from composing to high-tech, from organizational combination of all to total fragmentation, from studies of a totally theoretical and philosophical nature to the most hands-on of technicality, using tradition as a basis for innovation. In his American character, especially the grand sweep of his mind, his occasional incomprehensibility, his tendency to say simple things in complex ways, and his espousal of elite methods tinged with a brand of populism, he has been compared to the composer Charles Ives. His articles consistently provided new ideas as well as new contexts of presentation for established ideas.

So while Herzog insisted on the sacredness of the traditions from which he came, making new scholarship by combining them, Seeger sought for new methods, emphasizing their newness rather than their relationship to tradition. The two approaches were continued by students and successors, but for a short time at the meetings of 1950 I saw them brought together, for Seeger and Herzog were both present. At that time, one might have worked to establish a strong arm of the IFMC in North America. I have no idea about the personal relationships of the time, or of conversations that might have taken place, but this rather climactic moment in American musical scholarship was shortly followed by the establishment of the Society for Ethnomusicology (SEM), an event to which Charles Seeger's contribution was preeminent.

The Arrival of the SEM: Merriam and Hood

Joseph Kerman (1985, 163) presents American ethnomusicology during the early 1950s to the early 1980s as a dialogue between two viewpoints, an essentially anthropological one, represented by Alan Merriam, and a more conventionally musicological one, represented by Mantle Hood (for paradigmatic expositions, see Merriam 1964; Hood 1971). One might be tempted to see Hood as a successor to Seeger, the composer, practical musician, and generally practical man, and Merriam as a successor to the methodologically holistic anthropologist Herzog. I'm not sure this is the right interpretation. Whether one is more interested in music or in culture has never been much of an issue among the more intellectual of American ethnomusicologists. Mantle Hood's publications make clear his interest in music as a part of the culture from which it comes, and Merriam provided detailed analyses and transcriptions, telling us that the "sound" of music is certainly a part of that "music" which he wished to study as culture. The issue between these two scholars and the institutions they represented may have been more political. Curiously, while Seeger and Herzog, in 1950, seemed to support the IFMC wholeheartedly, neither Merriam nor Hood ever did so to a great extent.

One of the pervasive bits of oral tradition in the SEM is the story of the society's founders, who met at the end of 1952 more or less by chance and proceeded to plan a series of steps to further ethnomusicology in America and the world. The "four founders" were Alan Merriam, the most activist; David McAllester, like Merriam a recent Ph.D. in anthropology; Willard Rhodes, a long-time collector of American Indian music; and Charles Seeger, who seems to have acted as a kind of elder statesman. Their discussions first led them to send a newsletter to a group of presumedly interested scholars, including a number of Europeans, so as to establish communication on an international scale.

Soon thereafter, I asked Merriam why one could not have done the same thing through the IFMC. The tenor of his replies in our correspondence involved his perception of the IFMC as specifically interested in music alone; the notion that folk-music scholars were interested in only a small segment of the music of any society; and the idea that the IFMC included a substantial practical component, that is, was in large measure a society of folksingers and dancers. The beginning of the SEM was deeply rooted in the anthropological background of its most influential leaders.

So, while the American Musicological Society occasionally welcomed papers on non-Western and folk music, special panels in the field of ethnomusicology typically took place at meetings of anthropologists during the early and middle 1950s. The intellectual leadership in ethnomusicology rested (and to a substantial extent still rests) with scholars who have an anthropological background or at least considerable knowledge of anthropology. This surely results from the broad view of anthropology espoused by Franz Boas and his school. The field of ethnomusicology might have gone on for a long time as a kind of anthropological subspecialty, scorning the IFMC because it took a totally different viewpoint from the theory-oriented field of anthropology. Yet the situation was modified by another important event of the 1950s, the establishment of the UCLA ethnomusicology program by Mantle Hood.

Contrary perhaps to Merriam and Herzog, Hood wished to present ethnomusicology as a field whose practitioners do essentially what typical traditional musicologists do, or at least what they professed to do. This included a concentration on art music; a requirement that the scholar play a musician's role, even to the extent of performing or possibly composing the music studied; and an essentially culture-specific, noncomparative, positivistic stance. Ethnomusicology should become part of the world of music, helping cultures communicate through music. In this respect, Hood's viewpoint paralleled that of some of the folklorists who appeared in the 1950 meetings in Bloomington, including Alan Lomax—except that Hood wished to concentrate on art music, and Lomax, on the "favored song style," folk music (Lomax 1968, 133). Interestingly, these two scholars, who have clearly disagreed at various times, both continued to maintain a strong allegiance to Charles Seeger. Mantle Hood, enormously successful in establishing a teaching program and encouraging North American institutions to include ethnomusicology in their curricula, wanted to see the Society for Ethnomusicology become a truly international body. The 1950s and 1960s saw a certain amount of jockeying for cooperation and absorption, both internationally and within the United States.

Scholarly Societies, American Education, and American Culture

The question of an officially "international" status for the SEM was first raised formally in 1965, when a large number of non-U.S. residents were elected to the society's council in the belief that this would give the international membership a greater voice. The notion of internationalization, foreign chapters, and plenary meetings outside North America was still being raised in the 1980s. The "official" position of the SEM has always been neutral. It is a society of persons, their residence or citizenship irrelevant. Canadians have played a major role in any event, and there have been presidents who resided in Berlin and Belfast. And there were times of official cooperation with the IFMC; for instance, a program reducing dues for those who belonged to both organizations was attempted for a few years.

In the course of the 1960s and 1970s, many American ethnomusicologists welcomed the existence of two societies in their field, one principally though not officially North American, the other unabashedly international though with emphasis on European membership. The two organizations also behaved quite differently. The IFMC had a journal which until 1971 had many short contributions and a very large bibliographical and reviewing apparatus; the SEM provided other kinds of services in its journal. Curiously, the history of the IFMC since 1970 involves a greater approximation to the services and publications of the SEM and greater participation in the organization's management by residents of North America. American membership increased to over 200 personal memberships, by far the largest group, though not in proportion to population size. The notion that one could attract members to both organizations through reduced dues had not worked, but here, perhaps suddenly, many individuals were members of both. The reasons surely involve economics, but they must also include the general proclivity of Americans, a self-described nation of "joiners," to sign up in many organizations. But the large-scale participation of Americans in the ICTM (its name had changed from the IFMC in 1981) also resulted from changes in the services it provided, its movement from a partially amateur to an essentially professional organization, and the role that ethnomusicology plays in the American academy.

The relatively small role that the ICTM has played in American ethnomusicology seems to be related to the role of professional societies in American academic life and to the structure of American higher education. In the arts and humanities, research and scholarship are, as it were, owned by universities. A university teacher is generally paid a salary on which one can live and modestly support a family, and his or her official obligations include teaching and administrative work as well as research. For this reason, you will see the names of institutions attached to the names of authors of articles. And as is well known, failure to publish can cost us our jobs and certainly salary increases. At the same time, however, universities and colleges generally fund the necessary research and its underpinnings—at least in the humanities. Thus, most scholarly societies have homes with central offices at universities, and the editors of journals receive, ideally, some support in the form of personnel, computers, and released time from their departments. There is, therefore, a substantial incentive to attract societies, their offices, and organs to one's home institution and, by the same token, to establish as many organizations as possible. It is a development that fits well into the character of the Americans as a nation of club founders and joiners.

And so, even if there is an IFMC or ICTM available for us, we in the United States are likely to say, "Fine, but let's also have our own organization, our own journal, and let's encourage our members to create subdivisions. And let's have overlapping societies; they will increase our support from the institutions, which, albeit sometimes kicking and screaming, will give us financial help." And so we have not only the SEM, with its chapters, but also the Society for Asian Music; societies involved with Chinese, Indian, and African American music; several folklore societies (with interest in folk music); local and university societies of ethnomusicology; and more. The system encourages American scholars to live professionally through their organizations. The somewhat special role that the ICTM has played in the United States must be to some degree derived from the particular interrelationships of scholars, institutions, and organizations.

10

Arrows and Circles

Fifty Years of the ICTM and
the Study of Traditional Music

Introduction

It's an honor for me to have been invited to speak, here in the Slovak Republic, on this occasion of the golden anniversary of the ICTM (International Council for Traditional Music). Astonished by this invitation, I have sought for the program committee's motivations and have concluded that they asked me because they thought I am such a senior citizen that I probably helped Theodore Baker proofread his dissertation in 1882. Indeed, as I was present at the 1950 meeting of the IFMC (International Folk Music Council) in Bloomington, I may qualify as the person who has been attending IFMC/ICTM meetings longer than anyone else here today. In that summer of 1950, I had just begun to study seriously with the conference's local arrangements chair, Dr. George Herzog, and he asked me to be his errand boy. So I'll hark back several times today to those precedent-setting times. I also have the feeling that the program committee ended up with me because they associated me with the part of the world where we are meeting today, an area that was seminal, as well, to much of what happened later in our field. And so, in looking unsystematically at our history, I'll be pointing out how so much of significance happened within two or three hundred kilometers from Nitra, where I'm speaking. Also, while the concept of "keynote talk" suggests prediction and a perspective of the future, I always duck when students ask me what I think may happen someday, so I'll talk somewhat about the past and avoid prediction.

If we are an organization of people devoted to scholarship and research, looking back to the time of our origins, we should be asking what we have learned—or with a bit more bite, whether we have learned anything—in all that time. A book by Stephen Jay Gould, *Time's Arrow, Time's Cycle* (1987), suggested my title to me. It juxtaposes the resigned-sounding adage "history repeats itself," applied to academic disciplines, to the progressive notion of the history of science as punctuated by successive paradigms.

So I want to ask to what extent we in ethnomusicology have been following the circle of history, repeating, rediscovering, and maintaining consistency, and to what extent we have followed history's arrow. I'd like to draw your attention back about fifty years, and more, so that we can see how our organization and our profession has moved forward and how our history has been cyclic. I want to do this substantially by sharing some personal experiences and also by referring to some of the early publications of the ICTM or, more properly, the IFMC.

Déjà Vu?

But wait—isn't this, in the possibly apocryphal words of the famous American baseball player Yogi Berra, "déjà vu all over again?" In 1987, our fortieth anniversary, several spoke about the history of the ICTM, its relationship to the field of ethnomusicology as a whole, the interface between European and American styles of scholarship, and our institutional history (see, e.g., Christensen 1988; Nettl 1988; Stockmann 1988). Certainly we don't need to hear this again. That year seems in some ways ages ago. We met in East Berlin, behind the wall, and I very much felt the restrictions this suggests. Sharp distinctions were made among members on the basis of their home countries, and people associated with one another largely in terms of closed groups based on national or political orientation. At that moment, I certainly wasn't expecting the onset of perestroika and glasnost, for I experienced them only a year later in the USSR; nor did I expect, just two years later, the Velvet Revolution in my native country of Czechoslovakia, the tumbling of the Berlin Wall, and everything else that followed. But four years later we were again in Berlin, this time without the wall, and these two meetings seem to me to constitute a watershed in the history of our organization. As I said, the 1987 meeting behind the wall now seems ages ago. As we would say in America, "it has been some ten years." And even our earlier history may look rather different to us today than it did in 1987.

It has also, as we might say, "been some half a century" since the IFMC took its first steps. At its beginning, in 1947, ethnomusicology was barely there, at least as a field with a population. Philip Bohlman (1988) made a fine case for the eighteenth-century beginnings of ethnomusicology, and various histories of the field ascribe its onset to Guido Adler's (1885) seminal article, to the earliest field recordings of 1891, to the publication of the *Sammelbände für vergleichende Musikwissenschaft* in 1922, to Jaap Kunst's first edition of *Musicologica* (Kunst 1950), or the establishment of the Society for Ethnomusicology in 1955 or even the publication of *The Anthropology of Music* (Merriam 1964). Never mind, origins are always obscure. In any event, when the IFMC was founded, in 1947, the term *ethnomusicology* wasn't yet established, and when it was, perhaps a few years later, many of our members really wouldn't have felt comfortable with such a high-falutin' word. The difference between the folk music of European and European-derived societies and that of non-Western societies loomed large at the time.

A Bit of Autobiography

Being presented here as your official senior citizen, I feel entitled to be a bit autobiographical, especially as my own first experiences of what we now call ethnomusicology are closely associated with the part of the world in which I make these remarks. To establish a kind of baseline for questions, I want to ask about our first fifty years, and to do so I'd like to use three personal incidents that characterize our field in the period around or just before 1947. The first goes back to my early childhood in Prague and Walter Kaufmann (born, incidentally, in Karlsbad, or Karlovy Vary, not far from here). Kaufmann later became a distinguished scholar of

South Asian music, but I knew him because he studied under my father, Paul Nettl, and was a friend of the family. Walter floored me in 1934 by telling me that he was moving to India. At the age of five, I had heard of India and knew it was far away, and so I asked Walter why. "Ah," he said, "they have wonderful music." I hadn't yet started violin lessons, but living in a household of musicians, I had the idea that playing music meant playing compositions from notes on music stands. No, Walter said, "In India, they *improvise* their music." I can almost hear him saying it: "Sie spielen es gleich aus dem Kopf" (they play it right out of their heads). Never mind the arguable nature of that statement; it rather blew my mind, and I've never recovered, but what I learned from Walter that day was that music in other cultures differs fundamentally, in its basics (like notation), from the standard music of Europe, and I think this may indeed be one of the central notions promulgated by people who were working in what was then called comparative musicology. The conception at the time was, it seems to me, that non-Western music is fundamentally different from the "normal" music experienced by these scholars, who thus need special concepts and perhaps methods for understanding it.

A couple of years later, still in Prague, my father came home with an album of 78-rpm records titled *Musik des Orients*, later recognized as a discographic landmark, and began to play them; in particular I still can hear in my mind's ear these bits of gamelan music and a responsorial iterative song of the Egyptian Sufis. But my father used these records to begin a course on music history, and the message seemed to be this: there is something in this music that could shed light on the origins and early forms of music. The study of this kind of music, at the center of it the figure of Hornbostel, a man born near us, in Vienna, was mainly a kind of *Hilfswissenschaft*, a subject complementary, albeit essential, to the historical understanding of real music. Anyway, as I said, this happened not far from here, in Prague, and so I share with you these almost local memories.

For my third incident I mention taking a course in 1949 at Indiana University, in Bloomington. The course was taught by George Herzog (a man reared not far from here, in Budapest) and titled "Folk and Primitive Music." I won't bother discussing what this kind of title tells us about the attitudes of early ethnomusicology, but Herzog brought to this course the eclectic approach that characterized his work and also that of many in our field: the analytic folk-music study of Bartók and Kodály, with their emphasis on authenticity; the analytical paradigms developed by Hornbostel; the holistic view of culture characteristic of American anthropology of

Franz Boas; the folkloristics of the Scandinavian school and its historical-geographic method; and pre-Chomskian linguistics as taught by Leonard Bloomfield and Edward Sapir (see Nettl 1991).

These three aspects of the study of non-Western and folk music—the focus on the exotic and the special methods that requires, the attachment of non-Western music to the Western for suggesting a skewed chronology of world music, and the unification of an eclectic methodology—these three seem to me to constitute a baseline for the development of ethnomusicology in the fifty years that followed.

So, what have we learned in the last fifty years? Have we reinvented the wheel, or have we moved forward? Let me ask several questions and provide comments, though of course no answers: (1) What is ethnomusicology? (2) What is music? (3) What is *a* music—or rather, what is our conception of the world of music? (4) What kind of people are we? And finally, (5) have we done anyone any good? Again, I have no answers but want to comment briefly and selectively from the viewpoints of circle and arrow.

What Is Ethnomusicology?

In 1964 Alan Merriam began *The Anthropology of Music* (1964, 3) by saying, "Ethnomusicology today is an area of study caught up in a fascination with itself." Considering that we ethnomusicologists are not numerous, the number of publications that set out to define and conceptualize ethnomusicology is considerable. Compare that with musicology as a whole, or with physics or chemistry, whose practitioners don't worry much about defining their fields. Merriam's (1977) article on the subject documents a long history of discussion as to what the *ethno-* means and what the adjective *comparative* implies. I think we are still at it. This, then, constitutes one of our circles: we keep coming back to self-definition.

Comparing the program of today's meeting with those of the IFMC's earliest conferences (whose proceedings were published in the first four volumes of the IFMC's journal, 1948–51), I am struck by the congruence of interests. Let me offer you some of the topics of 1947–50, some of the principal subjects, and a sampling of papers. Peasant societies: a host of papers, such as Cvjetko Rihtman, "Les Formes polyphoniques dans la musique populaire de Bosnie," or Solon Michaelides, "Greek Folk Music, Its Preservation and Traditional Practice." Education: Charles Seeger, "Folk Music in the Schools of a Highly Industrialized Society," and Sándor Veress, "Folk Music in Musical and General Education." Music and ethnicity: Ayalah Kaufman, "Indigenous and Imported Elements in the New Folk Dance of Israel," or Sara Gertrude Knott's description of the U.S. National Folk Festival. Technology: there were no computers yet, but Charles Seeger's "Instantaneous Music Notator" appears here, as does Bertrand Bronson's "Melodic Stability in Oral Transmission," which explains his punch-card classification system. Relationship of music and dance: the first four volumes are full of articles on dance and music. "World Beat": our predecessors were concerned with its predecessors, though they worried about authenticity and about the effects of letting popular music get a foot in the door of folk traditions; nonetheless, Ben Lumpkin read a paper entitled "Traditional Folk Songs Available on Commercial Records." And boundaries of all sorts were there: Arnold Bake, "The Impact of Western Music on the Indian Musical System"; Patrick Shuldham-Shaw, "Folk Song and the Concert Singer"; several articles on folk and art music; George Pullen Jackson's "Native and Imported Elements in American Religious Folk Song"; Felix Hoerburger, "Correspondences between Eastern and Western Epics"; and Jonas Balys, "Lithuanian Folk Songs in the United States."

I give you these titles to display the heraldry of our anniversary celebration but also to point out the important consistencies in the interests of fifty years ago and those of today. But we also have the arrow. Our attitudes have changed enormously. For one thing, we worry less about authenticity and about preservation, though the attention paid to media, copyright, and archiving in this meeting and in the latest *Yearbook* suggests that we are still concerned about them, though in a new way. We believe, though sometimes we throw up our hands in frustration, that each society has some music it considers its own and with which it identifies itself—but to the nature of societies as nations or ethnic groups sharing a language, we have added generational, religious, gender-based, and occupational subcultures. More significantly, we have responded to the attitude of Jaap Kunst, who in 1959 told us that "Western art- and popular (entertainment-) music do not belong" in ethnomusicology (1959, 1). We now pay more attention to popular musics, variously defined, than to anything else. I won't try to comment further on what has changed. Instead I'll ask whether it's time for us to reconsider the disciplinary alignments that have served us well yet sometimes impeded us, too. Above all, just what does the ICTM mean by "traditional" music?

What Is Music?

I don't propose to define music, heaven forfend. But we ethnomusicologists understand music in a unique way. It's not Longfellow's "universal language of mankind," and it does not have Congreve's "charms to soothe a savage breast," nor is it Horace's "sweet and healing balm," or "the only sensual pleasure without vice," as Samuel Johnson would have it. Music has many forms, but ethnomusicologists have tended to look at it in dichotomies: oral/written, authentic/mixed, and most important, ours/not ours or normal/strange. "Do you also do research on normal music?" I was asked by a pianist visiting my American Indian music class. But the papers at the 1950 Bloomington meeting and in the early volumes of the *Journal of the International Folk Music Council* saw folk music principally as it contrasted with art music. During the early times of the IFMC, the division was between folk music and the rest, but from the beginning, IFMC members seem to have been uncomfortable with the concept of folk music, too. In 1955 they tried to establish a definition by resolution; I think it's time to quote it:

> Folk music is the product of a musical tradition that has evolved through the process of oral transmission. The factors that shape the tradition are: i) continuity that links the present with the past; ii) variation which springs from the creative impulse of the individual or the group; iii) selection by the community which determines the form or forms in which the music survives.
>
> The term can be applied to music that has evolved from rudimentary beginnings by a community uninfluenced by popular and art music and it can likewise be applied to music which has originated with an individual composer and has subsequently been absorbed into the unwritten living tradition of a community.
>
> The term does not cover composed popular music that has been taken over ready made by a community and remains unchanged, for it is the re-fashioning and re-creation of the music by the community that gives it its folk character. (IFMC 1955)

This dichotomy, between folk and art music, may be our oldest, the one that first drove our field. It goes back to the early nineteenth century, to Johann Gottfried Herder, Père Amiot, Sir William Jones, maybe even Beethoven and his arrangements of Scottish, Irish, and English folk songs. Yet listening to Beethoven's arrangements, one can easily imagine the discomfort of those members who wanted the category restricted to "Lord Randall" and "Barbara Allen," those who objected to the notion that highly professionalized repertories living in oral tradition should be called "folk," and those who agree with Big Bill Broonzy, who is said to have asserted, "All music is folk music; I've never heard a horse sing" (to which the more gluttonous ethnomusicologists might reply, "Yes, they do, or we can study the neighs as if they were song, just as we have looked at the sounds of whales and dolphins"). In any event, we continue to be fascinated by the great variety of the world's musical sounds, everything from gagaku to Plains singing to Tuvan throat singing, from the Sardinian *launeddas* to the didgeridoo. It is the logical successor to the exoticism of two centuries ago.

The question for the future is clear. Fortunately, we can cease going for the exotic because it is exotic. But what music will the ICTM take to be special in its next years? Will we define ourselves by a group of musics? Will we cease to be driven by the world's musical diversity?

What Is *a* Music?

The notion of a world of discrete musics is relatively new, and the change in terminology has various implications. From the beginning of the IFMC, however, and even earlier in the beginnings of "ethno," there has been the overwhelming conception that we must speak of Cherokee music, Persian music, or Slovak music and that in making, say, statistical statements about the world's music, we must use the world's musics as the units of counting. But what to include in *a* music?

Our colleagues in historical musicology have an easier time; their units of musical creation—their "default" unit, to use computer terminology—is the composer. Yes, they talk about English or Italian or Hungarian music, but there's no pretense that it's a single thing. When the chips are down, the units of musical thought are the composers. In folk-music studies, from the beginning—Herder or Bishop Percy—one talked about the music of *peoples*. Indeed, when pressed for an aesthetic justification for the study of Czech or Mambuti or Australian Aboriginal music, one used to say, "Well, I don't know whether this is as great music as is Bach, but after all, it's the music that all Czechs or Aboriginals know; it's *their* music more than Bach is any society's principal music." The first few volumes of our organization's journal contain many papers about the music of this or that nation: folk dances of Ireland, folk songs of Egypt, folk music of East Pakistan, Norwegian folk music and its social significance, the folk dances of Canada. These papers and others like them don't attempt to draw boundaries, but the boundaries are rather taken for granted; it's assumed that the folk songs of Sweden have important things in common. We still talk largely in these terms. The idea of the world of music as a set of musics is a paradigm of one of our circles, a concept to which we keep returning. But as we do, we see its difficulties and complexities.

When I studied with George Herzog, he, like Jaap Kunst, discouraged attention to popular music. Too commercial it was, it had no aesthetic justification, and perhaps most important, it played havoc with the notion of boundaries. Most of it was mixed, hybrid, polluted. Today it's that mixing, the cultural and stylistic layering, the polysemic quality, the recombination and reinterpretation, that fascinates many of us. And so one of the major changes in the attitude of ethnomusicologists is the abandonment of the notion of authenticity. In volume 3 of our journal, two articles deal with authenticity, but both authors, Maud Karpeles (1951) and Adnan Saygun (1951), conclude little as to what is "authentic" folk music. But several papers refer to the notion of a particular country's "true" folk music. Thus, volume 3 also has an extended discussion among Herzog, Richard Waterman, George Pullen Jackson, and Samuel Bayard as to what constitutes black versus white music and to what extent African American church music is distinctly African-derived. This now well-documented controversy finds its motivating force in the question of boundaries (Waterman 1951).

Today, curiously, we still talk about music largely in terms of cultural and social boundaries, but perhaps we have learned things about the interrelationships of music, ethnicity, and personal and group identity. Our predecessors were concerned with the preservation of unchanging folk music—unchanging among the people who practiced it—but they subscribed to a definition that emphasized the changeability of that music. We have vastly better technologies for preservation, but we also realize that if change is one of the characteristics of folk music, we had better leave it alone to undergo change, concentrating on how this change takes place and what it means.

But away from nostalgia. Looking toward the future, we should consider how to conceive the world of music. The analogy with languages has been helpful, but it goes only so far. Do we need a new theory of what is *a* music?

What Kind of People Are We?

I looked at the photograph, in volume 3 (opposite p. 1), of the participants in the 1950 meeting in Bloomington, and I marvel at the youngish appearance of figures now departed—Charles Seeger, Bertrand Bronson, Samuel Bayard, George Herzog, Albert Lord—and the middle-aged look of people now in the realm of legend—Maud Karpeles, Walter Anderson, Otto Andersson, Stith Thompson, Marius Barbeau. These are scholars on whose shoulders we now work. Absent at that particular meeting, by the way, were colleagues from Eastern Europe, Asia, and Africa, whose opportunities to travel to America were limited. But the people who were there—what were they like, as a group?

They are there in their Sunday best, wearing neckties and sometimes jackets in the sweltering heat of August in southern Indiana. But in the paper sessions, at their social events, and in their outings they were a pretty relaxed crowd, especially considering that most of them were, after all, teachers in higher education. It was interesting to compare them with members of the International Musicological Society and the American Musicological Society, who are much more formal and less relaxed, I felt. Still, they were not generally people who identified themselves directly with the "folk." They were doing something *for* the folk: preserving their art, studying it in ways that wouldn't occur to the "folk" themselves, and even doing things to help the folk maintain authenticity—whether they wanted it or not. They saw themselves as experts, not as pupils. But when they read papers, they showed humor and they sang their musical examples—even the revered Walter Anderson, author of the pathbreaking reconstructive work *Kaiser und Abt* (1923), sang a ditty. Memorably, Gertrude Kurath danced her way up the aisle to the podium as an introduction to her paper. And they argued with great conviction not just about scholarship but also about matters of a practical significance—broadcasting, folk music in education, or the maintenance of traditions in modernized society. They had practical goals; they wanted people to know folk songs, wanted to become established.

Are we still like those people at the Bloomington meeting? I'm not sure. We like to talk about world music in education, but we expect educationists to make it happen. We would like to maintain that our type of study, dealing as it does with music accepted by large populations, by music that carries relevant social messages, bears greater significance than does research on Brahms and Gounod, but we haven't developed a professional conviction, and we lack a holistic theory that integrates social and aesthetic factors.

It seems to me that we are a rather different kind of crowd from those of 1947 or 1950 in several ways. One of the most evident involves the number of nations represented today. In its earliest years, the IFMC comprised mostly Europeans, joined by some North Americans and the occasional Asian scholar. Later, participation by East Europeans, residents of the socialist nations, greatly increased—as did that of North Americans, who, as Dieter Christensen pointed out (1988), were seen as a threat because of their numbers and resources. Today one can identify several schools of researchers, best though only approximately designated by world area. I won't dare try to characterize lest I miscast you, my listeners in Nitra, but these groups of scholars differ in their conception of ethnomusicology—in North America, for example, it's the study of all music from an anthropological perspective, with emphasis on studying the foreign. In some other parts of the world, it is the study of the music of ethnic groups; elsewhere, it concentrates on uncovering the ancient; and elsewhere again, national minorities are the focus. Of course, this is the most cursory kind of typology. There are many overlaps, and I apologize if you feel you have been miscast. But while the greater inclusiveness of the ICTM, and of the field of ethnomusicology, is part of history's arrow, the lively interchange among different groups of scholars that characterized the discussions printed in volume 3 of our journal inspires hope. And speaking of history's circle: one may have heard a lot about authenticity fifty years ago, but one also heard, in papers such as Walter Wiora's (1949), plenty of misgivings about the concept and the way it might be used.

I am sorry to note that history's arrow has tended to move us away from dance. We still pay a lot of attention to it, more than do other societies with a central commitment to music, but less than we used to do. Of the ninety-five papers of substance in the first five volumes of our journal, twenty-six deal explicitly with dance—and in others, dance plays a bit of a role. Of the forty-seven articles in the last five issues of the *Yearbook of the International Folk Music Council*, I identified only four as being mainly about dance. The early IFMC, it seems to me, was an organization devoted to both music and dance, with virtual equality.

In its early years the IFMC represented fewer nations but more professions—scholars, teachers, singers, and dancers—as well as amateurs. In contemplating what kind of people we are, should we continue on the road to scholarly professionalism, or should we try to return to the broader and not always so academic orientation of 1947?

Have We Done Anybody Any Good?

It's tempting to make an occasion such as our fiftieth anniversary into an event of self-congratulation. The ICTM has grown into a major organization; the field of ethnomusicology has changed from the strange hobby of a few practitioners to a recognized profession. We may say smugly that the world must need us because it has provided jobs for at least a good many of us. But we should also ask whether anyone would notice if we all disappeared. Have we benefited musical life as a whole, or the place of music in higher education, or have we done something for the musicians who have been our teachers?

The world has grown in its consciousness of musical diversity, of the role music and dance play in ethnic identity. Many of the points that we used to make in teaching during the early days, points that students and other listeners greeted with surprise and skepticism, are now part of mainstream experience. We would like to claim responsibility, yet I think the profession of ethnomusicology and the efforts of organizations such as the ICTM have played only a minuscule role in the ordinary world of humanly organized sound. The attempts to speak to the wider public via our publications and some of our study groups cannot claim major impact.

Our influence has been largely in the academy, where we have helped to raise the consciousness of some of the world's music teachers and professors to the diversity of the world's music and the diversity of the approaches that might be followed to understand it. The number of people who teach ethnomusicology or have done some study of it is now very large. Musicians—everybody from the Grateful Dead to the Kronos Quartet—take our existence for granted and want to talk to us, even though they sometimes misunderstand what we are really about.

Have we done any good for the musicians of the world whose work we study but whom we have often treated more as exotic objects than as persons? That's more questionable, but at least we have talked about this obligation more than did our predecessors. We have engaged in some self-flagellation on that account, but only a few of us have taken an active role. In part, we aren't sure what that role should be, how we could do anyone any good. Should we maintain distance or become agents and advocates? I salute those of you who have made concrete decisions and become active, including, I may say, our new president, Anthony Seeger, who became famous for studying why the Suyá sing, as well as for helping them to maintain their culture. It raises a question for the future: should we, not just as individuals but as an origination, increase our emphasis on providing service to people who are not our members and who have never heard of us?

Well, to close, I don't know whether the denizens of the field of ethnomusicology and the organizations that represent them can claim to have succeeded in significantly changing the world's attitudes toward music or in having furthered the interests of the world's musicians. But in a parallel world, I feel, it would indeed have been noticed if those who in our world founded the IFMC and others like them had not taken up their swords or their pens in the late 1940s and early 1950s. We have certainly gone substantially beyond the modest aims of the IFMC as stated at its beginnings, and I venture to say that the field of musical learning and education would have developed very differently without us. I have said some things about the past and asked but didn't answer some questions for the future, and I kept my promise not to predict. Our first fifty years have seen lots of continuity and some change. Whatever the answers to my questions, and in the light of the objectives of the IFMC as stated in 1947, I hope that for its second fifty years, the ICTM and its members will continue to study and help disseminate, preserve, and practice the traditional musics and dance of the world's peoples, as arts and as essential domains of culture. They should change their approaches and methods as suggested by disciplinary, technological, and social developments, but they should also maintain a central purpose with curiosity, with energy and passion, and with concern for both substance and method, for scholarly and human values. Holding to these principles will nevertheless give us, I now feel safe in predicting, a hundredth anniversary meeting in 2047 whose content is totally beyond our imagination today.

11

We're on the Map

Reflections on the Society for Ethnomusicology in 1955 and 2005

I'm looking at the Society for Ethnomusicology (SEM) with one eye on the arrow, the other on the circle—trajectories leading from 1955 to 2005. We are still—or again—asking ourselves many questions. What is ethnomusicology, anyway? Are we satisfied with our name as a society? Are we national, regional, global? Who are our allies? What disciplines are setting precedents for us? What kinds of people do we as ethnomusicologists want to be, and how do we want our society to reflect this set of personal commitments? And what will we do with our ubiquitous visual emblem, the "little man" or "ethnoman"? History's arrow may show us to have made unbelievable progress, constantly leaving old ideas and approaches far behind. History's circle seems to be putting us back where we started, to revisit, constantly, the same fundamental issues.

Some of these questions were in the air back when the SEM was founded and beginning to establish itself, but they weren't discussed much, which meant that in various guises, they have had to be revisited periodically. I want to comment a bit about these questions in the context of our founding period's relationship to the present. But I wish to start by recalling some of the facts of the early days, putting them into a historical context, and to use as a starting point a kind of mythology that parallels and explains but also contradicts history and that we should both celebrate and challenge, an interesting, larger-than-life mythology.

Three Myths

MYTH 1: THE GRAND ENTRY Here is the story as it is often told. Alan P. Merriam, David P. McAllester, and Willard Rhodes attended a meeting of the American Anthropological Society during the 1952 Christmas season, decided that something ought to be done to further what would later be called ethnomusicology, and took a train to New Haven, where, at a meeting of the American Musicological Society (AMS), they met and consulted Charles Seeger, a senior colleague. The four then decided to try to get something started with a newsletter. This led to the publication of a set of mimeographed communications; issue number 5 (September 1955) began with an announcement of a meeting, to be held on November 18, 1955, at an American Anthropological Association meeting in Boston, "for the purpose of forming an ethno-musicological society." These things happened, but the sequence of events gets its aura of mythology because of the larger-than-life significance it came to possess. It's that 1955 meeting we're celebrating today. For long after that, and maybe even now, old-timers in the SEM such as myself have seen these events of 1952 to 1955 as a grand entry of something quite new.

But let me try to remember how it felt at the time. I found it all very exciting, but I think that I—and maybe others, too—saw these events more as revival than innovation, as one of a sequence of landmarks in our field's organizational and intellectual history. For one thing, the word *ethnomusicology* sounded odd to me. I acknowledge that the term was first used in a publication by Jaap Kunst (1950), but I am pretty sure that it was already used by American anthropologists who probably weren't aware of Kunst and had produced their own coinage, possibly as an informal analogue to the then-flourishing ethnolinguistics or maybe even as a slangy neologism. Clearly, *comparative musicology*, simply a blanket term for the study of all the music that Western scholars had neglected, already enjoyed a long history, having been used by a group of scholars closely associated with various schools of anthropology and with psychology and music history. After all, in 1955 we should have been celebrating the fiftieth anniversary of Hornbostel's article on the "problems of comparative musicology," which begins, "A new specialty within a discipline has the task of justifying its existence" (Hornbostel 1904–5, 85; my translation) and goes on to explain the need for a special methodology in the analysis of music. Hornbostel's article, by the way, was the published form of a lecture held in Vienna in March for the local chapter of the Internationale Musikgesellschaft, the predecessor to the International Musicological Society (talk about wishing to have been a fly on the wall), and it was delivered, it is worth noting, four days after President Theodore Roosevelt's inauguration, in the days of King Edward VII, Kaiser Bill, and—in Vienna—that symbol of Austro-Hungarian unity, Emperor Franz Joseph, a moment when work had just begun on the Panama Canal. It was a different world from ours, but still, Hornbostel's conclusions end with thoughts that we've continued to hear over and over for the next hundred years: "There is great danger that the rapid diffusion of European culture will eliminate the last vestiges of song and story of foreign cultures. We must save what can be saved, before cars and electric trains are supplemented with steerable aircraft and the musical world becomes totally homogeneous" (Hornbostel 1904–5, 97; my translation).

And Hornbostel too, in 1905, might well have been celebrating an important anniversary—the twentieth—of twin articles by a rather odd couple, the young firebrand Viennese Guido Adler and the distinguished elderly Englishman Alexander Ellis, with Adler giving ethnomusicology a (sort of) essential place in the newly minted discipline of musicology by suggesting it to be "ethnological study for comparative purposes" (Adler 1885, 14) and Ellis maintaining that the musical scales of all societies—and by implication, all musics—are equally natural and, one therefore must conclude, equally worthy (Ellis 1885). But while we're inundating ourselves in anniversaries, there is at least one other to be noted. This year, 2005, is the seventy-fifth (and in 1955 it was the twenty-fifth) anniversary of the founding, in Berlin, of the Gesellschaft zur Erforschung der Musik des Orients (Katz 2003, 32), which began to publish the predecessor to our journal, the *Zeitschrift für vergleichende Musikwissenschaft*, which would publish a number of eventually classic articles in English, German, and French by such scholars as George Herzog, Robert Lachmann, and Alexis

Chottin. So, in accordance with the Western custom of giving special significance to numbers divisible by five or ten, we should be celebrating several landmarks.

So as I said, inexperienced as I was in 1955, I think I remember perceiving the founding of the SEM less as a grand innovation than as a kind of revival—specifically, the revival of a great school of researchers who had been mainly working on parallel tracks in America and Europe, of research programs that had been developed and then stunted and almost obliterated by the Holocaust, World War II, and the Iron Curtain.

In truth, others, too, might qualify as founders of the SEM: the ten who signed the letter of spring 1953, the seventy who received it, the twenty-four who showed up at the founding meeting fifty years ago today, the fifty or so (I don't think there's a record) who attended the first annual meeting of 1956 in Philadelphia, or the two hundred or so in the first dues-paying class.

But the myth of the grand entry came to overshadow these details and to play an important role in the continued burgeoning of the SEM, and this anniversary celebration is a moment to toast the creators of the SEM. We often speak of the four founders—McAllester, Merriam, Rhodes, and Seeger—who met on December 31, 1952. We see them as a unified committee, but each deserves individual recognition for a unique contribution: Merriam, the youngest, who was the chief ball-carrier from 1953 to 1958; Seeger, mainly an adviser, a kind of Nestor, who provided overall direction and eventually drafted the society's constitution; McAllester, who took care of secretarial details and who persuaded his university to give us an institutional home; and Rhodes, who accepted the somewhat risky task of becoming the first president of a small society with an unclear function and uncertain future, an association that might not go anywhere. So the grand entry is an attractive myth, but history was a bit more complicated.

MYTH 2: THE BATTLE FOR ACCEPTANCE Here's what we sometimes heard: the founders of the SEM fought valiantly, and finally won, against great and determined opposition. Several times at our meetings, the four principal founders appeared as a panel to discuss what they did and to reminisce, and while I don't think they themselves complained, voices in the audiences sometimes expressed reactions such as, "Wow, how did you ever manage this?" or "What do you think might have happened if you hadn't been able to get the SEM started?" Many of us, especially students, felt that the field's academic existence was often under threat and siege and that establishing the SEM was a way for us as a group of teachers and research-ers to find our place in the sun.

No doubt these battles did go on here and there, probably most within certain institutions, and to those seeking jobs today, or trying to hold on to top jobs, these struggles continue. But I had the feeling—in 1953, when the mimeographed newsletter began, in 1955, when the SEM was founded, and in 1958, when the journal began in earnest—that as indi-viduals, our various colleagues in music departments and (maybe a bit less) in anthropology departments were inclined to welcome the coming of this new society, and we didn't have to fight the Battle of Saratoga or to avenge defeats of Karbalā or White Mountain. Some who questioned the establishment of the SEM thought that it would be better to maintain, maybe in a reoriented AMS, a united society for the study of all music from all perspectives (which, by the way, is how our web site describes the SEM's mission). They feared that the SEM would become isolated and in turn tend to isolate historians of Western art music; this may have happened to a degree. But a look at our membership list of 1957 (*Ethno-Musicology Newsletter* no. 11 [Sept.1957]: 39–53) may correct the view of the SEM as embattled. The roster contains a good many distinguished representatives of historical musicology—Allen Britton, Gilbert Chase, Edward Lowinsky, Irving Lowens, John Ward, William Lichtenwanger, Edward A. Lippman, Leonard Meyer, Alexander Ringer, Emanuel Winternitz, Carleton Sprague Smith—and also anthropologists, including William Bascom, Clyde Kluck-hohn, William Sturtevant, and of course Melville J. Herskovits. Individuals from other professions belonged, too: the music critic Edward Downes; the jazz historian Marshall Stearns; the famed writer on social issues and on jazz Nat Hentoff; the composers Chou Wen-chung, Henry Cowell, and Vladimir Ussachevsky; and of course the folksinger Pete Seeger. Through-out, I think our colleagues across disciplinary lines strongly supported the creation of our society. When the SEM applied for membership in the American Council of Learned Societies, its strongest supporter among the member societies, so I was told, was the AMS.

Educational institutions, schools and departments in universities, were sometimes slower to support ethnomusicology (I mean now the field, not the society). They sometimes saw research in ethnomusicology as inter-esting but rated courses in this field as something of a luxury impinging on curricula already full of explicit requirements; as teachers, many of us had to fight our own personal battles as bloody as that of Agincourt. In 1954, Alan Merriam asked me to compile a survey of institutions that taught courses in ethno and related fields (Nettl 1954b), and I came up with fourteen that could qualify, though sometimes barely—many of them, even those of George Herzog and Richard Waterman, still using the term *primitive music* in course titles. Clearly all these courses were electives or even extracurricular luxuries. (A European supplement as well as an annual German survey of musicology courses published in the journal *Musik-forschung* from 1950 on showed that there was more action in Europe than in America.)

The attitude in American schools was distilled in a remarkable experience of my own in 1953, when I was first looking for a teaching job. Like other aspiring college teachers in those days, I put in my papers with the music section of the Charles Lutton teacher's agency in Chicago. Mr. Lutton interviewed me and predicted that jobs for musicologists would never be numerous, adding, "But for that stuff you are doing, whatever you call it, there will never be any jobs!" For a while, it seemed he was right.

MYTH 3: AMERICAN LEADERSHIP   In the early years of the SEM, American leadership was essential in establishing the field of ethnomusicology. America was in the lead when the SEM was created, and some believed (see, e.g., Kerman 1985, 159–60) that ethnomusicology was a field virtually invented for Americans. Well, to be sure, after World War II, the United States was the only large country that hadn't suffered major economic losses, and all things considered, it had endured far fewer human losses than had others. But I believe those of us in the United States who were practicing ethnomusicology around this time saw ourselves not as innovators but as newcomers to an established scene, and one of our main tasks, we thought, was to make contact with European scholars. A number of comparative musicologists who matured in the 1920s and 1930s had come to North America—notably Herzog (but he came in 1925 as a student) and Kolinski, but I should also mention Ida Halperin, Walter Kaufmann, and Fritz Kuttner. Nonetheless, far fewer ethnomusicologists immigrated to the United States and Canada than did music historians, of whom some sixty-five arrived, fleeing the Nazis, Holocaust, and war. This diaspora was to change the picture of historical musicology in the United States rapidly and totally (see Brinkmann and Wolff 1999, 341–44).

To be sure, the four founders of the SEM were Americans, and they were all Americanists in their researches, but among their principal goals was making—well, reestablishing—contact with Europeans and, to a degree, with scholars elsewhere. I remember Herskovits, at the founders' meeting, urging that non-Americans be quickly included in the society's governing council and strongly recommending Professor J. H. Nketia, then in his early thirties. It didn't happen, I think, because the establishment of the council itself was put on the back burner. In 1957, though, about 25 percent (sixty-three) of our members were non-U.S. residents (and of those, only seven were Canadian), and this group included most of the well-known senior European scholars: Hans Hickmann, Ernst Emsheimer, Marius Schneider, Jaap Kunst, José Maceda, Giorgio Nataletti, Walter Graf, Edith Gerson-Kiwi, and many more. The organization certainly didn't start out trying to lead the ethnomusicologists of the world, but it wanted them in part to be our leaders. There have been repeated calls for "internationalizing" our society, but in fact it began more international than it came to be later on.

Hopes and Expectations

The attitudes of those who were involved in the beginnings of the SEM differ in interesting ways from the interpretations of these attitudes later on. A parallel relationship emerges if we recall the expectations of the early members of the SEM. I have no concrete data and so use myself as what I hope is a typical witness. What did we who were young in the 1950s and just getting into this field expect of our new scholarly society?

JUSTIFYING "OUR" MUSIC   For one thing, we thought the SEM would give us a place in the sun, that is, would justify our studies, which, though accepted by many music historians, were regarded as a bit outré. I was a member of the AMS, along with the SEM, and read several papers on Native American music at its meetings; and those present were kind, but there's no doubt they considered me and my subject area outside the center. "Do you also do research on normal music?" I was once asked. The implication was, I think, that only thus could I prove myself as a member of the musicological profession; having done so, I'd be permitted to pursue my exotic interests. There was certainly pressure on us to justify Native American music on aesthetic grounds. I'm afraid that I often resorted to defending, instead, the social theories to which my studies might contribute—admitting, in other words, that Native American music was interesting only because it helped us understand the function of music in human or American Indian societies, not because it, like Brahms or Verdi, was intrinsically interesting. I'm afraid that attitude is still around even now, certainly among academic musicians and other academicians who take an interest in music. But at the SEM, I thought—we all thought—we'd be among people who considered us totally normal. Well, generally speaking, we were.

A MISSIONARY ENTERPRISE   Some of us didn't get any respect at our home institutions; most typically we found ourselves allied with the other music-department Rodney Dangerfields, such as avant-garde composers, jazz musicians, and maybe violists. Salving our self-esteem, the SEM functioned as a kind of support group. We wanted the SEM to be an organization that would promulgate ethnomusicology in institutions where it wasn't known. Around 1960, Alan Merriam recommended that members of the governing council commit themselves to giving invited lectures without fees at institutions that were not yet teaching our field. The Society for Ethnomusicology was to be a kind of agency for advertising and arranging this service. I don't think the SEM actually did this, but a lot of us have spent time giving talks at institutions to stimulate the idea that exposing students in many fields to the materials and ideas of ethno is educationally and socially valuable. In the 1960s, Merriam was very much in the vanguard; in the 1970s, incidentally, John Blacking devoted much of his prodigious energies lecturing at various British universities in order, as he put it, to institutionalize ethnomusicology.

COMMUNICATION ABROAD   As did the senior founders mentioned previously, we thought that one of the SEM's important functions might be to foster contact with scholars abroad. Certainly many American ethnomusicologists now take North America to be the undisputed leader in this field. Many people elsewhere think so, too. At the same time, some of us think that we've been headed in wrong directions all along. But as people of what many in the 1950s considered a young country, we in America did often look to European scholars and models for inspiration. That's surely why one of the first items Merriam published in his mimeographed SEM newsletter was a bibliography of Hornbostel's works (Merriam 1954) and why international contact, as represented by the many news items from "abroad," was one of the newsletter's major functions during its early years.

As an example of the newsletter from this time, take number 3, from 1955. Like the others, this issue includes many "Notes and News" entries. About half the notices come from people abroad—Marius Schneider, Paul Collaer, Eta Harich-Schneider, and Kurt Reinhard wrote, and the editor reported on letters from Jaap Kunst, Fumio Koizumi, Maud Karpeles, José Maceda, Dov Noy, Walter Wiora, and others. It seemed to me then that this international contact could be one of the nascent society's most valuable assets, for we early members of the SEM really looked to the senior European scholars, who had actually studied with Hornbostel and his generation, for leadership and inspiration.

Incidentally, when I had the opportunity of teaching in Germany between 1956 and 1958, I tried to visit as many senior ethnomusicologists as I could and had the great pleasure and honor of being hosted by Jaap Kunst in the Netherlands; Ernst Emsheimer in Sweden; Arnold Bake, Maud Karpeles, and Peter Crossley-Holland in England; Kurt Reinhard, Fritz Bose, Hans Hickmann, and Marius Schneider in Germany; Walter Graf in Austria; Paul Collaer in Belgium; and others. I also had the opportunity to attend a meeting of the International Folk Music Council in Copenhagen in 1957. Everyone was extremely friendly and welcoming, especially considering that I was really quite young and inexperienced and without accomplishments; my hosts arranged for me to give talks about American subjects and were curious about what was happening in the United States. But they obviously were wondering just what this new "Society for Ethnomusicology" was up to, and some suspected it would become a kind of loose cannon. Clearly, they saw us as a colonial intellectual outpost with exotic qualities, promising but needing the solid leadership of the European establishment.

Nonetheless, for a time we Americans, and the SEM, maintained rather loose ties with our European colleagues, expecting them to seek our help rather than depending on them for leadership, and in any event, maintaining to some degree an attitude of splendid isolation from Europe. I believe we're now, in 2005, moving vigorously to get some of our international perspectives back.

During the early 1950s, while the SEM was being forged, I also thought about the IFMC—now ICTM—and the complementary roles of the two organizations. In the 1960s and 1970s, the cold war and the Iron Curtain played a major but unacknowledged role in defining these roles. Thus, the SEM was dominated by American- and British-style social anthropology, by fieldwork far from home, and by the concept of bimusicality in research and teaching. The IFMC was dominated by Europeans—but particularly by Eastern Europeans—working in the rural cultures of their own nations. With issue 9, the *Ethnomusicology Newsletter* began a series of articles describing other societies with similar purposes; the first of these, by Maud Karpeles (1957), covered the IFMC. Later on, there was discussion about combining the two organizations, and I suspect that to some extent the

SEM's national ambiguity got in the way. By now, the two organizations' memberships overlap significantly, and their meetings and publications cannot easily be distinguished by subject matter or methodology.

THE FUNDAMENTAL BIFURCATION?   What about musicology and anthropology as parent disciplines? I think the history of the SEM, and maybe of ethnomusicology in North America, started with the unreflective view that these two areas ran together in ethnomusicology. Eventually—maybe in the 1960s—the concept of two ethnomusicologies became widely accepted, an anthropologically derived one centered on the approaches of Alan Merriam and a music-oriented one best characterized as proceeding under the leadership of Mantle Hood. Part of the mythology of our history puts these two schools of thought at loggerheads, and certainly Merriam frequently emphasized the conceptual and theoretical distinctions between these two approaches. Indeed, at the 1962 meeting of the SEM, in Bloomington, celebrating the tenth anniversary of the four founders' meeting, Merriam—as program chair—organized three panels, each with a main speaker. Merriam himself led one, and Hood led another, the two men essentially presenting their views of ethnomusicology's fundamental character. The third speaker was Alan Lomax, who conceptually stood both between and aside from the others, discussing both analysis and "music-in-culture" in the somewhat idiosyncratic approach of cantometrics. These papers and the responses to them were published in *Ethnomusicology,* except that I, as the hapless editor, could never browbeat Alan Lomax into sending his essay (Hood 1963a; Merriam 1963b). As our history unfolded, we diversified further, beyond these two branches. Today, though, I see us returned to a version of what I conceived as the original, more unified perspective—at least in our training of students, all of whom seem to me to read a lot of anthropology and social theory, and almost all of whom study performance in the framework of the participant-observer approach.

In looking at the early history of the SEM, we see the participation of many individuals from almost everywhere. The letter that functioned as the first call to arms, sent to seventy people or so, was signed by a diverse group—Merriam and Sachs, Waterman and Bukofzer, Seeger and Densmore. It's a sad note that the person who sometimes was, and certainly should have been, a major intellectual leader of this group, George Herzog, was absent throughout, a psychological illness keeping him hospitalized some of the time and unable otherwise to get his act together very often. He might have provided a kind of cement between Europeans and Americans and among approaches suggested by several disciplinary inspirations. I often wonder how ethnomusicology would have developed had Herzog continued in the scholarly career he had begun in the late 1920s. As it is, he stopped productive work in his late forties. Because of all he had done, he was made a member-at-large of the executive board for several years beginning in 1955, but I believe he never attended a meeting.

HOW THE EUROPEANS SAW US   Finally, let me mention how I believe European scholars perceived the SEM in its infancy. As I mentioned before, I had the good fortune of living in Germany from 1956 to 1958, visiting many European ethnomusicologists during my stay. (The only one who used the term, though, was Jaap Kunst.) These European scholars were uniformly kind and welcoming to this junior American, and virtually all of them had joined the SEM, as our 1957 directory indicates. They weren't too impressed by what we were doing, though, and I got the feeling that on the whole, they thought the leadership of this field was and would remain in Europe. They did grant the Americans' special talents for organization. It's interesting to see that later on, the SEM did for a time assert a kind of world hegemony (John Blacking, when president of the SEM, tried unsuccessfully to promulgate the organization as officially "international" and to have meetings outside North America). But in recent years, with the resurgence of the ICTM, the establishment of the European Seminar in Ethnomusicology, the British Forum for Ethnomusicology, the Société Française d'Ethnomusicologie, and the Sociedad Ibérica de Etnomusicología, an intellectual and organizational pluralism has been reasserted (for further discussion, see Christensen 1988; Nettl 1988).

ACCOMPLISHMENTS AND CHALLENGES   Did the SEM do what we young members of 1955 hoped it would do? Well, in many ways, surely. It provided places to publish, to read and hear papers. It took its unifying role seriously, publishing the -ographies and emphasizing mechanisms for contact among the faithful. It provided the isolated a forum for togetherness, welcoming students as members and speakers more voluminously than did other societies. Whereas the society previously treated women scholars with offensive neglect, as documented by Charlotte Frisbie (1991), they now play a leadership role. The founders took enormous satisfaction in the society's success, and while I think young members now take the SEM for granted, newly arrived members in the 1950s and 1960s seemed to marvel at what had been wrought.

But we have a long way to go to fulfill the implied promises of 1955. We, the membership, don't look like the world, yet neither do we look like America. We haven't really figured out our intellectual contours, our essential goals as a profession, the central questions we wish to ask or answer. Our effect on the educational world has been considerable but sometimes misinterpreted. When we started, I confess that I wasn't comfortable with the name, the term *ethnomusicology*, though it now runs as a macro on my computer, and so I find it interesting that the term is again under scrutiny—along with the "little man" logo, first published in 1956, with which many of us have a kind of love-hate relationship.

When the SEM was founded, I had a good idea of what the notion of "ethnomusicology" meant, though maybe I couldn't articulate it well, and I found that there was a lot of difference between definitions of the word itself, what we actually did, and further, what we thought we should ultimately be doing. But fifty years later, the SEM itself hasn't figured out the answers—and maybe doesn't want to. Our mission statement says that the SEM aims to "promote the research, study, and performance of music in all historical periods and cultural contexts." The constitution says that we exist "to promote research and study in the field of ethnomusicology." Our journal says that it publishes articles in the field of ethnomusicology, "broadly defined." It's amazing that a society with such a vague notion of what it includes can have been so successful.

Some months ago, a colleague in another field of music, hearing that I was about to go to an SEM meeting, asked, "Are you still fighting the good fight?" "What fight?" I asked. "Well, putting ethnomusicology on the map." "We're on the map," I asserted, but then I asked myself, What's the map? And just what is it that we've put on the map?

IV

A Collage of
Commentary

12

Recalling Some Neglected
Classics in Musical Geography

For Tullia Magrini

In past decades, a simple way to distinguish historical musicology from ethnomusicology could have been to say that the first asks "when," and the second, "where." The two have tended to merge, even while the two fields increasingly declare academic and curricular independence, as music historians (of European classical traditions) cast their eyes toward colonies and postcolonial fusions and ethnomusicologists enjoy increasing access to recorded history. Nevertheless, for over a century, ethnomusicology has always included the study of location as a principal concern, asking what one can do with the findings of geographic distribution and what geography means in the life of music.

Tullia Magrini's work has contributed importantly to this area of research and interpretation, most, of course, through her devotion to the study of the cultures bordering the Mediterranean—both her own studies of Italian, Greek, and Cretan musical cultures and her encouragement of scholarship in all regions bordering that sea. She nurtured our field's interest in a geographical focus in many ways, organizing relevant conferences and publications and insisting that we should study and in some cases examine—without prejudice—what, if anything, these regions have in common, culturally and musically.

Magrini's edited collection *Music and Gender: Perspectives from the Mediterranean* (2003) has quickly become central not only to the study of issues concerning gender but also in efforts to understand how the study of geographic distribution can illuminate questions of culture and history. In this, her last publication on the subject, she summarizes but also criticizes arguments for contemplating the region as a unit, yet she refrains from a strong conclusion, implying that more study of the complexities will yield a picture of heterogeneity, not cultural and musical unity. It thus joins a large and diverse body of literature, coming from a variety of roots and using multiple approaches, whose history remains to be interpreted as an integrated whole. This literature's historical roots include models from other disciplines, including, but not limited to, the cartography of the so-called German school of diffusionists, also known as the Kulturkreis school (described by A. Schneider 1976); the classifications of multiple small societies in so-called culture areas by scholars associated with Franz Boas; the historic-geographic method of folklore developed in Finland and Scandinavia and brought to Germany by Walter Anderson (e.g., 1923) and to North America by Stith Thompson (1929, 1951); and the practices of linguistic geography and cartography used by students of language in general, such as Joseph Greenberg (1963), and of Native American languages in particular, such as C. F. Voegelin (1945).

The literature comprised within this intellectual history of musical cartography—the criteria for this kind of mapmaking and the interpretation of the results—is well known to ethnomusicologists. My purpose here is to revisit and comment briefly on a few seminal works that seem largely to be forgotten and that deserve attention because they were harbingers of significant developments.

Curt Sachs's Most Ambitious Work

The movement that took geographic distribution most seriously was manifested in the group of largely German and Austrian scholars often called the "Kulturkreis school," and its most prominent musical adherent was Curt Sachs, many of whose publications participate in its combination of geographic and historical analysis. The high-water mark of musical Kulturkreis study was Sachs's *Geist und Werden der Musikinstrumente* (1929), perhaps his most ambitious research project. On the basis of museum collections and ethnographic literature, Sachs proceeded to map the distribution of (he hoped) all musical instruments, a formidable task even for one with his comprehensive knowledge of the literature. He organized his findings in twenty-three areas, which he then placed in historical order according to distribution and technological level. For example, stratum 7, found in Polynesia and parts of South America, includes the whistling pot, double-row panpipes, and bone buzzers. Stratum 13, present in Indonesia and East Africa, includes the "earliest metal instruments," various kinds of xylophones, and board zithers. Stratum 18, found from Indonesia to Madagascar, dates from about the first century CE and is characterized by the tube zither.

Hornbostel (1933) used a similar approach to establish twelve instrument areas for Africa. Sachs later went on to simplify, combining most of his twenty-three strata into three groups (1940, 63–64), but he began to have doubts about the kind of detailed historical speculation in which he had engaged: "The geographic method, too, may prove fallacious. . . . Nevertheless, geographic criteria are safer than any other criteria" (63).

Leading to Cantometrics

Paul Collaer's far-reaching *Atlas historique de la musique* begins with a map of the musical world (1960, pl. 1). On the basis of a few societies, Collaer divided the world into several *zones musicales* based entirely on scalar structure, distinguishing "pre-pentatonic," "anhemitonic-pentatonic," "heptatonic," and others. Assuming the existence of a typical, central musical style for any large group of cultures, he ignored the obvious—for example, that Europe has both seven- and five-tone scales in great quantity and that seven-tone scales are found in China—and assigned Europe to the seven-tone area and China to the pentatonic category.

Alan Lomax's best-known work, *Folk Song Style and Culture* (1968), may be considered something of a successor to Collaer's; as did Collaer, Lomax required the problematic concept of centrality. A "favored song style" (1968, 133) is diagnostic for each of fifty-seven areas. He established a group of naturally or culturally determined areas and then described the musical style of each, testing its degree of internal homogeneity and its similarity to others. Interestingly, some of his areas are far more unified than others. Essentially, however, he describes the music of culture areas instead of providing musical areas.

Lomax's neglected classic, however, is a precursor to his publications on cantometrics. His article "Folk Song Style" (Lomax 1959) divides the world into ten musical styles, based largely on what is usually called performance practice. Lomax lists American Indian, Pygmoid, African, Australian, Melanesian, Polynesian, Malayan, Eurasian, old European, and modern European, some (but not all) of these styles correlating with geographic or readily recognized culture areas. The styles relevant to considerations of the Mediterranean include three varieties of European folk song: the Eurasian (which covers most of Asia, too), old European, and modern European. The distinctions among the European styles are insightful: the Eurasian is "high-pitched, often harsh and strident, delivered from a tight throat with great vocal tension" (1959, 936). Old European is "relaxed . . . [the] facial expression lively and animated . . . unornamented" (ibid.). Looking at Lomax's later attempts to map the world, it seems that his ten major areas may be the least unsatisfactory grouping of all the various musical globes and, in any event, served as the jumping-off point for the development of cantometrics as the study of style and of musical culture.

It is interesting to find a precursor to Lomax's work in a study by Bence Szabolcsi (1935)—a Hungarian music historian whose later work I discuss later—where he classifies ornamentation in European music (mainly but not exclusively applied to art music) in five geographic categories: Mediterranean, "Atlantic," Baltic-German, East European, and Northern European. Some of his boundaries are not distant from those suggested by Lomax.

Musics and Landscapes

Another theory of musical distribution appeared in an appendix to the history of melody by Szabolcsi (1959), who dealt there with the question of world musical geography more holistically than have most others. He did not confine himself to the presumably less volatile folk and tribal musics but considered classical systems as well. Relating musical styles to geographic factors such as river valleys and access to the sea, he saw the musical map as a combination of geographically bounded areas and a patchwork resulting from musical differences of locales with varying degrees of isolation. Generalizing about principles of musical distribution, he drew several conclusions: (1) Musical life is closely tied to the natural divisions of the earth. (2) Geographically "closed" areas preserve musical styles, while open ones favor change and exchange, providing a venue for the development of cultivated or classical systems. (3) The center standardizes and unifies materials developed throughout the area, while the margins develop and preserve diversity. (4) Diffusion of musical styles from the center is the typical process of music history; the longer a musical style exists, the further it becomes diffused. (5) The unity of archaic folk-music styles is evidence of the most ancient intercultural contacts (Szabolcsi 1959, 313). Here is a set of fundamental hypotheses on which one can build a cultural geography of music.

In the Footsteps of Clark Wissler

The part of the world most subjected to musical cartography is aboriginal North America, that is, the region as it was culturally and geographically before 1492. The "culture-area" concept was developed with Native American data in studies by Wissler (1917), A. Kroeber (1947), and Driver (1961), and I undertook, in the early 1950s, to develop musical areas (Nettl 1954a) analogous to but not coterminous with culture areas, a scheme that was revised and appropriately criticized. Helen H. Roberts (1936), however, produced the first serious attempt to map American Indian music. Her book was unjustly neglected because it appeared under an obscure imprint, but I used it as a starting point for some of my later studies. Her work depends substantially on Wissler's pioneering culture-area scheme—the others were not published until later, and in any event, Wissler's remains the most widely used.

Roberts, significantly, takes into consideration some factors and criteria with which my mapping did not deal. But rather than try to show how the geography of music differs from that of other domains of culture, she essentially described the musical styles and instrumentaria of culture areas, assuming, very logically, that nations that share a lifestyle probably also share musical style. Most of her monograph is devoted to the distribution of instruments. After discussing individual instrument types, Roberts identifies "instrument areas," enumerating five: Eskimo, Northwest-Coast-Plateau, California, Southwest and Plains, and the eastern part of the continent plus Mexico. For musical styles, she identifies a slightly different arrangement: (1) Eskimo, (2) Northwest-Coast-Plateau, (3) southwestern/Hokan, (4) Navajo, (5) southwestern Shoshonean, (6) Plains, (7) Iroquois or possibly eastern woodlands, and (8) a "polyphonic" area comprising Mexico with offshoots on the North Pacific and in the Midwest. While based on a small amount of data available in 1935, this is a comprehensive study that served as inspiration for future studies.

Touching on the Mediterranean

The early literature of ethnomusicology provides no book dealing explicitly with Mediterranean music; the area is seen, much more, as the meeting place of cultures, religions, language groups, and styles. Their cultural and linguistic diversity rendered the cultures surrounding the Mediterranean a poor fit with the earlier models of cultural geography developed by the Kulturkreis, by the culture-area approach, or by the historical-geographic method of folklore. Only in the 1980s did the study of gender relations and the pairing of the concepts of "honor and shame" lead to considerations of cultural homogeneity. Tullia Magrini (2003, 18–25) suggests that in terms of musical behavior patterns, music as culture, and music in gender relations, the Mediterranean is a kind of musical area; in addition, I believe that the explicitly musical components of her argument find further support in the significance of improvisation, of the use of modal systems, of extended soloistic singing, and of certain characteristic uses of the voice, as well as in the widespread distribution of certain plucked string and reed instruments.

The concept of the Mediterranean thus did not play an important role in the early literature contemplating the significance of spatial distribution. Let me mention, however, three early works that drew attention to this area of concern.

In 1918, a new musicological periodical, *Archiv für Musikwissenschaft* (with its sister journal, *Zeitschrift für Musikwissenschaft*), began a new era of German musicology; its first issue, full of significant articles by major figures, opened with a short piece by Curt Sachs, "Die Streichbogenfrage" (1918), which foreshadowed his participation in the Kulturkreis studies. Opposing a belief that plucked strings everywhere led to the more sophisticated bowing, he divided Europe into a plucking south and a bowing north, giving the Mediterranean area an identity as the heartland of lutes.

A decade later, Robert Lachmann published a short survey of Asian classical traditions, *Musik des Orients* (1929), which similarly, though not explicitly, points to a musically homogeneous Islamic and Islamic-influenced Mediterranean. Lachmann's work was one of the first to suggest a significant association within the cultures that developed elaborate modal systems in essentially monophonic structures, together with highly ornamented improvisation in nonmetric performance—cultures in an area that he saw stretching from India westward to the Middle East and the Balkans but that in the end encompassed southern Italy, North Africa, and Iberia.

Musical cartography with some reference to the Mediterranean also played a role in pioneering works of historical musicology. I'll mention two: Marius Schneider's attempt to conceive of the growth of polyphony as a single history in his monumental book *Geschichte der Mehrstimmigkeit* (1934) uses the Kulturkreis approach and suggests four culture circles (i.e., periods), the second of which encompasses southern France and Italy, a plan that sees the Mediterranean area as principally monophonic, with northern Europe dominating the development of polyphony. This interpretation of history may be related to the conclusions drawn by Sachs in his article on bowing.

The other pioneering work looks at European music history from a perspective not unlike that of the culture area of American anthropology, applied principally by A. L. Kroeber (1947) for establishing a classification and reconstructed history in the plethora of distinguishable cultures of Native American peoples, areas in which a "culture climax" functions as the point of both origin and diffusion of the area's most important features. I refer to Gustave Reese's *Music in the Renaissance* (1954), for decades the pioneering first-line reference on its subject, though now rarely consulted. Reese distinguished an area where the "central musical language" was developed—Italy, France, and the Low Countries—and then diffused to the outskirts of this area—Germany, England, Spain, and Eastern Europe.

The study of geographic distribution in music and in culture as a whole is perhaps becoming irrelevant, for modern technology makes it increasingly easy to communicate with anyone, anywhere, at any time. Much of Tullia Magrini's work began by considering relationships and commonalities that resulted from the geographical configuration of the Mediterranean lands. Her thought and publications thus take their place—more than a half-century later—among these venerable classics, and her analyses and critiques of the cultural and musical integrity of the cultures surrounding the Mediterranean join a significant strand of the history of ethnomusicology and of historical musicology.

13

. . . .

Minorities in Ethnomusicology

. . . .

A Meditation on Experience in Three Cultures

The Study of Minorities—or of Majorities?

In this chapter I use several perspectives to discuss the role minority studies have played in the history of ethnomusicology, but principally I explore three cultures with which I have had experience—Native American peoples, the musical society of Iran, and several minorities (of which I was a member) in the Czech lands before 1940. These groups illustrate three configurations: a culture marginalized by a surrounding immigrant and previously colonialist majority where music has become a primary ethnic marker; a society ambivalent about music, in which minorities are principal bearers of musical culture; and a confluence of coexisting societies, each a minority in some sense, interacting through music.

Most ethnomusicological literature may tend to evoke the concepts of "minority" and "minorities." Many ethnomusicologists, after all, have for decades seen themselves as students of the music of the world's downtrodden. At the same time, they have often seen themselves as a kind of minority among music scholars and musicians in Europe and North America. Looking back to my days as a student in the early 1950s, however, I find it ironic that in several important ways, we also saw ourselves as the defenders of majorities, perhaps labeled best as "neglected majorities." We considered ourselves foremost to be students of music shared by all people in a society. It was the music historians, we thought, who were interested in the exceptional—for example, in understanding the greatest composers or alternatively, as with my father, Paul Nettl, in discovering unknown and forgotten composers. Those who were devoting themselves to what we later called ethnomusicology wished to understand the music shared by all—"the" music "of" a "people," no matter whether this "people" implied the total population of a nation such as India, with its many millions, or of a village of six hundred in Romania, or of an American Indian tribe (or nation) of merely two hundred. Of course, delineations of this sort are complicated. It makes a great difference whether we look at that Indian tribe as a comprehensive unit and attend to the songs known to all within it; at the ways in which this tribe tries to hold on to its culture in the context, perhaps, of a reservation that it shares with other tribes in the American West; or at the members' strategies for coping with the increasing presence in their lives of music from the true majority, the millions of European and African Americans.

Just what a minority is, then, depends in part on the social and cultural relationship between a group of people and its environment, but it depends also on aspects of this environment that we—as academicians—are contemplating. So there's no doubt that the concept of minority, and the identification of minorities, is to some extent a construction of the observer.

But instead of pursuing the problem of perspectives in constructing a conceptualization, let me first go to the venerable *International Encyclopedia of the Social Sciences* for a definition: "A minority is a group of people—differentiated from others in the same society by race, nationality, language, or religion—who both think of themselves as a differentiated group and are thought of by the others as a differentiated group with negative connotations" (Rose 1968, 365). This may work as a starting point, but ethnomusicologists use the concept in broad and complex ways, with metaphorical extensions, because we also talk about music as if it had a life of its own. The literature of ethnomusicology contains some distinguished works (but only a few) that deal explicitly with minorities as minorities, but little in that literature doesn't somehow touch on the concept.

In the following paragraphs, I construe the notion of minorities a bit more broadly than does the *International Encyclopedia of the Social Sciences*. The concept's usefulness as an intellectual tool for ethnomusicology continues to expand. Allow me to offer three examples. First, minority status may be a function of something other than numbers. We may thus wish—in seeking insight into the interrelationships of peoples in a society—to analyze the music of certain population groups who may constitute a numerical majority, but who see themselves discriminated against and who are viewed by others as having undesirable characteristics. Examples are legion; blacks in pre-Mandela South Africa and Czechs in Habsburg-era Bohemia come to mind. Second, most of us feel that we belong to some sort of minority, that the sense of being surrounded by groups of people who have certain powers beyond ours is part of the human condition.

Third, it is important to point out that in the twenty-first century, the field of ethnomusicology has expanded the concept of minority—or perhaps moved into areas of concern not ordinarily associated with the concept of a "minority." In this respect, consider the studies that ordinarily fall under the term *medical ethnomusicology* and whose most prominent examples include research involving autistic children (see Bakan 2009; Bakan et al. 2008), elderly patients in nursing homes (see Allison 2008), and individuals suffering from HIV/AIDS (see Barz 2006). The research involved here may be classified as falling in the subdiscipline of "applied ethnomusicology," and in its practical applications, it should also be seen simply as an area of medicine, music therapy, or other areas of health-care science. Its literature is most adequately summarized in the *Oxford Handbook of Medical Ethnomusicology* (Koen 2008). My point here is that within ethnomusicology, the groups of people whose musical culture is investigated (often, though not exclusively, with hopes for practical result) fit into the scheme of ethnomusicological thought and method by being viewed as minorities, a category whose definition is appropriate to them. These are groups of people best understood as having a distinct culture and, typically, a distinct musical culture that may be best understood by seeing them as musical minorities.

Again, the musicological literature devoted explicitly to the minority status of societies is modest, but important histories and synthetic treatments have recently been published, most significantly, Ursula Hemetek's edited volume *Echo der Vielfalt* (1996) and her own large book *Mosaik der Klänge* (2001); an essay by Oskár Elschek and Alica Elscheková (1996) provides a comprehensive historical and conceptual background, laying out many questions and issues faced by anyone wishing to synthesize musical-minority studies. These authors demonstrate the complexity of this endeavor. For example, we should heed the Elscheks' warning that social and musical minorities may not be congruent—or even the same species of thing (1996, 26–27). Thus the concept of minorities among repertories rather than human populations played a significant role in the early era of ethnomusicological collecting, for many early collectors of folk music were motivated by the belief that this music, a minority among musics, would disappear if not preserved.

Speaking from a North American perspective, it strikes me that minorities seem to be the populations always on the way out. In the United States, at least, and maybe elsewhere, it is public policy (a policy explicitly endorsed among certain minorities) to absorb minorities and homogenize the larger society, to avoid the treatment and perception of certain groups as different and so avoid the negative characterizations that such perceptions often entail. But certain aspects of the traditional culture, particularly music and dance, are the subject of strenuous attempts at preservation, both by outsiders such as ethnomusicologists and national governments and by members of the minority society itself. How one maintains these opposing positions while also asserting that music and dance are integral to the rest of culture seems a problem to me. (For recent contributions to this issue, see the essays in Turino and Lea 2004.)

Studying and then working in the field of ethnomusicology, I have had the good fortune to experience many diverse musical cultures. Each of these cultures can, I believe, be profitably contemplated from the perspective of minority studies. I want to touch on several of them briefly from this perspective. Since it is, as already stated, difficult to identify cultural regularities in the musical lives of the world's minorities, internally and in their relationships to their cultural and demographic circumstances, each of my experiences provides a different set of lessons.

Overrun by a Majority: American Indian Cultures

The Elscheks' (1996) contribution outlines many kinds of minorities and ways to classify them. For one thing, one may distinguish them by the way they came to be minorities. Thus, for example, there are minorities whose members immigrated to a new area of the world and settled among a majority, whereas others were forcibly imported—various European and Asian groups settling in North America are an obvious example of the first kind; African Americans, of the second. There are population groups that, because of peculiarities of descent, religion, or occupation, came to have minority status—I think of Jewish populations in Europe, but also of castes or occupational descent groups in India, though some migration may have been involved here, too. Then there are groups who became minorities because of shifting borders, such as Hungarians in Slovakia or German speakers in the Italian Tyrol. And importantly, there are aboriginal peoples who were surrounded by powerful invaders and thus became minorities— examples that come to mind include Aboriginal Australians, south African Khoi-San, European Celts, and western Slavic peoples such as the Sorbs and Wends in what became eastern Germany. Among these, Native American peoples are the most prominent in the ethnomusicological literature.

In the aggregate, the literature on Native American music is frighteningly large, although the number of separate peoples or nations to be investigated leaves a thorough understanding very distant. And significantly, while American Indian peoples are clearly minorities in the total populations of the United States and Canada, their musical cultures have rarely been studied from this perspective, a perspective that would be expected to involve their musical relations to the surrounding majority. I have in mind issues such as these: how being a minority has affected an Indian tribe's musical culture, how the music of the majority has affected the group, how they may have used music in relating to the (white) majority, or how they affected the musical culture of the white majority. Typical studies of American Indians have essentially treated each culture or tribe in isolation, trying to reconstruct its musical life as it might have been before the coming of white people and their music.

My principal experience has been with the Blackfoot people of Montana, and I followed this conventional approach when I studied them, primarily in the small town of Browning and its surroundings (see Nettl 1989). Looking back now, I realize I could have come up with a somewhat different ethnographic and musicological picture had I viewed the Blackfoot people as a minority among the various cultures of North America. Let me give a few brief examples of the kinds of things on which I might have concentrated.

Basically, the Blackfoot say they have both Indian and white music and that although the former is a minority music for them, it has special functions in the modernized Blackfoot culture. Their most important musical activity occurs within the powwow, which is used to negotiate and to a degree resolve conflicts. For example, a large powwow will include a daily presentation of the U.S. flag with an American military color guard accompanied by unmistakably Indian music. Powwows are rather explicitly modern events, however; older and at one time central Blackfoot musical traditions have been wiped out, forgotten, or abandoned, but some of them are being reconstructed. There are some musical styles of white-Native fusion. The functions and uses of the traditional repertory have shifted in accordance with culture change. The participation of non-Blackfoot Native Americans, and also of white dancers and singers (usually referred to as "hobbyists"), in certain components of Blackfoot musical life, present important issues to study. I initially came from a tradition of scholarship that emphasized the purity and authenticity of the culture to be investigated, but I realize the shortcomings of that tradition, for it dismisses these issues as merely the result of corruption or pollution.

But the Blackfoot picture is made more complicated because their main town of Browning, Montana (pop. ca. 8,000), is not homogeneous but consists of several groups perhaps best labeled minorities. When I worked in Browning, between 1966 and 1983 or so, it was home to a small number of whites, including the majority of professionals and business owners—the wealthy. The majority of people called themselves mixed bloods; this category, which the difficulty of specifying descent made less biological than cultural, essentially indicates allegiance to a mixture of cultural values and practices. Finally, the town contained a smallish population of so-called full-bloods, largely poor people whose cultural interests were closer to older cultural traditions. They were treated like a minority by all the others, treatment that included the attribution of negative stereotypes—in this case, drunkenness, laziness, ignorance of modern ways—mentioned in the previously cited definition (Rose 1968). This kind of mix goes back to prewhite days, when the various and complex ways in which traditional Blackfeet divided themselves socially—including the special role of women—had its musical analogues.

And so, despite the tribe's small population, the musical culture of the Blackfoot, like that of most Native American peoples, was not homogeneous. To put it very simply, not all people knew all the songs. On the contrary, the Blackfoot repertory was divided according to formally constituted age groups, associations with different guardian spirits, differential winter residence patterns, gender, and more.

Very significantly, some of this changed as Native American peoples came to have a minority status among the white invaders (see Olson and Wilson 1984 for a historical perspective). The musical repertories experienced both centrifugal and centripetal forces. On the one hand, as the tribal allegiances of individual Blackfoot people began to diverge or for some to disappear, the typical musical idiolect (the individual's musical experience) became more varied (for a pioneering study of musical idiolects in Shoshone culture, see Vander 1988). Some people held on to many songs, even singing songs to which they traditionally would not have been entitled. Others forgot most Indian songs and learned "white" music—church music, vernacular music, folk music. On the other hand, as the extant repertories of most Native American peoples shrank because the songs' functions declined or disappeared, and as members of once separate tribes were thrown together on common reservations and in cities, some songs began to make up a core common property that, through the intertribal powwow circuit, came to be shared intertribally (for more detailed analysis of powwow music, see Browner 2002).

As do most American minorities of European origin, a large proportion of Native Americans in the United States today live in large cities, maintaining a tenuous, perhaps love-hate relationship to the reservations from which they came and on which relatives still live. Like the Europeans (more properly, European Americans), they have developed national festivals celebrating music, dance, and foodways, the most important being the already mentioned powwow. Thus, for example, about half the nation's Blackfoot people live in large cities in the North—mainly Seattle and Minneapolis—and many schedule annual visits to relatives in Montana to participate in the main four-day powwow. But while there are anthropological studies of urban Native American communities, not much has been done to learn about their musical culture. How is it like and unlike that of Italian Americans, Arab Americans, Mexican Americans, or Hungarian Americans? Although there are, perhaps surprisingly, interesting parallels, one is struck by the significant contrasts.

Briefly summarizing the history of the Blackfoot shows a picture typical of Native American peoples. Surrounded by invaders and treated far worse than European immigrants, they were not really encouraged to assimilate, to become part of the European culture. Yet they learned English, and by 1950 many knew no Native language. Except for certain egregious instances of proscription, however, as when Blackfoot children were put into boarding schools and forbidden to speak or sing Blackfoot, during the twentieth century the white majority unenthusiastically encouraged them to hold on to their traditional music, though perhaps to little else. Like many tribes, the Blackfoot began to try to recapture language, music, and folklore in the late twentieth century. Some youngish mixed-blood people began to reconstruct old, virtually forgotten musical ceremonies via recordings made by pioneer ethnomusicologists about and soon after 1900, and many young people have begun to revive the use of Blackfoot language by taking courses in it at a local community college and by establishing an archive of Blackfoot music consisting of recordings made by anthropologists and music scholars over the century. These recent developments parallel those found in certain minority populations in Europe and elsewhere.

Life in the Czech Lands

Now, allow me to speak as your "native informant." I was a native of this city (Prague), and as a child, I was a member, with my family, of several minorities: we mainly spoke German, but, unlike many German-speaking Prague people we knew, were quite fluent in Czech; in addition, we were ethnically Jewish, though totally secular. Given this configuration, no matter what the social context, somebody was probably thinking they were better than I was, and everybody—following Rose's definition of minority—thought I was a member of a group with undesirable qualities of some sort or other. The only exception might have been the occasional Roma one might see on the street, the people whom scholars of the area often regard as the minority par excellence. Had I lived a few decades earlier, I might have added to my burdens of minority that of being a Bohemian in an essentially Austrian-German cultural and political environment. It is interesting to look back and see how one individual may need to negotiate several different kinds of minority status. In certain respects, in my experience, this negotiation was done through music.

In the United States, the state of Tennessee and the city of Nashville claim to be "music country," and the Tennessee quarter has an engraving of a guitar, a violin, a trumpet, and a piece of sheet music. Born Czechoslovakian, however, I feel that the Czech lands have a better claim on this title. Indeed, before 1939 Bohemia was inhabited by peoples who all tended to claim, or in whose behalf it was claimed, that they maintained a kind of primacy in the art of music: (1) Czechs, formerly often called Bohemians, to whose nationalist movements in the nineteenth and twentieth centuries music was incredibly central (during the eighteenth century Charles Burney [1775, 131] praised them as capable of excelling even the Italians in musical ability); (2) Germans (including Austrians), whose composers so dominate the world of classical music that Pamela Potter (1998) titled her book about German musicology *Most German of the Arts* and Vladimir Karbusicky sarcastically titled one of his *Wie deutsch ist das Abendland?* (1995; How German is the West?); (3) Jews, who are traditionally associated with music in both Christian and Muslim worlds—in the many nations of Europe, the Americas, and the Middle East; (4) and the Roma, whom many see as quintessential musicians, almost like some of the South Asian hereditary musician castes. All were minorities of a sort: Roma and Jews, obviously; Czechs, a cultural if not numerical minority under long periods of German hegemony; Germans—or Deutschböhmen—a twentieth-century minority within a resurgent Czech culture, a minority because they didn't really associate themselves with the true Germans or Austrians but retained a Bohemian separateness, at least until the Nazi period. Even as a child, I kept noting that these societies negotiated their cultural space by different attitudes toward folk and classical music.

Conflicts among these groups since the fourteenth century have often been violent; I don't have to remind you of the dates remembered by all, 1412, 1620, 1918, 1938, 1948, and 1968, or of the history of defenestrations, of pogroms and anti-Semitic riots, of assaults on and ostracization of Roma. But there were also long periods of relative calm, and in these the competition among the ethnic groups was often musical, noted even in the experience of individual families and persons.

How was it played out? Let me mention a few areas for further consideration. One involves the importance of classical or art music, with which ethnomusicologists have rarely been concerned, and the significance of certain composers or genres in the estimation of various minorities. A second is the notion that each individual has, in his or her musical life, a configuration of allegiances to various musical concepts, each associated with a kind of (social or musical) minority. A third area concerns how the various population groups see one another in music or conceive of one another's music. All this involves the interface between an individual's music (we might call it a musical idiolect) and music—style, repertory, genre—as something belonging to a society. I'll try briefly to reconstruct my own early experience and that of my social circle in Prague, suggesting that studying personal repertories—the music performed, known, and loved or hated by the society's individuals—would be helpful in learning how minorities negotiate their interrelationships through music.

The musical relationships among ethnic groups, the sharing of musical markets and the competition in music, go far back in the Czech lands. An early work by Paul Nettl (1923) described policies regulating the activity of Jewish musicians in the late seventeenth century. To keep them from competing unfairly with Christian musicians at events such as Christian weddings, they were permitted to teach no more than two of their children to become musicians.

Living in twentieth-century Prague (see Nettl 2002b for more detail), however, in a middle-class family of German, secular Jewish, and Czech components, I was inevitably brought up in an atmosphere of classical music; even folk music was classicized, imbued with characteristics of classical music such as harmony and standardization. But what was the structure of the musical culture? There was a central music, maybe best identified by its main composers: Mozart head and shoulders above others, Schubert, Chopin, and Haydn, but not much emphasis on Bach, Beethoven, Brahms, or Wagner. There was the Czech component, whose main, most important characteristic was an association with folk music—Smetana and Dvořák, seen more as "Czechs" than as universally valid musicians, and a large body of folk songs typically accompanied by elaborate piano arrangements. So I learned Czech folk songs, while German folk songs were largely ignored. The Czechs were the "people of folk music." There was, I think, a Jewish sector in this construct of musical life, but it did not consist of any liturgical music or Jewish folk songs—for someone to sing a Yiddish song, such as "Auf dem Pripetchek," was regarded as exotic and mildly embarrassing. It did, however, include special attention to composers of Jewish background, such as Mendelssohn, Mahler, Schoenberg, and Zemlinsky.

The characteristics of this divergence in the musics of my life can be found also in some writing about music. For example, Helmut Boese (1955), in a generally sympathetic 1955 dual biography of Smetana and Dvořák, titles the work *Zwei Urmusikanten*, using the rather condescending *Musikant* instead of *Musiker* (see Komma 1960 for a German-oriented interpretation). Czech makes a similarly value-laden distinction with the terms *muzikant* and *hudebnik;* in American English the closest equivalents might be "vernacular musician" and "classical musician." For Boese, and I think for ethnic Germans in and outside Bohemia before 1939, Czechs were, as in my family, seen quintessentially as the people of folk music; even in their art music, the role of folk song and folklore is paramount. This attitude prevailed despite the fact that in the eighteenth century, ethnic Czechs (some no doubt German speakers) populated the orchestras of Europe. Despite their numerical majority, they were assigned a stereotype best represented by the good soldier Švejk.

But I began to note even at age eight, and later came to realize more fully, that while all population groups in Prague more or less shared the international classical repertory and had, despite being urban, some knowledge of folk song, each group had its own approach toward these and constructed a unique configuration of attitudes. Interestingly, the German-speaking residents of Prague, I think, understood their particular music to be different from that of the Germans in Germany or the Austrians (see Nettl 2002b). There is a certain amount of cross-cultural appropriation: Czech musicians and music-lovers even now seem to me to treat Mozart almost as a local composer, with an important Czech music magazine named *Bertramka,* while Germans make a great deal of the fact that for parts of his life, Smetana evidently felt more at home speaking German than Czech.

The point is that most German-speaking Bohemians, especially in Prague and particularly in the late nineteenth century (see Cohen 1981), saw themselves not as true Germans but rather as a distinct culture labeled as "Deutschböhmen" (literally, "German Bohemians") coexisting with, and I think valuing, the strong Czech influence, and until the 1930s, they largely had no wish to join either Austria or the German Reich. Admittedly, these attitudes changed after 1932. So it was clear to me, growing up in the 1930s, that I was a member of a kind of hierarchy of minorities whose relationships could be traced through musical allegiances and emphases. It was not so much that each ethnic group had its distinct repertory but that each emphasized and privileged different parts of a shared repertory. In my family and their circle, it seems to me, Austrian, Jewish, and Czech elements were favored. No doubt Czechs, ethnic Germans, and perhaps observant Jewish families, all residing in Prague, even if devoted to the same art music repertory, would have given various portions of it different emphases.

I am sorry to have to present this material from a strictly personal and speculative perspective. This approach to the interaction of minorities deserves more detailed study.

The Music Makers?

I went to Iran in 1968 hoping to learn something about improvisation in the Persian classical tradition, but the issue of minorities presented itself to me again, in ways significantly different from those in the European and North American situations. In contrast to the United States, Iran does not include a large population of recent migrants, but minorities are important to musical life there, just as they are in America and the Czech lands, and understanding the relationships is important to understanding the musical culture. There are many minorities, and this seems to have been the case for a long time. Relief sculptures in the ancient capital of Persepolis show representations of twenty-eight ethnicities over whom the emperor ruled, and some 2,500 years later, in the days of the Pahlavi shahs (1923 to 1978), certain minorities competed with the Shiite Muslim majority for positions of power (Wilber 1976, 162–63), these groups including ethnic minorities, such as Kurds, Turkomans, and Baluchis; religious minorities, such as Zoroastrians and Baha'is; and minorities who were both ethnic and religious, such as Jews and Armenians. All these minorities tried to find niches and get a bit of special influence, and the shah's government used and manipulated these unstable relationships to maintain power.

But back to music—and what I say comes from my experience in the late 1960s and early 1970s. I was interested to note that music was carried out more by minorities than by Muslim Persians, enough so that I began to think of a slogan, "minorities are the people of music" or "the music-makers," which reminded me of the situation in the Czech lands and, in yet another way, in the United States, where successive immigrant groups (minorities, naturally) were stereotyped as particularly musical and tended to play disproportionate roles in the field of music entertainment—in this case, Germans, Italians, African Americans, and Jews. But in considering Iran, an important caveat must be inserted. Traditional Iranians define music more narrowly than do most Europeans, for they exclude certain genres such as chanting the Koran and related liturgical performance. Devout Shiites question the appropriateness of hearing certain kinds of music—in certain contexts, by certain people, or at all. I believe that the key to the role minorities play in music lies in the need to reconcile the devout Muslims' ambivalence about music with the larger population's interest in having a full musical life. Most obvious may be the idea that musicians are themselves a minority. Professional musicians in both the vernacular and the classical music sectors lived a life apart; they espoused values that conflicted somewhat with the majority's, they behaved differently, and they kept their activities somewhat under cover, staying home from work on minor holidays and not admitting that their main livelihood came from music.

But more important, when I was there, before the revolution, music was to a disproportionate extent carried on by ethnic and religious minorities—I'm talking not about hereditary musician castes, as one might in Afghanistan or India, but about disproportionate representation. In the traditional urban musical culture, classical and popular, musicians would often be Jews, and Armenian Christians were the outstanding instrument makers; in villages and small towns of northern Iran, musicians were often Kurds and Baluchis (Blum 1974). In the modernized music culture of prerevolutionary Iran, musicians performing Western or Western-derived music, such as members of the symphony orchestra, were often Jews, Zoroastrians, and Baha'is.

These ethnic minorities had their own internally defined musical cultures, and I know hardly anything about these. I am referring to the contribution minorities made to a mainstream musical culture—in other words, to Christians and Jews providing music for Muslims and tribal people providing music for Persians. So the ideas of music as an activity of low respect and of minorities as people not widely respected are easily correlated. Disrespect for both minorities and music also helps explain why urban Muslims who are experts in music often did not wish to be considered professional musicians but rather prefer (or preferred, before 1978) to be regarded as learned amateurs. In addition, they sometimes associated this attitude with the concept of freedom, a concept essential in the most respected kind of music, the nonmetric modal improvisation; a great musician of classical music could thus say that he had freedom to make decisions not available to professionals—he could play when he wished and what he wished and could improvise as he wished. Further, being an amateur, he was not primarily associated with a disapproved activity, not a member of a barely legitimate profession associated with undesirable stereotypes such as drug addiction and unreliability, and also not suspected of being a member of a despised ethnic or religious minority.

One can speak of a Persian diaspora after about 1965, as members of minorities moved to the Americas, France, and importantly, Israel. After the 1979 revolution, when the government tried for about a decade essentially to stamp out music, centers of Persian classical-music culture developed in Paris, London, New York, and Los Angeles. The rather large population of Iranian Jews in Israel, in which I briefly worked with Amnon Shiloah (Nettl and Shiloah 1978), had a number of musicians who practiced Persian classical music and who, in a kind of diaspora, preserved but also departed from or changed the tradition. Interestingly, immigration changed their minority status from Jewish to Persian.

While the Iranian situation is unique and perhaps exceptionally complex, it bears comparison with many cultures in which isolated social groups—minorities of an important sort—specialize in music.

Coda

It is difficult to do extensive work in ethnomusicology without coming face to face with the roles and problems of minorities.

Introducing the subject matter of Hemetek's *Echo der Vielfalt,* Oskar and Alica Elschek show the world's minorities to be incredibly varied in their interrelationships and in relation to other cultures, and this variety is reflected in a great variety in musical behavior, in uses, functions, values, and concepts. We need to study further some of the conclusions drawn decades ago. For example, do minorities behave musically in a predictable way? Are there patterns or regularities in preservation, abandonment, reconstruction, and revival? Are concepts frequently used to describe cultural interrelationships, such as syncretism and marginal survivals, valid for explaining musical cultures? We want to look further at music as the medium in which you can protest and contradict with relative impunity.

In closing, I wish to touch on an area where certain tentative conclusions have been drawn in a variety of publications: the close relationship between the existence of minorities and the processes of migrancy and what is now broadly called diaspora. Many minorities have emerged through either in- or out-migration. To the extent that ethnomusicology is in certain respects the study of minorities, it has also, especially in recent years, become fundamentally concerned with musical issues resulting from migrations. The world may now be full of peoples who live in a diasporic state, but music—musics—can migrate, now more than ever, without human bearers. We in ethnomusicology have not given up certain interests of our predecessors—searching for survivals, for parent tunes and (we hope) ancient styles, for peoples who preserve abroad what has disappeared at home. But we have also taken into account the behavior of music in the era of globalization, at a time when musical dissemination no longer depends on the oxcart or even on our ability to send LPs by airmail, but where all communication is possible in an instant.

Most people in the world can now access virtually all music in recorded form, and we can claim a certain global homogeneity for the world of music. But the world of music can alternatively be seen as consisting of innumerable small groups of people—they include conventionally defined minorities but ought also to include groups defined by gender, age, class, and occupation, along with traditional markers of ethnicity—who continue to insist on maintaining their own music, identifying themselves by their specific repertories, genres, styles, instruments, and ideas about and attitudes toward music, often more than by anything else.

Riding the Warhorses

On the Ethnomusicology of Canons

The concept of "canon" and the term have a long history in the contemplation and evaluation of literature, and to a smaller extent, they have had their place in the world of classical music, as described by Samson (2001) in *The New Grove*, second edition. After 1950 or so, when musicology came increasingly to contemplate its own nature and history, its denizens began to note how canonic concepts affected their approaches to their work. Samson credits Walter Wiora (e.g., in his *Four Ages of Music* [1965]) as one of the first to pay attention to the canonic in musicological thought, and a few major figures, particularly Carl Dahlhaus (1977), contributed to a rather sparse dialogue (see Komara 2007 for an account). But the canons that musicologists themselves use did not become a subject for extended research until the late twentieth

century (see Bergeron and Bohlman 1992). Musical canons became an issue of greater currency in the early twenty-first century, constituting, for example, the subject of an issue of *Notes* (2007; see particularly Danielson 2007) and of a special conference (2008) at the University of Illinois, the latter devoted to canons in ethnomusicology specifically.

Canons have played a role in ethnomusicology in a number of ways—ethnomusicologists have used canons, studied extant canons, and fought off canons throughout their field's history. The following paragraphs discuss my personal experience with three types of canons: those that play an important role in education, those established by scholars for aesthetic or ideological reasons, and those discovered in the course of fieldwork and thus possibly indicating that, in some form, the canonic concept appears in all musical cultures and thus perhaps constitutes a cultural universal.

When I was a student ("pupil" is better—I was not yet ten), the concept of the canonic dominated my musical education. Perhaps it is still essential in classically oriented Western music teaching and learning. It started with piano lessons: "Have you started the Bach Inventions yet?" I was asked by a slightly older girl—I couldn't tell whether she was sympathetic and informative or proud of being ahead. She quickly reinforced my understanding that there was no way to bypass learning these short pieces (I and others saw them as a kind of torture) if I was to retain my place as a respectable beginner. Later, the Inventions were succeeded by the "Gradus ad Parnassum" of Clementi and Bach's "Well-Tempered Clavier."

There are, I know, many versions of this scene, different in place, time, and person. But here were the elements of canonicity—the corpus of undebatably great music, a repertory that all involved in music are assumed to know; a kind of unquestioned center of music; the epitome of normalcy; the idea that there is a right way to proceed in study.

This playbook continues in higher education. Let me illustrate with three scenes. First, there are the "names on the building"—on a good many campus music buildings and concert halls. Not all buildings have the same names, although Beethoven seems always to be there, but the very fact that one finds them there conveys the concept of a central repertory. Second, there are theory classes, in which the common-practice style is first and central and becomes the norm to which one compares everything earlier and later and foreign. But at the center of this "common practice" is its system of harmony, and other parameters of music receive far less attention. The major scale and its triads are absolutely the first thing to learn. But can the typical teacher or student imagine anything else? The emphasis on harmony and the primacy of major define the normal. That's what makes it canonic.

In my days as a college student, during the late 1940s and early 1950s, teachers complained that students were ignorant of musical works they needed to know, and to remedy this situation they developed the system of "music-literature" classes that we still have. We now have far more ways of teaching music-literature courses, but I remember in the piano-literature classes having to listen to (or enjoying listening to) performances and explanations of a number of major works: Bach's "Forty-eight," a couple of Mozart sonatas, a middle-period Beethoven sonata, the *Diabelli Variations*, Schumann's *Carnaval*, and some Chopin etudes. Again, the idea was of a central repertory, both an elevated center of the whole and a distillation of its principal values, that all professional pianists must know well and other music students should recognize. We students tended to take a cynical view, and one of us coined a name for the course—"Riding the Warhorses."

At my institutions and others like it, students and teachers today are probably much less focused on convention. Still, when I taught a course required of all first-year music majors, "Basic Music Literature," and was trying to convert it from a survey of the standard Western concert repertory to a kind of world music cum Western music survey approaching music from a number of perspectives, I was confronted by a couple of students who complained, "I thought this course would teach me the works of music that I would need to know during my four years here." This was perhaps a rather good practical definition of a canon.

I encountered another relevant, perhaps memorable, example only a few decades ago at my institution in the context of the music-theory examination required for entrance into the graduate programs. The examination included a number of generalized tests—on harmony, counterpoint, and ear training—but the last one required the candidate to write the exposition of a fugue, or at least the beginning, in Bach's style. Evidently few students could do this, and the requirement was changed to the analysis of a fugue. Being skeptical, I asked why the fugue form was given this unique and exalted place, why students should have to deal with it rather than other genres or styles, such as twelve-tone technique or modal counterpoint. My question exceeded the comprehension of some faculty members, who replied in such diverse ways as, "After all, it's the most perfect music" and "But they've always had that requirement at Harvard."

Standard dictionaries present us several definitions of canon, and the relevant publications, including the previously mentioned *Disciplining Music* (Bergeron and Bohlman 1992) and Jim Samson's (2001) article, point to a set of historical periods in Western music, each of which makes its own use of something that could be called a canon. But leaving aside the technical use of the concept, as in "the Beethoven canon"—meaning all the works that Beethoven himself composed—and looking at canons that somehow relate to a total musical culture, it's clear that a canon elevates a distinct body of music, a methodology, or a way of thinking about music, above the rest. There are many different ways of making practical use of the canon concept, extending from the strict educational use mentioned at the beginning of this essay to the rather extreme group of essays in Chris Washburne and Maiken Derno's collection *Bad Music: The Music We Love to Hate* (2004), whose contributors single out and contemplate various musics for their "badness." And certainly the concept of the canonic extends to our system of education in musicology—the notion that there is a certain sacredness about particular concepts, theories, and written works; the requirement that one know or be able to do certain things, no matter what else one also controls; possibly even the notion that certain musics somehow hold together a discipline concerned with the multimusical world. Thus, at one time, it seemed that most American ethnomusicologists, whatever their far-flung specialties, tended to know something about certain privileged repertories whose presence in this canon was based not on intrinsic characteristics or values but on special relationships to American culture or American musical culture: gamelan music (non-Western orchestral music analogous to the highly valued large ensemble in Western music), Indian classical traditions (music with a theoretical system both analogous and complementary to Western theory), West African drum traditions (the source, perhaps, of African American musical values), and Native American music (the music of the local "other"). The discourse about these, fortuitously, became something like a *lingua franca* for these scholars.

Ethnomusicology can seem tailor-made to represent the anticanonic side; it ought to be, one may think, the profession of canon-busters. To some degree ethnomusicologists have done this, becoming the nay-sayers or deniers about generalizations and conventional wisdom.

As Don Randel (1992) described it in an important essay, musicology itself has a toolbox of canons of various sorts as part of its arsenal. In ethnomusicology, we can distinguish among various kinds of canons. First, there are those discovered in the field; more about these later. There is the notion of a prescribed and once considered universally valid methodology, a prescribed order of activities. At one point, this methodology consisted of fieldwork, transcription, analysis, and other steps to the complete project (for example, some institutions required transcriptions as part of acceptable dissertations); later, fieldwork had to include performance study. There is, third, the development of a canon of musical cultures privileged over others as a kind of common ground—I've already mentioned them (Javanese, Indian, West African, Native American), but I might add Anglo-American folk music, Japanese gagaku, and the Middle Eastern *maqam* system as a second tier. My list is hardly definitive, though this canon's existence is palpable (I won't go into the reasons), and I admit that I'm only partly sure of my ground here. There are canons developed for education and canons meant to integrate a field with a population of widely divergent and varied interests and knowledge.

Most important, though, are canons of the first sort I listed, those we discover as part of the ethnographic enterprise. We ask whether canons exist, in some form, in all musical cultures; whether the division of a repertory into a general and a somehow privileged part is a cultural universal; and how we can discover canons without simply transferring our Western ideas of canons to other systems of musical thinking. Let's also consider the other side: scholars construct canons to organize their data, to make the musics of other cultures compatible with ours and thus digestible, as when they divide music into elements such as melody, rhythm, and texture. We develop canons, too, for a mix of aesthetic and ideological reasons. Sometimes one wonders how they came about but marvels at their strength and persistence.

Let me comment on an example from folklore: the Child ballads (Child 1956). Folklorics now defines itself largely as the study of certain processes and as a collection of approaches from particular perspectives, but its adherents in the first sixty years of the twentieth century saw themselves more typically as students of a particular body of orally transmitted literature and music. In the United States, one of its centers was Anglo-American folk song, and a considerable body of its publications took the form of regionally oriented collections, with or without analysis or commentary. Beginning with Cecil Sharp's (1932) collection of English folk songs from the southern Appalachians and going on to Belden's (1940) folk songs of Missouri, Davis's (1929) of Virginia, Flanders's (1960–65) of New England, Schinhan's (1937) of North Carolina, Brewster's (1940) of Indiana, Eddy's (1939) of Ohio, and lots more, these collections typically begin with ballads and go on to other genres ("songs"); within the group of ballads, they begin with Child ballads, move on to others of English origin, and continue further with ballads of American origin. Minor differences appear—Schinhan segregated the ballads in a special volume, and Davis included only Child ballads—but in all these collections, the Child ballads are set forth as the canon, and indeed, folkloristic discourse often referred to them as "the Child canon."

Francis James Child believed that these ballads were of considerable age, originated in an anonymous folk culture, told stories that had broader rather than local significance, and finally, were just better literature than other ballads and songs. To Child, it was important that these ballads came from England or Scotland and exhibited high literary quality, and he saw them as possessing a high degree of "authenticity," a concept that has canonic implications. And although text groupings and tune groupings were only partially congruent, the tunes to which the ballads were sung also became a unit, as demonstrated by Bronson's monumental collection *The Traditional Tunes of the Child Ballads* (1958–72). These tunes, as collected by Bronson, do have a certain kind of unity. For example, of the 141 versions of "Lady Isabel and the Elf Knight" (Child no. 4) for which Bronson found tunes, 97 were sung to variants of one family or type, and the rest, to a second. To be sure, this unity and the proposed congruence is disturbed by two factors. The tunes serve as settings for non-Child ballads and other songs, and the story of Lady Isabel, like those of most Child ballads, was used in songs in many other nations, as documented by Iivar Kemppinen (1954). We find further reason to doubt the Child ballads' status as canon in the fact that while scholars separate them from other ballads and songs, putting them at the head of collections, the folk community (i.e., the singers from whom they were collected and who presumably sang them at their leisure for themselves, their families, and friends) did not consider them a separate category—not, that is, until they discovered that the collectors did this and wanted them to do so, too.

Well, here's a canon created by and for folklorists, and it's hard to justify its existence, but it sometimes influenced the "folk." The notion that Appalachian singers divided their songs in a way that might allow us to identify a canon—a group of favored songs—seems unlikely, but the fieldworkers didn't really say whether they did that. I suggest that perhaps they did, because many musical cultures structure their music in ways that identify a central repertory, a favored group of songs. And the ethnomusicologist's and folklorist's impact on the folk? Well, that's a subject for another conference.

But if the concept of canon is one of our tools or part of our arsenal, and if we were to make an axiom of the belief that every culture has something like a canon, that every culture privileges some music, then how would we identify one? We might ask such questions as, What are the best songs?

Who are the best musicians? What music does everyone know? What is the most sacred? What music never changes? Perhaps all cultures have musical canons, but each individual cannon will be identified by distinct criteria and serve unique purposes.

Nonetheless, looking in the world's musics for a paradigmatic example of a canon, one that satisfies the various criteria in my list, one would likely come upon the Persian *radif,* the body of music that is learned by each musician and becomes a point of departure for virtually all improvisation and composition in the traditional sector of Iranian classical music. It is used, further, for musical reference of various sorts in Iranian-Western fusion. It is a canon in several senses, satisfying a number of the criteria I listed earlier. It is the common pedagogical device; everyone learns it as a way of becoming a musician. It is thus like the Bach inventions and the Kreutzer etudes; indeed, it is even more central than they are—for many musicians, it was the only body of music they studied before being considered competent. In conversations with musicians, it became clear to me that the *radif* is central. When asked questions such as, "What actually is the true music of Iran," musicians typically replied that it is the *radif* (described, e.g., in Zonis 1973; Farhat 1990), which they considered a repertory of music, a theoretical construct, a somewhat abstract guide, and measuring device for authenticity. Musicians would be evaluated in part by how well they were thought to control it. And musicians would also describe the *radif* as the crowning achievement of the musical system, somewhat as the works of the great composers might be considered the greatest accomplishment of Western music, the music one has to know to go through the educational system, perhaps.

Looking at the *radif* as the epitome of the canon concept leads to some unexpected observations. The *radif* as it exists now was created (more properly, organized, for it is a codification of widespread practices, not universally accepted and probably not very homogeneous) in the late nineteenth century. Some of its components—certain *dastgahs* and even some *gushehs*—are said to be very old, and their names are evident in older literature, although there is no evidence of the way they sounded. But the *radif,* though central to Persian musical culture, is widely understood to be only a little more than a century old (Zonis 1973, 39). Indeed, both Western scholars and Persian musicians agree that it was created so that Persian music would have a canon. In fact, the Western notion of canonical classical music, of a body of literature that would unify education, provide a central repertory everyone knew, and serve as an ideal—a notion introduced to Iranians by European musicians who had been invited to modernize mainly military musical life—probably provided an important stimulus to the Persian musicians. Some of them, such as Mirza Abdollah, considered the *radif* to be a preserving device, while others, such as Ali Naqi Vaziri, saw its function more as the modernization of the system (see Khoshzamir 1979; Zonis 1973, 39–40).

During my time in Tehran, I often heard musicians insist that while there is such a thing as "the" *radif*, all musicians develop their own *radifs*. All students learn their teachers' *radifs* precisely but then develop their own variants. Some students' styles diverge more from their teachers', and some less, but my point is that the individual association was important. To each musician, the *radif* was the canon but also his own expression and understanding of it.

For a time, after the revolution of 1979, musical life in Tehran declined and became, at most, a practice carried out in private homes. After 1989 or so, classical music was revived and emerged again into public view. Interestingly, education and scholarship were first given relatively free rein. The last fifteen years have thus seen publication of various versions of the *radif*, some in transcription but most in recorded form. Older recordings made by the Ministry of Fine Arts under the shah were rediscovered and issued on tapes and CDs, and so now comparative study of *radifs* can be carried out at various levels. To me, they are indeed amazingly similar, and I suspect they have always been. The various pieces, the *gushehs*, differ more in the terminology attached to them than in their musical content. Significant for the concept of "canon," however, is the degree to which their unity is now stressed, whereas emphasis lay on their individuality in the 1960s. This unity is not affected by the large amount of theoretical study many Iranian scholars now pursue; their work seems to concentrate on finding new ways to understand and interpret the material that they all accept as their common heritage.

I can only guess at the reason for this change in attitude. Perhaps the government's cultural policy, supporting a requirement of unity and conformity (in a culture I always saw, and that also described itself, as highly individualistic), moved musicians toward emphasizing conformity. Perhaps music is more acceptable if one can claim that it relates, directly and in a straight line, to a period preceding the execrable Pahlavi dynasty. In any event, it is interesting to see, in a period of canon-busting in many of the world's musics, this example of a canon carefully preserved and strengthened. But then, Iranian musicians have a strong emotional attachment to the *radif*. Their hearts warmed toward me when I showed even a slight knowledge of it. My teacher, Dr. Boroumand, often said something like,

"It is really something great, something especially fine, this *radif* that we have created here in Iran."

During a short stay in Madras, now Chennai, a lot of my time was devoted to looking at similarities and differences between the classical music cultures of Persia and southern India. The one in Madras was much larger, with many more musicians and audience members. The structure of the musical culture paralleled that of Western cities somewhat, probably because of conscious attempts to compete, and so there were public concerts, newspaper criticism, a system of star performers, and so on. But of course, since the music is a combination of composed works and improvisations, there were differences. A canon was surely present; one could identify it by noting behavior, choices, and practices and also by asking musician questions such as, "What is the most important component of your music?" For what it's worth, I got a few different answers. Some identified it as the seventy-two *melakarta* ragas, the ragas that are central to the music theory because both the ascending and descending forms have the seven scale degrees in the same order. Interestingly, these are not necessarily the most widely performed ragas. Others pointed to the great *kritis,* or composed pieces, that everybody knows. Still others took the central component to be the great composers, mainly the so-called trinity of Tyagaraja, Dikshitar, and Syama Sastri. Indeed, these three composers were by far the ones I saw performed most often while I was there. But it was difficult to find a concert that did not include at least one work of Tyagaraja, whom, in his dominant role in the musical culture, Indians often compared to his close contemporary Beethoven. So I think that Carnatic and Western classical canons are parallel, but in part because Carnatic musicians wanted to relate to, and to compete with, European music.

These canons—Western, Persian, Carnatic—presented themselves to me on their own, as it were; and this is true of the Child ballads as well, though they are a canon of scholarship, not of the cultures to which the scholars addressed themselves. I would like to test the hypothesis that a canon in some sense of the word can be identified in the structure of every musical culture by looking briefly at the music of the Blackfoot people, with whom I studied in the late 1960s and 1970s (see Nettl 1989), though I didn't specifically address the question in my fieldwork. The individualism characteristic of Blackfoot culture and music in earlier times, resulting from the human's association with an individual song-giving guardian spirit, seemed to suggest a negative conclusion. In recent times, the importance of intertribal songs in the powwow culture, also, militates against a central Blackfoot repertory. I was told that many new songs entered the repertory annually, and many were forgotten as well. Trying to get three singers to sing their entire repertory for me, as they could construct it in a short period, yielded little overlap.

Still, conversations indicated that certain songs were singled out for greater respect, including songs of the most important ceremonies. But were these songs the most widely known? Had people heard them? On the one hand, special respect was bestowed on personal songs that were to be sung only in moments of crisis, perhaps with no one present; theoretically, these songs might never be sung. Might there be a kind of canon— or anticanon—of songs regarded as special because they were not widely known and rarely heard? On the other hand, there were songs—social songs performed at powwows or gatherings—that were said to be known by everybody. But they were not taken very seriously. Walter McClintock (1968), describing an encampment of 1910, indicates that lots of singing was always going on, reporting that one could hear songs emanating simultaneously from various tents and from the outdoors, and suggested that some songs were particularly popular and widely known. And at powwows more recently, one might hear the master of ceremonies refer to "one of the favorite songs of our people."

This suggests that the concept of canon might be found everywhere, but if so, we are certainly talking about canons of very different sorts. As ethnomusicological fieldworkers, we are obliged to learn about the world's musical canons as part of comprehending the world's musical cultures. As ethnomusicologists interested in theory, we might need canons of our own to communicate with one another, though these might be canons of theory, method, concept, or procedure rather than collections of repertories, cultures, or works. In this regard, we might wish to look critically at the tendency to change allegiances to authors and theories at the drop of a hat and to mistake new verbal formulations for conceptual changes. As ethnomusicologists in the academy, we should also continue to take a dim view of canons that have been developed simply from received knowledge, to continue contradicting facile generalizations, and to question conventional wisdom.

A Stranger Here?

Free Associations around Kurt Weill

Several Kinds of Strangeness

"*You?*" exclaimed my wife. "He [the editor of the *Kurt Weill Newsletter*] asked *you* to write something about Kurt Weill?" She was no more incredulous than I had been when this invitation came to me—an ethnomusicologist with principal experience among Native Americans of Montana and musicians in Tehran, who loves but knows only little of the music of Weill and is thoroughly ignorant of scholarly issues surrounding this major but idiosyncratic figure in twentieth-century music history. "I'm a Stranger Here Myself"—so ends one of Weill's best-known songs, and on these pages, "stranger" is surely the right designation for me.

But I am struck by this interesting coincidence: the gradual recognition of Weill's significance by musicologists, after his death, involved erasing boundaries, and the history of ethnomusicology since 1950, too, is marked by the deleting of unnecessary conceptual borders. Kurt Weill certainly has to be sort of a stranger in this essay and the world of ethnomusicology in which it is based, but recently developing interests of that field, and the burgeoning of Weill scholarship, have eradicated some of the distance.

My own memories of Weill go back to my teenage family home in Princeton, around 1942, where my father once played a catchy-sounding tune about somebody called Messer, but the most important thing about it at that moment seemed to be its relationship to *The Beggar's Opera*. Later, when a young student in the Jacobs School of Music at Indiana University, I had begun to learn something about what would later be called ethnomusicology, a field that at the time rather rigidly divided the musical world into categories such as "classical," "popular," and "folk," wherein the concern with folk music was much about "authenticity." My teacher, George Herzog (1901–82), an immigrant from Hungary who had lived in New York in the 1930s and most of the 1940s and had met Weill (the two were nearly exact contemporaries), considered these categories real and their maintenance important. Herzog's message, as I perceived it, was this: seek out and study authentic folk music, as had his idol Béla Bartók; avoid cultural mixes such as popular music (e.g., the kind that combines African American and European styles or that draws on both folk and classical sources); maintain respect for, but in your scholarship eschew, Western classical music, remembering that it has its own scholarly discipline. Well, Dr. Herzog wasn't really that rigid, but in midcentury this was the ethnomusicological view of the musical world. In such a world, Kurt Weill's oeuvre would surely be a stranger.

Actually, ethnomusicologists in America and Europe are themselves generally seen as strangers in the world of music, concerned with the "other" in various respects. But until recently, they didn't want to hear about strangeness within the cultures they were studying. Originally, they wanted to know what was typical in the music of India, or in an Aboriginal tribe, or Appalachia, what was "normal" and acceptable (in this field that most people see as the home of abnormal musical taste). They didn't care about the Indian who had learned to play ragas on the cello, or the folksinger who was inserting Mozart songs into his repertory, or the Cheyenne peyote religionist who was accompanying his songs on the guitar—or for that matter, the kind of composer who would write both "September Song" and the 1921 *Berliner Symphonie*. The musical public and its critics were similarly narrow-minded, feeling obliged to choose among the "German" Weill of the *Dreigroschenoper* and *Mahagonny*, the "serious" Weill of chamber music, or the "American" Weill of *Street Scene* and *One Touch of Venus*. They were uncomfortable when they found that Weill swimmingly straddled musical worlds, just as did my cello-playing Hindu.

A Foray into the History of Ethnomusicology

Because of the way people and peoples have been forced to move from place to place, as well as the technological advances that allow us to move around the world easily—physically and now also virtually—strangeness has been a kind of leitmotiv for life since 1950, the era of modern diasporas. Ethnomusicologists began their studies by trying to find music as it existed, or as it might have once existed, in cultures that were self-contained, to contemplate music uncontaminated by intercultural influences. This was how they perceived the cultural norm of the past eras, but I think they knew that this quest would ultimately be frustrated, and still they sought the unspoiled, emphasizing the concept of authenticity. They avoided the impact of colonialist cultures on the world's musics, of hybridization, mass mediation, the multicultural nation-state, and the processes that led to what is now widely called globalization. The music of indigenous peoples and village folk and uncorrupted classical systems were their favorite subject matter. This kind of focus hasn't quite disappeared, but after World War II many began to realize that the sort of unspoiled authenticity previously sought just wasn't around anymore—and maybe had never been, for the "pure" of today was usually the "hybrid" of yesterday. While scholars everywhere participated in this sea change in attitude, I think it was concentrated in the United States and Canada, and incidentally also Israel, nations significantly shaped by diasporas—I'm using the term broadly to refer to large-scale movement and dispersal of populations and cultures.

Following this virtual turnaround, ethnomusicologists became (and now are) much concerned with concepts that help us to understand the role of music in enabling individuals to negotiate and maintain various kinds of identity—ethnicity (the group of which you're most essentially a part), nationality (membership in a larger, imagined community), hybridity (recognition of simultaneously holding several identities), gender, class, and age group. The notion of ethnicity is (following the analysis of Martin Stokes [1994]) concerned with establishing boundaries; thus, a social group may use music and other cultural domains to erect boundaries between "us" and "them," using concepts such as authenticity to justify these boundaries (Stokes 1994, 6). Of these various concepts, ethnicity is the least related to specific, predictable criteria such as physical borders, language, or culture. Its contents are fluid and debatable. But all these concepts could be helpful in interpreting the relationship Kurt Weill had to the cultural contexts in which he lived and worked. I say this realizing that the question of Weill's personal and musical identities, as seen by himself and by his audiences and critics, has been a major issue in the burgeoning literature, both critical and documentary (e.g., Taylor 1991; and Symonette and Juchem 2000).

I first heard the term *ethnic group* in early 1950s Detroit. The society at large was beginning to recognize the cultural diversity of American cities, and an organization, the International Institute, had been established to encourage ethnic groups to practice their traditions but also to share and mix them, traditions such as those involving music, dance, holiday customs, or foods. When I joined the faculty at Wayne State University to teach about folk music, I found that music was indeed an important ethnicity marker. People who had become thoroughly "Anglo" nevertheless knew some songs from the old country; for example, they could perhaps sing them but not understand the words. Moreover, I realized that when vernacular musicians played at, say, Polish and Serbian weddings, they exhibited what Stokes calls a "magpie attitude toward genres" from different national sources, picking up, digesting, and reinterpreting in various ways (for further details and bibliography, see Nettl 2002a).

After about 1960, American ethnomusicologists began to take seriously the task of analyzing the music of ethnic groups, and this meant taking into account how these societies related, musically, to other groups—those who were like themselves, their relatives elsewhere (perhaps in their places of origin), and their immediate neighbors.

Well, to make this more concrete, ethnomusicologists of this stripe would have done fieldwork among Hungarian Americans in Detroit, some of whom had arrived in the 1890s, finding individuals who remembered and sang traditional Hungarian folk songs. They would have compared these songs to the repertory collected in Hungary, thus studying how the traditional repertory had been preserved in America, how it had been changed, and perhaps also how—while the home tradition had undergone change—it had preserved older forms. But they would also examine the sociocultural context to see how, for example, the functions and uses of traditional songs would have changed as they moved from a rural agricultural to an urban industrial society, how they came to be performed by professional musicians with instruments taken from the jazz world, or how their function changed from accompanying traditional rituals to maintaining cultural identity in a culturally hybridized world. Although earlier ethnomusicologists, keeping their focus on authenticity, occasionally collected such music, this approach to understanding the musical culture of America became almost the norm for ethnomusicological studies after about 1980. Interestingly, because of the confluence of Jewish populations from many parts of the world in Israel, their musical interactions reflected developments in North America. In all these studies, though, the concern focused on groups who agreed, not with idiosyncratic individuals. (For background and illustrations, see Erdely 1979.)

This kind of research came into existence because of the way the cultures of the United States and Canada grew, through immigration from everywhere, to form in some respects a melting pot, in others, a kind of cultural mosaic, as well as other relational configurations. It's the result of hundreds of separate waves of immigration and hundreds of ways in which immigrant groups settled and negotiated their relationships to their places of origin and their new environments. Using the term now very loosely, it's the result of hundreds of separate diasporas, and they provided food for study and thought to a substantial population of music scholars. Considering the life and work of Kurt Weill motivates us to see whether the ethnic group of which Weill was a member, Germans and Central Europeans of Jewish background fleeing the Nazi threats, differed from the others and to ask whether those who came to America were like those who went to Palestine/Israel.

Ethnicity, Diasporas, and Music

The heterogeneity of the Jewish population and the variety of musical traditions was noted early on by Abraham Zevi Idelsohn and also by Robert Lachmann in the 1930s, and the increased immigration triggered first by the Holocaust and then by the founding of the state of Israel gave further impetus to a view of Israel's musical culture as a microcosm of Jewish traditions from everywhere, as well as of Christian and Islamic musical traditions in which Jews had participated. A large number of scholars, significantly beginning with Edith Gerson-Kiwi and continuing with Ruth Katz, Dahlia Cohen, and Amnon Shiloah, among others, made studies that in some ways paralleled those being carried out in North America. But of course the situation was more complex, for while the American scene involved people who left their traditional and permanent home for something they hoped to be better, Israel gathered in people who, though also looking for something better, saw themselves as coming home, bringing music traditions from abroad while trying to integrate themselves in the traditions they found. The German-speaking (and Czech and Hungarian) immigrants developed a musical culture that, according to Philip Bohlman (1989), duplicated and even extended the experience of the original home, a musical life based on Mozart, Beethoven, Schubert, and so on. Composers coming from Europe began to use Middle Eastern and Eastern European folk styles as resources but worked hard to remain composers of "art music." While Kurt Weill blended into the vernacular musical culture of the United States, Israeli composers, and many others who came to America (e.g., Schoenberg and Hindemith), did not effect this kind of blend.

In the literature on Kurt Weill, one doesn't read much about experiences he might have had with music his generation of German musicians would have labeled as "exotic"—for example, Arabic music he might have heard during his visit to Palestine—but he drew on a great variety of musical traditions. In today's world, where the musical norm includes multicultural roots and polysemy, he might have felt quite at home, more than in Berlin of the 1920s. Some of his correspondence from the late 1940s, however, suggests that while he considered issues of authenticity and the appropriation of music from various sources, he was not all that comfortable with or sympathetic to "exotica." In working on *Lost in the Stars,* he became acquainted with examples of South African music but in the end decided that it wouldn't be appropriate as source material.

Music's primacy as an index of ethnic identity became clear to me in many of my field experiences, particularly when I was trying to learn something about the classical-music culture of South India, in Chennai. The emblem of ethnicity for the whole culture seems somehow to have been the classical music, Carnatic music. It is a complex system; few people, I think, knew it well, and very few went to live concerts—although there were plenty of those. It was principally the music of the intelligentsia and the associated caste groups. Even so, pride in this great music, its great composers, such as Tyagaraja and Muttuswami Dikshitar, and its great performers was a kind of hallmark of Madras society as a whole. It's a bit as if the emblem of American ethnicity were Aaron Copland (which is probably not imaginable) or that of Austrian ethnicity were Mozart and Schubert (which definitely is). Here the purpose of presentation to the outside world was to show parity; one was told that there are two great musical systems, and two great cultures, European and Indian. Indian music is melodic, and European, harmonic; Indian, vocal, and European, instrumental. But each had its trinity of great composers. Music thus symbolized the superiority, in a world context, of Hindu society and culture (Nettl 1984).

As ethnomusicologists ceased paying much attention to the boundaries delineated by the George Herzog generation, some of them began to look at the Viennese trinity, and at the whole group of Great Masters, not as historical figures but as a kind of pantheon ruling our world of classical music today, and I undertook to examine them through a study of university schools of music. A pantheon indeed—it is clear who the principals are; they are the composers whose names are emblazoned on our music buildings and whose music you must unquestionably respect. Some at the borders (Berlioz, Bruckner, Liszt) might have a kind of associate status, like certain demigods in ancient Greece. Can one imagine Kurt Weill joining such a pantheon? It's not that no one in this pantheon reached out. Take Mozart; one thinks of the incredible variety of genres, his multinational sources of inspiration, his ability to appeal to audiences not particularly learned in music. He's not the only one. But the uniqueness of Kurt Weill and his existence on several sides of too many borders may keep him a stranger.

What Are You, Anyway?

In the modern world, deciding one's ethnic identity and one's cultural allegiance has not always been an easy matter. According to the anthropologist Anya Royce, people manipulate their identities to attain satisfaction in different contexts; identity is less a matter of external ascription or biological or cultural pedigree than of the conscious decisions individuals make when presenting themselves to others in a variety of situations (Royce 1982, 19). When I first came to the United States, in 1939, my father frequently went to a pastry shop on New York's Seventy-second Street called Eclair, where recent émigrés from Germany, Austria, and Czechoslovakia gathered; sometimes I got to go along. Much of the vigorous but also desperate-sounding conversation revolved about the speakers' relationships to Europe and America. All were happy to have escaped with skin largely intact, but only a few seemed to love America, while others were critical and disappointed—no gold in the streets, no jobs, no proper "culture," the few words of British English they had learned unintelligible to New York doormen, and so on. A few were determined never to return to their nations of origin and even in their homes conversed in heavily accented English. Some were clearly disoriented, thinking they had better leave the refugee beehive of New York City for the hinterlands but afraid it would be just too strange. A good many thought they would hold on and, when it was again safe, return to Europe.

My parents arrived from Czechoslovakia (they had lived in Bohemia, in its incarnations first as an Austro-Hungarian province and then as a Czechoslovakian one, all their lives), but they chiefly spoke German, with Czech as a second language, and came from a Jewish background, though one without religious participation. They arrived with no knowledge of America and no plan of action, typical refugees; they then turned into exiles who hoped eventually to return, but near the end of the war, they turned into immigrants, becoming citizens (for more detail and interpretation, see Nettl 1999). Even so, around 1946, I witnessed a curious conversation my father had with a German who asked him, "Was ist eigentlich Ihre nationale Einstellung?" perhaps best translated as, "What do you consider yourself to be?" (Maybe he just said, "Was sind Sie eigentlich?"— "What are you, anyway?"—I don't remember for sure.) Mentally weighing the alternatives—was he Jewish, German, Czech, Sudetendeutsch, *Deutschböhme,* American—my father answered, "Well, when all is said and done, I think I am a kind of Austrian," going back to what he would have had to say in his youth, before World War I, and at the same time confessing to his identification with Germanophone culture without uttering the then negative word *German.* Indeed, our household language continued to be German, with English words thrown in to bridge the culture gap and with Czech largely neglected. The whole business of identity made him uncomfortable, though. Although he traveled a great deal in Europe in his old age, he never returned to Czechoslovakia, where he was born, and he never visited Israel, which would have tied him to his roots in a significant way. I mention all this to illustrate the problems that others in Kurt Weill's shoes might have had (Nettl 2002a, 12–18, 33–39).

I have no survey of statements of identity made by émigré intellectuals in the late 1930s, but I suspect that my father's attitude was not atypical. Many of them opted to stay strangers, seeing that this nation consisted of people who could easily survive by remaining strangers, a country of diverse ethnic groups with no ethnic majority. This was an aspect of the cultural context in which Kurt Weill lived during the World War II period, but when it came to deciding how to present himself, he may have been a bit of an exception, a man who came to America and decided with little difficulty that it was the right place for him. Reading the biographical literature, one sees Weill coping with his multiple identities in a pretty straight-forward way. He did much the same with his musical identities, not worrying about whether he was doing the right thing by composing light or heavy, classical or popular, E or U music, taking refuge in the somewhat simplistic cliché that there's only good and bad music. It's my impression that Weill adjusted personally better than most émigrés; maybe it had to do with his ability to adapt musically, especially to the American musical culture.

Meeting a "Folk Opera"

During this period of my life, when I was absorbing the musical worldview that my teachers then espoused, I also had the good fortune of being asked to play, in 1948, in an orchestra that was rehearsing for the stage premiere of Weill's *Down in the Valley* during the incunabular portion of the eventually famed Indiana University opera program (Logan 2000, 152–53). Being a type of work, sometimes labeled as *Gebrauchsmusik* (a term that Paul Nettl is sometimes credited with originating; see P. Nettl 1921–22, 258), that could be staged rather quickly, the opera was produced on a couple of months' notice. The score—written to be accessible to high-school orchestras, with many violin players but few who had yet shifted down the perfect fifth to embrace the viola, which was more respectable than second violin—included three violin parts. I was assigned to third violin and played under the watchful eye of Ernst Hoffmann, the conductor who built the IU orchestra from a scraggly bunch of amateurs into a pretty disciplined crew before being killed in an early morning car crash in 1953 and about whom I remember particularly his strategic use of rubato both to produce a dramatic effect and to help us get through difficult passages. I recall sitting in the pit and hearing the high-pitched, intense voice of the distinguished Hans Busch, son of the conductor Fritz, directing the singers, trying to get them to act and not just to sing. It was the first time I played in the pit of a real opera house, the Indiana University Auditorium, with its 3,800 seats, where I had seen Metropolitan Opera productions.

A few days before the performance, Kurt Weill appeared, with Lenya (not yet so famous in the Midwest); Marion Bell, who sang the lead; and her husband, Alan Jay Lerner. I wish I could say I had actually met Weill—it was less than two years before his death—but I only saw him from a distance as he observed the dress rehearsal. He made some encouraging remarks to Hoffmann and Busch and waved to us in the pit in a friendly fashion, but I have the feeling that he was otherwise monopolized by the university's administrators. I have the feeling, too, that some of those people in Indiana didn't quite know what to make of a German composer who wrote Broadway musicals and film music. After all, "popular music" was something of a no-no to the orchestra, whose members had been ordered by the dean to avoid dance-band gigs and such.

Most of all I remember the heartbreaking story of *Down in the Valley,* of the falsely accused hero escaping from death row to visit his girl. At the same time, I found it pretty curious that someone was trying to combine opera and folk music, and I was bemused at this way of injuring the authenticity of folk music by the intrusion of the operatic genre, wondering whether this was a proper "opera" and whether the song that gave it its title was still a proper "folk song."

What should ethnomusicologists do with *Down in the Valley?* They might look at it as an outcropping of the Anglo-American folk-song tradition or see it as part of a minority movement in the turbulent history of twentieth-century opera or an aberration in the canon of the Broadway musical. They could view it as a contribution to a genre that never got off the ground in America, serious but accessible music for young musicians, a kind of *Gebrauchsmusik.* Or, looking at it within the theoretical frameworks used by ethnomusicology, they could find in it an example of syncretism or hybridization—in contemporary terms, globalization (see Nettl 1985; Turino 2000). Might it be best related to the history of musicians in Europe, America, and the Middle East, looked on with suspicion and to some extent viewed as outsiders, who—like the Jewish musicians in Middle Eastern villages, the Bohemian musicians throughout eighteenth-century Europe, or the 1990s Peruvian musicians in the world's cities—make music for their audiences, music maybe strange to their own ethnicity or perhaps exaggerating the traits of their ethnicity?

The creation of *Down in the Valley* at about the same time as ethnomusicological interest began its great reversal may be just an interesting coincidence. But it's probably more significant that it also came at the time when the so-called second folk-song revival came into its own, spearheaded in Weill's time by Woody Guthrie and Pete Seeger, who broke down the barriers between popular and folk with their particular ideas of the authenticity and modern role of folk music (Rosenberg 1993). Although ethnomusicologists have tried to avoid being labeled as the musicologists whose job it is to study and evaluate the use of folk and indigenous music by composers of art music, I can imagine examining *Down in the Valley* as part of a movement in which American folk music moves into several mainstreams of American musical culture. Certainly the sources of the songs that Weill used were a step or two away from their forms as recorded by folklorists and sung by untutored miners or farmers' wives.

Contemplating *Down in the Valley* and Kurt Weill's work at large enriches my sense of the wealth of our twentieth-century musical culture and reinforces my sense that the boundaries we draw among various kinds of music are worthless. While others may argue about the proper conceptual category for his music and look critically at the variety of his interests, Kurt Weill himself, who might hold the record among composers for participation in the most genres, classes, and types, seems to me, in his life, to have made his peace with being a stranger everywhere and might perhaps have been willing to be culturally at home anywhere.

16

Music — What's That?

Commenting on a Book by Carl Dahlhaus and Hans Heinrich Eggebrecht

As this essay was written for a conference honoring the memory of the distinguished music historian Hans Heinrich Eggebrecht, I must begin by admitting that unfortunately I met Professor Eggebrecht only two or three times. I greatly admired the many-sidedness of his work, his numerous publications, and the many areas of interest to which he devoted his lectures and his writings; I was, in addition, always impressed by his rhetorical eloquence and by the large number of scholars to whom he was "Doktorvater." Since I find myself here in a crowd of Eggebrecht's former students, virtually all historians of European music, I must admit that, being an ethnomusicologist, I should probably have chosen as my title the well-known song by Kurt Weill "I'm a Stranger Here

Myself." However that may be, Professor Riethmüller assigned me the task of speaking from an ethnomusicological perspective about the concept of music, with reference to the approaches toward and definitions of music Eggebrecht himself used, ones he proposed and debated.

Well now, is there such a thing as a specifically ethnomusicological position on the concept of music, a notion of music that characterizes ethnomusicology as a field and that has particular utility for the tasks we set ourselves? One that comes to mind is Alan Merriam's tripartite model, according to which music consists of activities, ideas, and sound—the music "itself" (Merriam 1964, 1967). Merriam is not cited as often as formerly, but this model, though expressed variously and not always explicitly, has become a kind of starting point for us all. But we also take the following into consideration: we ethnomusicologists come to our contemplations from two directions. For one, we are impressed by the unity of human music and its universality, but this viewpoint is actually rather ethnocentric, for we base it on the assumption that each society possesses something that reminds us of music (Wachsmann 1971, 382) as we imagine it. If we imagine this unity, however, we are overwhelmed by the multitude of musical sounds extant in the world and perhaps even more by the variety of ideas about music, the variety of ways to conceive of (what we in our culture call) music, promulgated by the world's peoples and the components of any one society.

To pursue these directions in reference to Eggebrecht's thought, I have chosen to deal with the ten themes, perhaps better described as "questions," that Dahlhaus and Eggebrecht (1985) used to analyze their fundamental ideas about music. To honor and memorialize the broad perspectives of these two authors, I wish to view each of the ten questions from a third perspective, hoping to compare their views with what seems to me to be the norm of—perhaps most typically, North American—ethnomusicological thought. I will focus my discussion through frequent references to three musical cultures with which I have had some personal research experience. I thus approach my assignment with two tasks in mind: to reflect the view of my academic colleagues and to elucidate how members of these three non-Western societies—the musicians of the Persian and Carnatic classical-music cultures and the Blackfoot people of Montana—traditionally think and speak about music.

Ten Themes

1. IS THERE SUCH A THING AS MUSIC? When music came into existence, was it in fact music? Was it, as Dahlhaus and Eggebrecht asked further, a unitary phenomenon? And has it remained so? Terminology provides some insights. We (English and German speakers) are used to the idea of defining music as a single comprehensive concept, but not even in Europe is it always so simple. There is, in German, the difference between *Musik* and *Tonkunst*. The former is the more comprehensive; "the latter, as used by scholars and writers on music, refers more specifically to art music, though examining the actual usage one may find it applied most to German, perhaps Italian and French, rarely English, and hardly ever Chinese musics. Here is a better example. In the Czech language, *huda* is the general term, but it refers mainly though not exclusively, to art music, and *muzika,* which refers mainly to vernacular and folk-derived music. The Blackfoot people of Montana have two words—*niinshchin,* which is glossed as "song," and *saapup,* which refers to song, dance, and ritual. They have no single word that directly translates the English term *music.* In Persian, one distinguishes between *musiqi,* glossed as "music" but principally indicating secular, composed, metric, instrumental sounds, and *khandan,* which includes the reading of the Koran or other sacred texts and vocal sounds similar to this, or performance possessing a certain sacredness—texted, nonmetric, and improvised. The many kinds of Persian music can be placed along a continuum between the two extremes of *musiqi* and *khandan.* Other peoples, too, have these kinds of dichotomies.

Now, relating these considerations to the debates on the ultimate roots of music, one may ask whether these cultural and terminological distinctions result from recent historical developments or suggest a branching off from a single, unitary origin of music. Contrary to the belief in a single point of origin, there may once have been several nonlinguistic ancestors of music, predecessors that, in certain societies, came eventually to be combined in the unitary concept of "music" while their individual descendants remained separate in other cultures. In the latter case, these separate categories of sound may well have retained their independence. In some non-European cultures, clearly, the unification occurred only when the European concept of music as a single phenomenon was introduced.

Let me offer an example. In the early decades of ethnomusicology, one frequently contrasted "art music" to "functional music." More recently, this division has sometimes been succeeded by the concepts of "presentational" and "participatory" music (Turino 2000, 47–49). In many cultures, one finds both; here and there, perhaps only one or the other. It is possible, however, that these two kinds of performance—in early human or prehuman times—had their origins in quite different functions, conceptions, and sounds. Conceivably, the one may go back to the need for attracting a mate by symbolically exhibiting flexibility, energy, skill, intelligence, and imagination—qualities necessary for supporting and protecting a family. The second suggests an activity that helps the members of a society to co-operate in work and perhaps to defend the group against enemies (Nettl 2006a, 65–66).

2. THE MUSIC CONCEPT AND EUROPEAN TRADITION   Defining the notion of music in the *Riemann Musik Lexikon,* Eggebrecht said, "Music is—in the realm in which it is relevant, the West—the artistic shaping of the audible, which, as natural and emotional sound, symbolizes both world and spirit in the realm of hearing in absolute concreteness" (Riemann 1967, 601; my translation). It's a particularly eloquent statement but also a very specialized definition. One may criticize it as ethnocentric, but for Eggebrecht, that kind of music exists only in Western culture. No other part of the world possesses music in the same sense; that, I think, is his assertion. (I'll return to that thought.) I find it interesting that other societies, too, regard music—all of music as a concept—to be something only they possess. Not only do they claim that their own music, both style and repertory, is essential to their culture, but sometimes they also claim that it is the only proper music. Only they truly "have" music.

One of my teachers in Madras expressed his belief that there are really only two classical-music traditions in the world, the European, which is the music of harmony, and the South Indian, quintessentially the music of melody. One is composed, the other, mainly improvised; one principally is vocal, the other, instrumental. Each has—and they are equal in this respect—a trinity of great composers. "Yes, but how about Chinese music?" I asked. "That's not a proper classical tradition to us; it has, for example, no seven-tone scale." He might as well have said, "For us, that's not truly music." Or he could have echoed Eggebrecht, saying, "Music, in the realm in which it is relevant, namely, South Indian culture . . ." (for contextual comments, see Nettl 1985).

My acquaintances among the Blackfoot people in Montana considered their culture to have two kinds of music, Indian and "white." In general, they took white music to be difficult: one has to know all kinds of technical stuff to understand it, there is a huge amount of this music, it requires many instruments, and people have to read music to perform it—it's all very complicated. But with all that, they viewed it as superficial. Indian music, on the contrary, directly reflects Blackfoot culture; it is much more essential to life than is this music of the Anglos, who don't regard their own music as something so essential. "Yes," they might say, "we can make (perform) white music, too, but you, as a white American, you will never understand our Indian music. We can understand your culture, but you can't understand ours." This assertion isn't far distant from the opinion of some early ethnomusicologists. I'll cite Carl Stumpf, who took a similar view about the songs of the Bella Coola: "On the evening of one of the days on which my friend Nutsiluska [Bella Coola singer] had sung for me, I heard, in Leipzig, a performance of Bach's great Mass. Nutsiluska would have had difficulty enjoying this music; I, on the other hand, had found many of his melodies approachable and listened to them for days on end without discomfort, and kept these tunes in my mind. This is an advantage of our culture" (Stumpf 1886, 25–26).

3. WHAT IS NONMUSICAL?   What is nonmusical? That was the next question Dahlhaus and Eggebrecht posed, a question more easily answered by the music historian than by the ethnomusicologist. We ethnomusicologists exclude almost no sounds made by humans (and maybe other species) from being potentially accepted as music. Within any one culture—for example, that of the West—the issue may be complicated by aesthetic and functional considerations. I remember the 1958 congress of the International Musicological Society, in Cologne, which included an interesting concert of electronic compositions by Herbert Eimert and Karlheinz Stockhausen. As we exited the studio, I overheard remarks in a conversation between two older scholars: "That was really ugly. Is it even music? Does something like this belong in a musicological conference?" The basic assumption was that one must be able to understand sounds to have them count as music. But one could have heard similar outbursts, at various times in history, about many works, from Monteverdi to Stravinsky and on, perhaps not always expressed so vehemently. Whether society deems a sound to belong to the realm of music, whether the music concept has wide or narrow boundaries—these decisions may depend on the strength and energy of music among the domains of culture. Narrowly conceived music may be illustrated by the Persian tradition, in which relatively few sounds are considered as proper and acceptable or even regarded as music (the two may not be the same).

The opposite viewpoint may be illustrated by the Havasupai of the Grand Canyon, as explained by Leanne Hinton (1968); this group does not limit music to human song. In prehuman times, when only spirits inhabited the world, all communication, as far as the Havasupai were concerned, was by song. The problem ethnomusicologists face is this: what is musical or nonmusical for our world of scholarship, and how do the peoples whom we study draw such boundaries? In 1982, Steven Feld (1982, 20–43) presented the musical taxonomy of the Kaluli, which he reported to include human singing, birdsong, speech, weeping, and poetic recitation, along with other systems of sound production. The Shuar of Ecuador have (or had) various kinds of singing but also ceremonial speech similar to song though not counted as music. One such form of speech, *auchmartin,* is a kind of ceremonial conversation between two strangers who meet on a mountain path; another, *enermartin* (Belzner 1981), comprises the calls and cries of a group of men who are preparing for a battle between tribes or bands. What may this mean to us ethnomusicologists? What should we consider to belong to our purview? Whatever Iranians consider as belonging properly to music, that is, *musiqi?* Or do we address everything that seems similar to music from our perspective? Birdsong, for example, or the calls of whales? (See Wallin, Merker, and Brown 2000, where animal sounds are subsumed under the concept of music.) The generally used term *music* is quite broad, we agree. We in ethnomusicology, however, in imitation of politicians and missionaries, have been stretching the envelope of music as far as possible. For my colleagues, then, almost nothing would be nonmusical.

4. GOOD AND BAD MUSIC   Like many before him, Kurt Weill asserted that only two kinds of music exist, good and bad. (I last heard that sentiment expressed in an interview with Ray Charles.) Weill (ctd. in Taylor 1991, 116) wanted to say that he recognized no other boundaries—between "E" and "U" music, "serious" and popular; between European and American music; between Broadway musical and opera—and that there was, in each category, good and bad music. Some music historians worry about the greater or lesser quality of the music with which they are individually concerned. On the one hand, they wish to comprehend all music they encounter; on the other hand, they wish to prove that the music to which they devote themselves has a high value. For ethnomusicologists, an analogous question arises—namely, whether this or that music, this genre or that style, is authentic, belongs properly to the music of its people. We are also concerned with the standards and criteria of every society—that's the obligation of the fieldworker when it comes to good and bad music. But it's known, too, that in many societies, the concepts of "good" and "bad" are not applicable, have no meaning. I'll return again to my colleagues among the Blackfoot people. When I asked whether a particular song was a good one, the man with whom I was speaking said, "Yes, okay, but I'd rather say it's a powerful song." Of another, he answered, "Yes, of course; my grandmother gave it to me." I asked further whether that song was therefore better than the first. "What do you mean?" was the reply. (I suspect he meant to say, "That's a stupid question." I often heard the expression "stupid white man," probably pointed in my direction.) Well, one can always tease something out of a friendly informant; he knows how white people talk (and perhaps he himself talks) about rock music and such. But how do Blackfoot people characterize music, songs, and singers when they talk among themselves? Songs are all good. There can be no "bad" songs, for they come from guardian spirits, such as animals, that appear in dreams and visions. That such a being would sing a specifically "bad" song is not really conceivable, and while this viewpoint and its associated beliefs belong to an earlier era in Blackfoot history, its remnants persist. "Yes," they may say, "we know this today. Human singers make up songs, and maybe it has always been so"; nevertheless, the association of the origin of songs with the supernatural is essential to the concept of music. Who now is a good singer? That's something one can talk about. Knowing a large number of songs is important, but performance practice is also a consideration. A good performance of a song? When I asked, "Did he do a good job singing that song?" the reply concerned mainly the accuracy of reproduction. What people did talk about a lot was the relative quality of the singing groups, or "drums," seen as units.

It was similar among Persian music masters, who evaluated themselves largely by their knowledge of the *radif*, the corpus of music learned by all as the point of departure for improvisation (for detailed information on the *radif*, see Zonis 1973; Farhat 1990; Nettl 1992). Does the *radif* include superior or inferior parts? The question didn't mean anything to my teacher. Some parts were, indeed, more important than others, but the basis for the distinction surprised me. Metric structure and memorable melody were less important than was material of an undefined sort that could lend itself to far-flung improvisation. But within this canon, nothing could be regarded as better or worse; only performance could be judged in this way. Is music in general a good or bad thing? The debates on this subject have occupied much of the theoretical literature on music for a millennium. But let me cite an interview with Ayatollah Khomeini from 1979 or so: "Music is no better than opium, it affects the senses so that one cannot think about anything else, music and sensual matters. One should abolish all this music and replace it with something more insightful" (ctd. in Hart and Lieberman 1999, 109).

5. THE OLD AND NEW IN MUSIC   Is this theme significant to ethnomusicologists? Those who love and study Western art music see the history of music as a series of eras, each one ending with the appearance of something new, something that we construe as innovation. A composer within an era, too, must be innovative, not only in the content of his or her work (e.g., in its original themes), but also in terms of style and method. One often might be inclined to say, "This 'new' piece has nothing 'new' in it." In our current culture, though, the body of music, even of "old" music, is constantly growing. We appreciate the new. Newly composed music must be innovative, but even so, the old music generally remains in some sense the "best." Now I've presented that in extremely simple terms, but I guess that an ethnomusicologist from a strange planet would give these findings as a summary of our music culture: one must innovate, but paradoxically, the old remains the most valued. I, however, an ethnomusicologist from this planet, have always been astonished by the number of ways that the world's musical cultures conceive of old and new. I once asked a Blackfoot colleague whether music had changed in his town during the previous two or three years. "Yes, indeed," he replied. "About a hundred new songs have come into our reservation, and we have also 'forgotten' [dropped or eliminated] a good many." But can one distinguish this group of new songs, together, from the old ones? Only if one knows them individually.

In the other hemisphere, a well-known musician and music critic in Madras told me, "There is no room for innovation in Carnatic music." What did he mean? One kept hearing new songs, *kritis*, and he himself was a composer. He explained: new social contexts for performance, new instruments—he saw none of that as innovation. For him, it was the influences from the outside, from Western music and perhaps even more from North Indian (Hindustani) music. Innovative would mean a change in the entire musical system, perhaps the substitution of a mixed musical culture for a unified and locally based one. To John Blacking (1979), incidentally, the term *musical change* also meant explicitly a society's adoption of a new musical system, replacing an older one. Thus, defining "new" and "old" in music is one of the most challenging issues ethnomusicology faces.

6. AESTHETIC SIGNIFICANCE AND SYMBOLISM   Non-Western peoples like and even love their music, and music has significance for them. This must have been clear even to the earliest ethnomusicologists. But the concept of aesthetics rarely plays a role in ethnomusicological literature. One of the earliest attempts to include it is found in Alan Merriam's *Anthropology of Music* (1964), which devotes a chapter to aesthetics, but in the context of the interrelationships among the arts. I searched in vain for the term *aesthetics* in later literature. Naturally, though, my colleagues are interested in the issue of evaluation of music in general, as well as its created components and their performance, and so one may well ask why they almost always limit the term *beauty* to literature about Western music. When Merriam asked his acquaintants among the Flathead people, "Is this—or that—song beautiful?" they would answer with something such as, "I like it" or "It's a good song." But beauty, in the sense that one might describe a painting as beautiful—that they seemed to find amusing (Merriam 1967, 43–46). Now designations of beauty ordinarily occur in a comparative context, with other items in the same category potentially designated as nonbeautiful or perhaps ugly. But Merriam's consultants could not accept or even perhaps imagine that a song at least putatively bestowed by supernatural sources could be ugly. Truly, though, things are not always so different in the culture of European or American music lovers (I'm not talking about musicologists). There, too, the greatest music is also a gift of the supernatural. At least that's the way it was in my childhood home. I wasn't ever permitted, if, for example, I wasn't enjoying my piano practicing, to complain that a piece by Mozart or Beethoven was not beautiful or that I didn't like it; that would have been considered some kind of sin.

7. THE CONTENT OF MUSIC   Is there an ethnomusicological perspective to the theme of musical content? Of what does music truly consist? Perhaps we can answer this only if we consider two related questions. Let me comment by giving a few relevant quotations. The first comes from Merriam: "All people, no matter of what culture, must be able to place their music firmly in the context of the totality of their beliefs, experiences, or activities, for without such ties, music cannot exist" (1967, 3). I take the next from Christopher Waterman: "An adequate analysis of 'the music itself'—a classic example of scholarly animism—must be informed by an equally detailed understanding of the historically situated human subjects that perceive, learn, interpret, evaluate, produce, and respond to musical patterns. Musics do not have selves; people do" (C. Waterman 1990, 6). And finally, this one is by John Blacking: "In this world . . . it is necessary to understand why a madrigal by Gesualdo or a Bach Passion, a sitar melody from India or a song from Africa, Berg's *Wozzeck* or Britten's *War Requiem,* a Balinese gamelan or a Cantonese opera, or a symphony by Mozart, Beethoven, or Mahler may be profoundly necessary for human survival." For ethnomusicologists, the most significant aspect of music, of its content in the broadest sense, is the need to contemplate it as integrated with all components of culture ("culture" in the anthropologist's sense). The character of each culture somehow gives birth to the culture's particular music. Music comes from the core of culture, but music can itself also affect the culture's other domains (Blacking [1973, 116] presents this viewpoint eloquently).

8. ON THE BEAUTIFUL   Is music fundamentally something of beauty, the "holde Kunst" of Schober's poem and Schubert's Lied "An die Musik," and can one system or kind of music thus be more "beautiful" than another? Does that question make sense, or does the concept of beauty mean something only in our Western culture, and if so, did that unique characteristic lead Eggebrecht to speak of the West as the only realm in which music has relevance? Add to that the tendency of intellectuals in other cultures, who are conversant with such problems, to comprehend our culture in these terms. Would they perhaps say, "Yes, to those Europeans who love to go to concerts and operas, the idea of musical beauty, beauty like that of a human body or a mountain, is the most important thing about music"? I have stated the claim here with utter simplicity, but I think something other than beauty provides the center of gravity in the way these foreign intellectuals think Europeans evaluate their music. Let me paraphrase some comments.

Consider first my teacher in Madras, who said something like, "The Western musicians have always concentrated on creating something grand and large—long musical works, gigantic orchestras and choruses. They want to impress with size; they want to overwhelm us." The Blackfoot Indians whom my colleague Robert Witmer interviewed (1982) expressed in various ways a related idea: For the white man, music must be complicated. In order to master it, one must learn and know a lot. The most important thing about it is its complexity (see Witmer 1982). The speaker meant not classical music but vernacular and popular music and jazz. And finally, let me cite the Arabic traveler in medieval Europe Ibrahim ben Yakub, cited by B. Lewis (1982, 262), who compared the singing of North Germans unfavorably to the barking of dogs. We are concerned, so said my outsiders, with grandeur and difficulty; beauty itself doesn't interest us.

9. MUSIC AND TIME   Dahlhaus and Eggebrecht rightly complain about the immensity of this theme. Time is everything; no wonder that Stephen Hawking chose, for a survey of his history of the cosmos, the title *A Short History of Time*. When I once attempted to organize a synthesis of Blackfoot ideas about music (Nettl 1989) in two categories—music in society of humans and supernatural beings—and also music in the realm of time, I came to a series of categories, or perhaps questions, that might mean something to my teachers. They were all rooted in the concept of time. First, I wanted to know how the Blackfoot pictured the origin of music at large and the origins or sources of individual songs. Continuing in that vein, I considered how they understood the passing of time within the dreams in which songs are said to have been learned; on the more mundane side I included the concept of history itself and the prehistory of music, as well as music's ability to change (or be changed)—both music in general and the content of individual songs. At the most specific end of the spectrum were questions about the appropriate times for performing various kinds of music, as well as the appropriate tempo or speed for a song or a dance. In discourse about music, everything makes one consider time, but one will labor in vain if looking for entries under *time* in the indexes of various musical ethnographies published over the last several decades. My colleague ethnomusicologists didn't develop a unitary concept of time in the way they organized their field; they (we) also don't as yet have an adequate method for dealing with temporal components such as tempo, for example, to provide a template for intercultural comparison, a theme Mieczyslaw Kolinski (1959) and Dieter Christensen (1960) famously debated in the 1960s.

How does the Blackfoot notion of time with respect to music differ from our Western attitude? I don't think I can generalize, but let me give two interesting illustrations. The first concerns their idea of music history, which I tried to tease out of conversations and narratives. They see it consisting in three epochs. In the first, a time of the mythic, humanlike animals and supernatural spirits teach music to humans (music and everything else truly important). By *music* I mean the ability to sing and the impetus for singing, as well as individual songs. Second came an era of normal life, the true culture of the Blackfoot, in which music had the function of reflecting culture and life, where every activity had its appropriate songs. The third era, leading into the present, began when the whites arrived, bringing their music into the life of the Blackfoot nation, a time when the concept of music, and of song, changed dramatically—indeed, the concept changed more than musical style did. Significantly, the Blackfoot conception of music history differs from the Western version in focusing on changes not in musical style but in the way humans use music in their relationship to the outside world. The first period is dominated by the supernatural beings; the third, by the white outsiders.

The second illustration concerns the possibility and permissibility of changing a song's melody. In principle, one cannot do that, or so I was told. Songs are unchangeable units that the spirits have taught; one can give them away and even sell them, but a song is something you learn in one hearing. Songs are units, as are other ceremonial objects; once they have come into existence, they cannot be re-created. But, I asked, does this mean that when you sing a song repeatedly, it is always exactly the same? What if you make a mistake? "That's not supposed to happen," I was told; "perhaps the song will lose its power if you sing it wrong, and if I make a bunch of mistakes, then it's no longer the same song." "But imagine," I asked further, "that two medicine men learn the same song in their individual dreams, sung by the powerful beaver figure. What about that?" I was then told that, yes, they would sound like the same song, but in a way they would not be identical, for they came about in two separate creative processes at different times. It's perhaps unnecessary to suggest that the differences among musical cultures may be largely based on differences in their conceptions of time.

10. WHAT THEN IS MUSIC?   Finally, the fundamental question: What then is music? The following remark in Eggebrecht's final chapter is of special interest, for it concerns music's superior position among the other arts. Music, he says, "is incomparable in its nature, and in its ambivalence, it is the reflection of the cosmos, creator as well as destroyer of the good and the evil" (Dahlhaus and Eggebrecht 1985, 191). Eggebrecht meant this to apply, surely, to European music, and I imagine that this description was intended to emphasize its uniqueness. But in the parts of the world with which I have some experience, one could also come upon the uniqueness of the concept of music, and particularly the uniqueness of the music of one's own culture. One musician in Madras asserted to me that the world needed two things for peace to be established—the literature of Europe (but he meant the English) and the classical music of South India, Carnatic music, which can achieve and express anything of which music might be capable. Carnatic music, he said, was the most significant music of humanity. Then, once more, let me turn to my Blackfoot teacher, who said, "The right way to do something is to sing the right song with it." Then he corrected himself: "The right *Blackfoot* way to do something is to sing the right song with it." Is it like that among other peoples, I asked him; could he imagine that? He didn't know, but he didn't imagine it could be so, because this was a way in which the Blackfoot differ from other peoples.

Finally, let me turn once more to my teacher in Iran, the distinguished Ostad Nor-Ali Boroumand, who had once studied medicine in Berlin before he became blind and who frequently compared Persian music to other musics of the world, few of which impressed him. Persian music, he maintained, could express everything of which music was capable; it had the perfect system of twelve modes, the *dastgahs*. It could—I interpret him thus after many conversations—reflect accurately, actually narrate, the world of Persian culture and its history. Western music, with its two modes, major and minor, is poor by comparison. Arabic music is even worse—he was an enthusiastic Iranian nationalist—for it basically has only one tonality. "And how about Indian music, with its many ragas?" I asked. "That's too exotic for us," he replied with a smile.

Music as reflection of the Cosmos, creator and destroyer of good and evil, as Eggebrecht thought, clearly referring to Western art music—it's just possible that this is how my friends among the musicians of three cultures, and perhaps many other musicians of the world's nations, might also have characterized their own music.

References

Abraham, Otto, and Erich M. von Hornbostel. 1906. "Phonographierte Indian-ermelodien aus Britisch-Columbia." In *Anthropological Papers Written in Honor of Franz Boas,* 447–74. New York: Stechert.

Adam, Nina, Florian Heesch, and Susanne Rode-Breymann. 2002. "Über das Gefühl der Unzufriedenheit in der Disziplin." *Musikforschung* 55:251–73.

Adler, Guido. 1885. "Umfang, Methode und Ziel der Musikwissenschaft." *Viertel-jahrschrift für Musikwissenschaft* 1:5–20.

———. 1916. *Gustav Mahler.* Leipzig: Universal.

———, ed. 1924. *Handbuch der Musikgeschichte.* Berlin: Keller.

Agawu, V. Kofi. 1995. "The Invention of African Rhythm." *Journal of the American Musicological Society* 48:380–95.

———. 2003. *Representing African Music.* New York: Routledge.

Allison, Theresa. 2008. "Songwriting in the Nursing Home." In *The Oxford Hand-book of Medical Ethnomusicology,* edited by Benjamin Koen, 218–45. New York: Oxford University Press.

Ambros, August Wilhelm. 1862. *Geschichte der Musik.* Vol. 1. Breslau: F. E. C. Leuckart.

Amiot, (Père) Joseph. 1779. *Mémoire sur la musique des Chinois.* Paris: Chez Nyon l'aîné.

Anderson, Walter. 1923. *Kaiser und Abt.* Helsinki: Academia Scientiarum Fennica.

Andrade, Mario de. 1936. *Cultura musical*. Sao Paulo: Guaíra.

Anttila, Raimo. 1972. *An Introduction to Historical Linguistics*. London: Macmillan.

Aretz, Isabel. 1991. *Historia de la etnomusicología en América Latina*. Caracas: Ediciones FUNDEF.

Arom, Simha. 1985. *Polyphonies et polyrhythmies instrumentales d'Afrique Centrale: Structure et méthodologie*. Paris: SELAF.

Arom, Simha, and Frank Alvarez-Péreyre. 2007. *Précis d'ethnomusicologie*. Paris: CNRS Éditions.

Bakan, Michael. 2007. *World Musics: Traditions and Transformations*. New York: McGraw-Hill.

———. 2009. "Measuring Happiness in the 21st Century: Ethnomusicology, Evidence-Based Research, and the New Science of Autism." *Ethnomusicology* 53:510–18.

Bakan, Michael, et al. 2008. "Following Frank: Response-Ability and the Co-creation of Culture in a Medical Ethnomusicology Program for Children on the Autism Spectrum." *Ethnomusicology* 52:163–202.

Baker, Theodore. 1882. *Über die Musik der nordamerikanischen Wilden*. Leipzig: Breitkopf und Härtel.

Barbeau, Marius. 1934. "Asiatic Survivals in Indian Songs." *Musical Quarterly* 20:107–16.

———. 1962. "Buddhist Dirges of the North Pacific Coast." *Journal of the International Folk Music Council* 14:16–21.

Barkechli, Mehdi. 1960. "La Musique iranienne." In *L'Histoire de la musique: Encyclopédie de la Pléiade*, edited by Roland Manuel, 9:455–523. Paris: Pléiade.

———. 1963. *La Musique traditionelle de l'Iran*. Tehran: Secreteriat d'État aux Beaux-Arts.

Barnett, H. G. 1953. *Innovation: The Basis of Cultural Change*. New York: McGraw-Hill.

Barnouw, Victor. 1971. *Ethnology*. Vol. 2 of *An Introduction to Anthropology*. Homewood, Ill.: Dorset.

Bartók, Béla. 1931. *Hungarian Folk Music*. London: Oxford University Press.

Barz, Gregory. 2006. *Singing for Life: HIV/AIDS and Music in Uganda*. New York: Routledge.

Barz, Gregory, and Timothy Cooley, eds. 2008. *Shadows in the Field*. 2d ed. New York: Oxford University Press.

Basso, Ellen. 1985. *A Musical View of the Universe: Kalapalo Myth and Ritual Performance*. Philadelphia: University of Pennsylvania Press.

Bayard, Samuel P. 1950. "Prolegomena to a Study of the Principal Melodic Families of British-American Folk Song." *Journal of American Folklore* 63:1–44.

Beals, Ralph L., and Harry Hoijer. 1965. *An Introduction to Anthropology*. 3d ed. New York: Macmillan.

Beattie, John. 1964. *Other Cultures*. New York: Free Press.

Becking, Gustav. 1928. *Der musikalische Rhythmus als Erkenntnisquelle*. Augsburg: B. Filser.

Belden, H. 1940. *Ballads and Songs Collected by the Missouri Folk-Song Society*. Columbia: University of Missouri Studies.

Belzner, William. 1981. "Music, Modernization, and Westernization among the Macuma Shuar." In *Cultural Transformations and Ethnicity in Modern Ecuador*, edited by Norman Whitten, 731–48. Urbana: University of Illinois Press.

Bergeron, Katherine, and Philip V. Bohlman, eds. 1992. *Disciplining Music: Musicology and Its Canons*. Chicago: University of Chicago Press.

Blacking, John. 1971. "Towards a Theory of Musical Competence." In *Man: Anthropological Essays in Honor of O. F. Raum*, edited by E. J. Jaeger, 19–34. Cape Town: Struik.

———. 1972. "Deep and Surface Structures in Venda Music." *Yearbook of the International Folk Music Council* 4:91–108.

———. 1973. *How Musical Is Man?* Seattle: University of Washington Press.

———, ed. 1977. *Anthropology of the Body*. London: Academic Press.

———. 1979. "Some Problems of Theory and Method in the Study of Musical Change." *Yearbook of the International Folk Music Council* 9:1–26.

———. 1989. "Challenging the Myth of Ethnic Music." *Yearbook for Traditional Music* 21:17–24.

Blum, Stephen. 1974. "Persian Folksong in Meshed, Iran, 1969." *Yearbook of the International Folk Music Council* 6:86–114.

———. 1991. "European Musicological Terminology and the Music of Africa." In *Comparative Musicology and Anthropology of Music*, edited by Bruno Nettl and Philip V. Bohlman, 3–36. Chicago: University of Chicago Press.

Boas, Franz. 1888. *The Central Eskimo*. Bureau of American Ethnology. Annual Report. Vol. 6. Washington, D.C.: Smithsonian Institution.

———. 1927. *Primitive Art*. Oslo: Kuturforskning Forlaget.

———. 1938. *General Anthropology*. Boston: Heath.

Bock, Philip K. 1969. *Modern Cultural Anthropology*. New York: Knopf.

Boehme, Franz Magnus. 1886. *Geschichte des Tanzes in Deutschland*. Leipzig: Breitkopf und Härtel.

Boese, Helmut. 1955. *Zwei Urmusikanten: Smetana—Dvořák*. Zurich: Amalthea-Verlag.

Bohannan, Paul. 1963. *Social Anthropology*. New York: Holt, Rinehart.

Bohlman, Philip V. 1988. "Traditional Music and Cultural Identity: Persistent Paradigm in the History of Ethnomusicology." *Yearbook for Traditional Music* 20:26–42.

———. 1989. *The Land Where Two Streams Flow*. Urbana: University of Illinois Press.

———. 1996. "Pilgrimage, Politics, and the Musical Remapping of the New Europe." *Ethnomusicology* 40:375–412.

———. 2002a. "World Music at the 'End of History.'" *Ethnomusicology* 46:1–32.

———. 2002b. *World Music: A Very Short Introduction.* Oxford: Oxford University Press.

———. 2007. "Becoming Ethnomusicologists: On Colonialism and Its Aftermaths." *SEM Newsletter* 4 (1): 4–5.

Bose, Fritz. 1952. "Messbare Rassenunterschiede in der Musik." *Homo* 2 (4): 1–5.

———. 1953. *Musikalische Völkerkunde.* Zurich: Atlantis.

Brewster, Charles. 1940. *Ballads and Songs of Indiana.* Folklore Series. Bloomington: Indiana University Publications.

Brinkmann, Reinhold, and Christoph Wolff, eds. 1999. *Driven into Paradise: The Musical Migration from Nazi Germany to the United States.* Berkeley: University of California Press.

Bronson, Bertrand H. 1958–72. *The Traditional Tunes of the Child Ballads.* Princeton, N.J.: Princeton University Press.

———. 1959. "Toward the Comparative Analysis of British-American Folk Tunes." *Journal of American Folklore* 72:165–91.

Browner, Tara. 2002. *Heartbeat of the People.* Urbana: University of Illinois Press.

Bücken, Ernst, ed. 1927–31. *Handbuch der Musikwissenschaft.* Wildpark-Potsdam, Germany: Athenaion.

Burney, Charles. 1775. *The Present State of Music in Germany, the Netherlands, and United Provinces.* 2nd edition. 2 vols. London: printed for T. Becket; J. Robson; and G. Robinson.

———. 1776–89. *A General History of Music.* 2 vols. London: Author.

Capwell, Charles. 1987. "Sourindro Mohun Tagore and the National Anthems Project." *Ethnomusicology* 31:407–30.

———. 1991. "Marginality and Musicology in Nineteenth-Century Calcutta: The Case of Sourindro Mohun Tagore." In *Comparative Musicology and Anthropology of Music,* edited by Bruno Nettl and Philip V. Bohlman, 228–43. Chicago: University of Chicago Press.

Caron, Nelly, and Dariouche Safvate. 1966. *Iran: Les traditions musicales.* Paris: Buchet-Chastel.

Caton, Margaret. 1983. "The Classical Tasnif: A Genre of Persian Vocal Music." Ph.D. diss., University of California at Los Angeles.

Chailley, Jacques. 1961. *40,000 ans de musique.* Paris: Plon.

Child, Francis James. 1956 [1898]. *The English and Scottish Popular Ballad.* Reprint. New York: New York Folklore Press.

Christensen, Dieter. 1960. "Inner Tempo and Melodic Tempo." *Ethnomusicology* 4:9–13.

———. 1988. "The International Folk Music Council and 'The Americans': On the Effect of Stereotypes on the Institutionalization of Ethnomusicology." *Yearbook for Traditional Music* 20:11–18.

Chrysander, Friedrich, ed. 1863–69. *Jahrbuch für musikalische Wissenschaften.* Leipzig: Breitkopf und Härtel.

Clayton, Martin. 2003. "Comparing Music, Comparing Musicology." In *The Cultural Study of Music,* edited by Martin Clayton, Trevor Herbert, and Richard Middleton, 57–68. New York: Routledge.

Cohen, Gary B. 1981. *The Politics of Ethnic Survival: Germans in Prague, 1861–1914.* Princeton, N.J.: Princeton University Press.

Collaer, Paul. 1958. "Cartography and Ethnomusicology." *Ethnomusicology* 2:66–68.

———. 1960. *Atlas historique de la musique.* Paris: Elsevier.

Collins, John J. 1975. *Anthropology: Culture, Society, and Evolution.* Englewood Cliffs, N.J.: Prentice-Hall.

Cook, Nicholas, and Mark Everist, eds. 1999. *Rethinking Music.* Oxford: Oxford University Press.

Cowdery, James R. 1990. *The Melodic Tradition of Ireland.* Kent, Ohio: Kent State University Press.

Crawford, Richard. 1984. *The American Musicological Society 1934–1984, an Anniversary Essay.* Philadelphia: American Musicological Society.

Dahlhaus, Carl. 1977. *Grundlagen der Musikgeschichte.* Cologne: H. Gerig.

———, ed. 1980–92. *Neues Handbuch der Musikwissenschaft.* Laaber, Germany: Laaber Verlag.

Dahlhaus, Carl, and Hans Heinrich Eggebrecht. 1985. *Was ist Musik?* Wilhelmshaven, Germany: Heinrichshofen.

Danckert, Werner. 1939. *Das europäische Volkslied.* Berlin: J. Bard.

Daniélou, Alain. 1959. *Traité de musicologie comparée.* Paris: Hermann.

———. 1973. *Die Musik Asiens zwischen Misachtung und Wertschätzung.* Wilhelmshaven, Germany: Heinrichshofen.

Danielson, Virginia. 1997. *The Voice of Egypt: Umm Kulthum Arabic Song, and Egyptian Society in the Twentieth Century.* Chicago: University of Chicago Press.

———. 2007. "The Canon of Ethnomusicology: Is There One?" *Notes* 64:223–31.

Darvishi, Mohammad-Reza. 2001–5. *Encyclopedia of the Musical Instruments of Iran.* Tehran: Mahoor Institute of Culture and Art.

Davis, Arthur Kyle. 1929. *Traditional Ballads of Virginia.* Cambridge, Mass.: Harvard University Press.

Driver, Harold E. 1961. *Indians of North America.* Chicago: University of Chicago Press.

Driver, Harold E., and William C. Massey. 1957. "Comparative Studies of North American Indians." *Transactions of the American Philosophical Society* 47:165–456.

Dundes, Alan, ed. 1968. *Every Man His Way.* Englewood Cliffs, N.J.: Prentice-Hall.

During, Jean. 1984. *La Musique iranienne: Tradition et évolution.* Paris: Recherche sur les Civilisations.

Eddy, Mary O. 1939. *Ballads and Songs from Ohio.* Hatboro, Penn.: Folklore Associates.

Egger, Kurt. 1984. *Ethnomusikologie und Wissenschaftsklassifikation.* Vienna: Böhlau.

Ellis, Alexander J. 1885. "On the Musical Scales of Various Nations." *Journal of the Society of Arts* 33:485–527.

Elschek, Oskár, and Alica Elscheková. 1996. "Theorie und Praxis der Erforschung der traditionellen Musik der Minderheiten." In *Echo der Vielfalt; Echoes of Diversity,* edited by Ursula Hemetek, 17–30. Vienna: Böhlau.

Ember, Carol, and Melvin Ember. 1985. *Anthropology.* 4th ed. Englewood Cliffs, N.J.: Prentice-Hall.

Engel, Carl. 1864. *The Music of the Most Ancient Nations, Particularly of the Assyrians, Egyptians, and Hebrews.* London: William Reeves.

———. 1866. *An Introduction to the Study of National Music: Comprising Researches into Popular Songs, Traditions, and Customs.* London: Longmans, Green.

Erben, Karel Jaromír. 1862. *České pisně a řikadla.* Prague: A Hynek.

Erdely, Stephen. 1979. "Ethnic Music in America: An Overview." *Yearbook of the International Folk Music Council* 11:114–37.

Erk, Ludwig, and Franz Magnus Boehme. 1893–94. *Deutscher Liederhort.* Leipzig: Breitkopf und Härtel.

Erlanger, Baron Rodolphe d'. 1930–59. *La Musique arabe.* Paris: Librairie orientaliste Paul Geuthner.

Farhat, Hormoz. 1990. *The Dastgah Concept in Persian Music.* Cambridge: Cambridge University Press.

Feld, Steven. 1982. *Sound and Sentiment.* Philadelphia: University of Pennsylvania Press.

Firth, Raymond. 1973. *Symbols, Public and Private.* Ithaca, N.Y.: Cornell University Press.

———. 1990. *Tikopia Songs.* With Mervyn McLean. Cambridge: Cambridge University Press.

Flanders, Helen Hartness, ed. 1960–65. *Ancient Ballads Traditionally Sung in New England.* Philadelphia: University of Pennsylvania Press.

Fletcher, Peter. 1997. *World Musics in Context.* Oxford: Oxford University Press.

Födermayr, Franz. 1971. *Zur gesanglichen Stimmgebung in der aussereuropäischen Musik.* Vienna: Stiglmayr.

Freeman, Linton C., and Alan P. Merriam. 1956. "Statistical Classification in Anthropology: An Application to Ethnomusicology." *American Anthropologist* 58:464–72.

Freilich, Moris. 1968. "S. F. Nadel." In *International Encyclopedia of the Social Sciences,* edited by David Still, 11:1–3. London: Macmillan.

Frisbie, Charlotte. 1991. "Women and the Society of Ethnomusicology: Roles and Contributions from Formation through Incorporation (1952/3–1961)." In *Comparative Musicology and Anthropology of Music,* edited by Bruno Nettl and Philip V. Bohlman, 244–65. Chicago: University of Chicago Press.

Garfias, Robert. 2004. *Music: The Cultural Context.* Senri Ethnological Report no. 47. Osaka: National Museum of Ethnology.

Goldschmiedt, Walter, ed. 1977. *Exploring the Ways of Mankind.* New York: Holt, Rinehart and Winston.

Gould, Stephen Jay. 1987. *Time's Arrow, Time's Cycle.* Cambridge: Cambridge University Press.

Gourlay, K. A. 1978. "Towards a Reassessment of the Ethnomusicologist's Role in Research." *Ethnomusicology* 22:1–36.

Grauer, Victor. 2006. "Echoes of Our Forgotten Ancestors." *World of Music* 48 (2): 5–58. With responses by Bruno Nettl (59–72), Jonathan Stock (73–93), and Peter Cook (93–100).

Greenberg, Joseph, ed. 1963. *Universals of Language.* Cambridge, Mass.: MIT Press.

Greve, Martin. 2002. "Writing against Europe: Vom notwendigen Verschwinden der 'Musikethnologie.'" *Musikforschung* 55:239–51.

Gronow, Pekka. 1978. "The Significance of Ethnic Recordings." In *Ethnic Recordings—a Neglected Heritage,* edited by Howard W. Marshall, 1–50. Washington, D.C.: Library of Congress.

Hall, Edward T. 1961. *The Hidden Dimension.* Garden City, N.Y.: Anchor Books.

———. 1983. *The Dance of Life: The Other Dimension of Time.* New York: Anchor Books.

Hammond, Peter B. 1975. *Cultural and Social Anthropology: Introductory Readings in Ethnology.* 2d ed. New York: Macmillan.

Harris, Marvin. 1968. *The Rise of Anthropological Theory.* New York: Crowell.

———. 1971. *Culture, Man, Nature.* New York: Crowell.

Harrison, Frank L. 1973. *Time, Place, and Music.* Amsterdam: Knuf.

———. 1977. "Universals in Music: Towards a Methodology of Comparative Research." *World of Music* 19 (1–2): 30–36.

Harrison, Frank, Mantle Hood, and Claude Palisca. 1963. *Musicology.* Englewood Cliffs, N.J.: Prentice-Hall.

Hart, Mickey, and Fredric Lieberman. 1999. *Spirit into Sound: The Magic of Music.* Petaluma, Calif.: Grateful Dead Books.

Haviland, William A. 1974. *Anthropology.* New York: Holt, Rinehart and Winston.

Hawkins, Sir John. 1776. *A General History of the Science and Practice of Music.* London: Payne.

Haydon, Glen. 1941. *Introduction to Musicology.* New York: Prentice-Hall.

Hemetek, Ursula, ed. 1996. *Echo der Vielfalt; Echoes of Diversity.* Vienna: Böhlau.

———. 2001. *Mosaik der Klänge.* Vienna: Böhlau.

Henry, Jules. 1963. *Culture against Man.* New York: Random House.

Herder, Johann Gottfried. 1807 [1778–89]. *Stimmen der Völker in Liedern.* (original title of *Volkslieder,* vol. 1). Tübingen: Cotta.

Herndon, Marcia. 1974. "Analysis: The Herding of Sacred Cows?" *Ethnomusicology* 18:219–62.

———. 2000. "The Place of Gender within Complex, Dynamic Musical Systems." In *Music and Gender,* edited by Pirkko Moisala and Beverley Diamond, 347–59. Urbana: University of Illinois Press.

Herndon, Marcia, and Norma McLeod. 1980. *Music as Culture.* Darby, Penn.: Norwood.

Herskovits, Melville J. 1941. *The Myth of the Negro Past.* New York: Harper.

———. 1945. "Problem, Method, and Theory in Afroamerican Studies." *Afroamerica* 1:5–24.

Herskovits, Melville J., and Frances Herskovits. 1936. *Surinam Folk-lore.* New York: Columbia University Press.

Herzog, George. 1930. "Musical Styles in North America." In *Proceedings of the 23rd International Congress of Americanists,* 455–58 (New York: International Congress of Americanists).

———. 1936a. "A Comparison of Pueblo and Pima Musical Styles." *Journal of American Folklore* 49:283–417.

———. 1936b. *Research in Primitive and Folk Music in the United States.* American Council of Learned Societies Bulletin 24. New York: The Council.

———. 1938. "Music in the Thinking of the American Indian." *Peabody Bulletin* (May 1938): 1–5.

Hinton, Leanne. 1968. Personal communication and unpublished paper, University of Illinois.

Hoebel, E. Adamson, and Everett L. Front. 1976. *Cultural and Social Anthropology.* New York: McGraw-Hill.

Hood, Mantle. 1960. "The Challenge of Bi-musicality." *Ethnomusicology* 4:55–59.

———. 1963a. "Musical Significance." *Ethnomusicology* 7:187–92.

———. 1963b. "Music, the Unknown." In *Musicology,* by Frank Harrison, Mantle Hood, and Claude Palisca, 215–325. Englewood Cliffs, N.J.: Prentice-Hall.

———. 1971. *The Ethnomusicologist.* New York: McGraw-Hill.

Hopkins, Pandora. 1977. "The Homology of Music and Myth: Views of Lévi-Strauss on Musical Structure." *Ethnomusicology* 21:247–81.

Hornbostel, Erich M. von. 1904–5. "Die Probleme der vergleichenden Musikwissenschaft." *Zeitschrift der internationalen Musikgesellschaft* 7:85–97.

———. 1906. "Phonographierte tunesische Melodien." *Sammelbände der internationalen Musikgesellschaft* 8:1–43.

———. 1933. "The Ethnology of African Sound Instruments." *Africa* 6:129–57.

———. 1976. *Hornbostel Opera Omnia.* 7th ed. Edited by Klaus Wachsmann et al. Vol. 1. The Hague: Brill.

———. 1986. *Tonart und Ethos: Aufsätze zur Musikethnologie und Musikpsychologie.* Leipzig: Reclam.

Hornbostel, Erich M. von, and Otto Abraham. 1904. "Über die Bedeutung des Phonographen für die vergleichende Musikwissenschaft." *Zeitschrift für Ethnologie* 36:222–33.

Hornbostel, Erich M. von, and Curt Sachs. 1914. "Systematik der Musiksinstrumente." *Zeitschrift für Ethnologie* 46:553–90.

Hungarian Academy of Sciences, Institute for Musicology. 1992. *Catalogue of Hungarian Folk Song Types Arranged according to Styles.* Vol. I. [by Lászlo Dobszay and Janka Szendrei.] Budapest: The Academy.

International Folk Music Council (IFMC). 1955. "Resolutions. Definition of Folk Music." *Journal of the International Folk Music Council* 7:23.

Jackson, Helen Hunt. 1881. *A Century of Dishonor.* New York: Harper.

Jardanyi, Pal. 1962. "Die Ordnung der ungarischen Volkslieder." *Studia Musicologica* 2:3–32.

Jessup, Linda, Andrew Nurse, and Gordon E. Smith, eds. 2008. *Around and about Marius Barbeau.* Gatineau, Quebec: Canadian Museum of Civilizations.

Jones, William. 1792. "On the Modes of the Hindoos." *Asiatick Researches.* Repr. in Sourindro Mohun Tagore, *Hindu Music from Various Authors* (1964), 88–112. Varanasi: Chowkhamba Sanskrit Series Office.

Karbusicky, Vladimir. 1995. *Wie deutsch ist das Abendland?* Hamburg: Von Bockel.

Karpeles, Maud. 1951. "Some Reflections on Authenticity in Folk Music." *Journal of the International Folk Music Council* 3:10–16.

———. 1957. "The International Folk Music Council: Its Aims and Activities." *Ethno-Musicology Newsletter* 9:15–19.

Kartomi, Margaret. 1990. *On Concept and Classifications of Musical Instruments.* Chicago: University of Chicago Press.

Katz, Ruth. 2003. *The Lachmann Problem: An Unsung Chapter in Comparative Musicology.* Jerusalem: Hebrew University Magnes Press.

Keesing, Felix M. 1958. *Cultural Anthropology: The Science of Custom.* New York: Rinehart.

Keesing, Roger M., and Felix M. Keesing. 1971. *New Perspectives in Cultural Anthropology.* New York: Holt, Rinehart.

Kemppinen, Iivar. 1954. *The Ballad of Lady Isabel and the False Knight.* Helsinki: Kirja Mono-Oy.

Kerman, Joseph. 1985. *Contemplating Music.* Cambridge, Mass.: Harvard University Press.

Khaleqi, Ruhollah. 1955–60. *Sargozasht-e musiqi-ye Iran.* Tehran: Chapkhane-ye Ferdowsi.

Khatschi, Khatschi. 1962. *Der Dastgah.* Regensburg, Germany: Bosse.

Khe, Tran Van. 1967. *Vietnam: Les Traditions musicales.* Paris: Buchet-Chastel.

Khoshzamir, Mojtaba. 1979. "Ali Naqi Vaziri and His Influence on Music and Music Education in Iran." Ph.D. diss., University of Illinois, Urbana-Champaign.

Kiesewetter, Raphael. 1842. *Die Musik der Araber.* Leipzig: Breitkopf und Härtel.

Kingsbury, Henry. 1988. *Music, Talent, and Performance.* Philadelphia: Temple University Press.

Kishibe, Shigeo. 1966. *The Traditional Music of Japan.* Tokyo: Ongaku No Tomo Sha Edition.

Koen, Benjamin, ed. 2008. *The Oxford Handbook of Medical Ethnomusicology.* New York: Oxford University Press.

Kolberg, Oskar. 1991. *Dziela wszystkie.* [Complete works.] Poznan: Polskie tow.

Kolinski, Mieczyslaw. 1959. "The Evaluation of Tempo." *Ethnomusicology* 3:45–57.

———. 1961. "The Classification of Tonal Structures." *Studies in Ethnomusicology* 1:38–76.

———. 1962. "Consonance and Dissonance." *Ethnomusicology* 6:66–74.

———. 1965a. "The General Direction of Melodic Movement." *Ethnomusicology* 9:240–64.

———. 1965b. "The Structure of Melodic Movement—A New Method of Analysis." *Studies in Ethnomusicology* 2:95–120.

———. 1973. "A Cross-Cultural Approach to Metro-Rhythmic Patterns." *Ethnomusicology* 17:494–506.

Koller, Oswald. 1902–3. "Die beste Methode, volks- und volksmässige Lieder nach ihrer melodischen Beschaffenheit lexikalisch zu ordnen." *Sammelbände der internationalen Musikgesellschaft* 4:1–15.

Komara, Edward. 2007. "Culture Wars, Canonicity, and 'A Basic Music Library.'" *Notes* 64:232–47.

Komma, Michael. 1960. *Das böhmische Musikantenthum.* Kassel, Germany: Hinnenthal.

Koskoff, Ellen, ed. 1987. *Women and Music in Cross-Cultural Perspective.* New York: Greenwood.

Kottak, Conrad Phillip. 1974. *Anthropology: The Exploration of Human Diversity.* New York: Random House.

Krader, Barbara. 1956. "Bibliography: George Herzog." *Ethnomusicology Newsletter* 6:11–20.

———. 1993. "Southern and Eastern Europe." In *Ethnomusicology: Historical and Regional Studies,* edited by Helen Myers, 160–86. New York: Macmillan.

Kroeber, Alfred Louis. 1947. *Cultural and Natural Areas of Native North America.* Berkeley: University of California Press.

———. 1948. *Anthropology.* New York: Harcourt, Brace.

Krohn, Ilmari. 1902–3. "Welche ist die beste Methode, um volks- und volksmässige Lieder nach ihrern melodischen (nicht textlichen) Beschaffenheit lexikalisch zu ordnen?" *Sammelbände der internationalen Musikgesellschaft* 4:643–60.

Kuhn, Thomas. 1970. *The Structure of Scientific Revolutions.* 2d ed. Chicago: University of Chicago Press.

Kunst, Jaap. 1950. *Musicologica*. Amsterdam: Royal Tropical Institute.

———. 1955. *Ethno-Musicology*. [*Musicologica*, 2d ed.] The Hague: M. Nijhoff.

———. 1959. *Ethnomusicology*. 3d ed. The Hague: M. Nijhoff.

Kuper, Jessica, ed. 1977. *The Anthropologists' Cookbook*. New York: Universe Books.

Lach, Robert. 1924. *Die vergleichende Musikwissenschaft, ihre Methoden und Probleme.* Vienna: Akademie der Wissenschaften.

———. 1925. *Vergleichende Kunst- und Musikwissenschaft*. Vienna: Österreichische Akademie der Wissenschaften.

Lachmann, Robert. 1929. *Musik des Orients*. Breslau: F. Hirt.

Lang, Paul Henry. 1941. *Music in Western Civilization*. New York: Norton.

Leaf, Murray J. 1979. *Man, Mind, and Science: A History of Anthropology*. New York: Columbia University Press.

Lee Hye-ku. 1986. *Korean Music and Instruments*. Seoul: National Classical Music Institute of Korea.

Lévi-Strauss, Claude. 1969. *The Raw and the Cooked: Introduction to a Science of Mythology*. Vol. 1. New York: Harper and Row.

Lewis, Bernard. 1982. *The Muslim Discovery of Europe*. New York: Norton.

Lewis, Oscar. 1941. "Manly-Hearted Women among the North Piegan." *American Anthropologist* 43:173–87.

———. 1942. *The Effect of White Contact upon Blackfoot Culture, with Special Reference to the Role of the Fur Trade*. Monographs of the American Ethnological Society, no. 6. Seattle, Wash.: The American Ethnological Society.

———. 1956. "Comparison in Cultural Anthropology." In *Current Anthropology: A Supplement to Anthropology Today*, edited by W. L. Thomas, 259–92. Chicago: University of Chicago Press.

Linton, Ralph. 1936. *The Study of Man*. New York: Appleton-Century.

List, George. 1979a. "The Distribution of a Melodic Formula: Diffusion or Polygenesis?" *Yearbook of the International Folk Music Council* 10:33–52.

———. 1979b. "Ethnomusicology: A Discipline Defined." *Ethnomusicology* 23:1–6.

Livingston, Tamara, Melinda Russell, Larry F. Ward, and Bruno Nettl, eds. 1999. *Community of Music: An Ethnographic Seminar in Champaign-Urbana*. Champaign, Ill.: Elephant and Cat.

Logan, George. 2000. *The Indiana University School of Music: A History*. Bloomington: Indiana University Press.

Lomax, Alan. 1959. "Folk Song Style." *American Anthropologist* 61:927–54.

———. 1962. "Song Structure and Social Structure." *Ethnology* 1:425–51.

———. 1968. *Folk Song Style and Culture*. Washington, D.C.: American Association for the Advancement of Science.

———. 1976. *Cantometrics*. Berkeley: University of California.

Lortat-Jacob, Bernard, ed. 1987. *L'Improvisation dans les musiques de tradition orale*. Paris: SELAF.

———. 1995. *Sardinian Chronicles*. Chicago: University of Chicago Press.

Lowie, Robert H. 1935. *The Crow Indians.* New York: Rinehart.

———. 1937. *History of Ethnological Theory.* New York: Rinehart.

Maceda, José. 1986. "A Concept of Time in a Music of Southeast Asia (a Preliminary Account)." *Ethnomusicology* 30:11–53.

Magrini, Tullia, ed. 2003. *Music and Gender: Perspectives from the Mediterranean.* Chicago: University of Chicago Press.

Mahillon, Victor. 1880–1922. *Catalogue descriptif et analytique du Musée Instrumental du Conservatoire Royal du Bruxelles.* Ghent, Belgium: A. Hoste.

Malinowski, Bronislaw. 1929. *The Sexual Life of Savages.* London: Routledge.

———. 1967. *A Diary in the Strict Sense of the Term.* New York: Harcourt, Brace, and World.

Malm, William P. 1967. *Music Cultures of the Pacific, the Near East, and Asia.* Englewood Cliffs, N.J.: Prentice-Hall.

Marcel-Dubois, Claudie. 1941. *Les Instruments de musique de l'Inde ancienne.* Paris: Presses universitaires de France.

———. 1946. *Instruments et musique populaire d'Europe.* Paris: Presses universitaires de France.

Massoudieh, Mohammad Taghi. 1968. *Âwâs-e šur.* Regensburg, Germany: Bosse.

———. 1976. "Die Musikforschung in Iran." *Acta Musicologica.* 43:12–36.

———. 1978. *Radif vocal de la musique traditionelle de l'Iran.* Tehran: Vezarat-e Farhang va Honar.

———. 1996. *Manuscrits persans concernant la musique.* Munich: Henle.

May, Elizabeth, ed. 1980. *Musics of Many Cultures: An Introduction.* Berkeley: University of California Press.

McAllester, David P. 1954. *Enemy Way Music.* Peabody Museum Papers, vol. 41, no. 3. Cambridge, Mass.: Harvard University, Peabody Museum.

———. 1959. "Whither Ethnomusicology?" *Ethnomusicology* 3:99–110.

McClary, Susan. 1991. *Feminine Endings.* Minneapolis: University of Minnesota Press.

McClintock, Walter. 1968 [1910]. *The Old North Trail.* Lincoln: University of Nebraska Press.

McLean, Mervyn. 1979. "Towards the Differentiation of Music Areas in Oceania." *Anthropos* 74:717–36.

———. 2006. *Pioneers of Ethnomusicology.* Coral Springs, Fla.: Llumina.

Mead, Margaret. 1928. *Coming of Age in Samoa.* New York: Morrow.

———. 1930. *Growing Up in New Guinea.* New York: Morrow.

Meintjes, Louise. 2003. *Sound of Africa! Making Music Zulu in a South African Studio.* Durham, N.C.: Duke University Press.

Merriam, Alan P. 1954. "Erich Moritz von Hornbostel." *Ethno-Musicology Newsletter* 2:9–15.

———. 1960. "Ethnomusicology: Discussion and Definition of the Field." *Ethnomusicology* 4:107–14.

———. 1963a. "Melville J. Herskovits, 1895–1963." *Ethnomusicology* 7:79–82.

———. 1963b. "The Purposes of Ethnomusicology: An Anthropological View." *Ethnomusicology* 7:206–13.

———. 1964. *The Anthropology of Music.* Evanston, Ill.: Northwestern University Press.

———. 1967. *Ethnomusicology of the Flathead Indians.* Chicago: Aldine.

———. 1969. "Ethnomusicology Revisited." *Ethnomusicology* 13:213–29.

———. 1977. "Definitions of 'Comparative Musicology' and 'Ethnomusicology': An Historical-Theoretical Perspective." *Ethnomusicology* 21:89–204.

———. 1982. "On Objections to Comparison in Ethnomusicology." In *Cross-Cultural Perspectives on Music,* edited by Robert Falck and Timothy Rice, 174–89. Toronto: University of Toronto Press.

Middleton, John, ed. 1970. *Black Africa Today.* London: Macmillan.

Miller, Terry, and Andrew Shahriari. 2006. *World Music: A Global Journey.* New York: Routledge.

Mithen, Steven. 2005. *The Singing Neanderthals.* London: Weidenfels and Nicolson.

Moisala, Pirkko, and Beverley Diamond, eds. 2000. *Music and Gender.* Urbana: University of Illinois Press.

Die Musik in Geschichte und Gegenwart. 1994–2007. Rev. ed. Edited by Ludwig Finscher. Kassel, Germany: Bärenreiter.

Myers, Helen, ed. 1992. *Ethnomusicology: An Introduction.* New York: Norton.

———. 1993. *Ethnomusicology: Historical and Regional Studies.* New York: Norton.

Nadel, S. F. [Siegfried]. 1930. "The Origins of Music." *Musical Quarterly* 16:531–46.

———. 1931. *Marimba Musik.* Vienna: Österreichische Akademie der Wissenschaften.

———. 1942. *A Black Byzantium: The Kingdom of Nupe in Nigeria.* London: Oxford University Press.

———. 1951. *Foundations of Social Anthropology.* London: Cohen and West.

Nanda, Sarna. 1994. *Cultural Anthropology.* 4th ed. New York: Rinehart and Winston.

Nattiez, Jean-Jacques. 1990. *Music and Discourse: Towards a Semiology of Music.* Princeton, N.J.: Princeton University Press.

———. 1999. "Inuit Throat-Games and Siberian Throat Singing: A Comparative, Historical, and Semiological Approach." *Ethnomusicology* 43:399–418.

Nettl, Bruno. 1954a. *North American Indian Musical Styles.* Philadelphia: American Folklore Society.

———. 1954b. "A Survey of Courses in Ethno-Musicology and Related Subjects." *Ethno-Musicology Newsletter* 3:5–6. Continuation in 5 (Sept. 1955): 7; 6 (Jan. 1956): 10–11; and 8 (Sept. 1956): 6–10.

———. 1965. *Folk and Traditional Music of the Western Continents.* New York: Prentice-Hall.

———. 1984. "A Tale of Two Cities." *Asian Music* 15 (2): 1–10.

———. 1985. *The Western Impact on World Music.* New York: Schirmer Books.

———. 1988. "The ifmc/ictm and the Development of Ethnomusicology in the United States." *Yearbook for Traditional Music* 20:19–25.

———. 1989. *Blackfoot Musical Thought: Comparative Perspectives.* Kent, Ohio: Kent State University Press.

———. 1991. "The Dual Nature of Ethnomusicology in North America: The Contributions of Charles Seeger and George Herzog." In *Comparative Musicology and Anthropology of Music,* edited by Bruno Nettl and Philip V. Bohlman, 266–76. Chicago: University of Chicago Press.

———. 1992. *The Radif of Persian Music.* Rev. ed. Champaign, Ill.: Elephant and Cat.

———. 1995. *Heartland Excursions.* Urbana: University of Illinois Press.

———. 1998. "Arrows and Circles: An Anniversary Talk about Fifty Years of ictm and the Study of Traditional Music." *Yearbook for Traditional Music* 30:1–11.

———. 1999. "Displaced Musics and Immigrant Musicologists." In *Driven into Paradise,* edited by Reinhold Brinkmann and Christoph Wolff, 54–65. Berkeley: University of California Press.

———. 2002a. *Encounters in Ethnomusicology: A Memoir.* Warren, Mich.: Harmonie Park.

———. 2002b. "Ethnicity and Musical Identity in the Czech Lands." In *Music and German National Identity,* edited by Cecilia Applegate and Pamela Potter, 269–87. Chicago: University of Chicago Press.

———. 2005. *The Study of Ethnomusicology: Thirty-One Issues and Concepts.* Urbana: University of Illinois Press.

———. 2006a. "Response to Victor Grauer: On the Concept of Evolution in the History of Ethnomusicology." *World of Music* 48 (2): 59–72.

———. 2006b. "Was ist Musik? Ethnomusikologische Perspektive." In *Musik— Zu Begriff und Konzepten,* edited by Michael Beiche and Albrecht Riethmüller, 9–18. Munich: Max Steiner Verlag.

Nettl, Bruno, and Philip V. Bohlman, eds. 1991. *Comparative Musicology and Anthropology of Music: Essays on the History of Ethnomusicology.* Chicago: University of Chicago Press.

Nettl, Bruno, Charles Capwell, Thomas Turino, Isabel K. F. Wong, Philip V. Bohlman, and Timothy Rommen. 2007. *Excursions in World Music.* 5th ed. Upper Saddle River, N.J.: Prentice-Hall.

Nettl, Bruno, and Ronald Riddle. 1974. "Taqsim Nahawand: A Study of Sixteen Performances by Jihad Racy." *Yearbook of the International Folk Music Council* 5:11–50.

Nettl, Bruno, and Amnon Shiloah. 1978. "Persian Classical Music in Israel: A Preliminary Report." *Israel Studies in Musicology* 1:142–58.

Nettl, Paul. 1921–22. "Beiträge zur Geschichte der Tanzmusik im 17. Jahrhundert." *Zeitschrift für Musikwissenschaft* 4:257–65.

———. 1923. *Alte jüdische Spielleute und Musiker.* Prague: Joseph Flesch.

Nettle, Daniel, and Suzanne Romaine. 2000. *Vanishing Voices: The Extinction of the World's Languages.* Oxford: Oxford University Press.

Neuman, Daniel, Shubha Chaudhuri, and Komal Kothari. 2006. *Bards, Ballads, and Boundaries: An Ethnographic Atlas of Music Traditions in Western Rajasthan.* Oxford: Seagull Books.

The New Grove Dictionary of Music and Musicians. 1980. Edited by Stanley Sadie. London: Macmillan.

The New Grove Dictionary of Music. 2001. 2d ed. Edited by Stanley Sadie and John Tyrell. London: Macmillan.

The New Oxford History of Music. 1957–65. Edited by J. A. Westrup et al. 10 vols. London: Oxford University Press.

Nketia, J. H. Kwabena. 1954. "The Role of the Drummer in Akan Society." *African Music* 1:34–43.

———. 1974. *The Music of Africa.* New York: Norton.

O'Brien, James Patrick. 1977. *Non-western Music and the Western Listener.* Dubuque, Iowa: Kendall/Hunt.

Olsen, Poul Rovsing. 1974. *Musiketnologi.* Copenhagen: Berlingske Forlag.

Olson, James S., and Raymond Wilson. 1984. *Native Americans in the Twentieth Century.* Urbana: University of Illinois Press.

Ortiz, Fernando. 1952–55. *Los instrumentos de la música afro-cubana.* Havana: Dirección de Cultura de Ministerio de Educación.

The Oxford History of Music. 1901–5. Edited by Sir Henry Hadow. London: Oxford University Press.

Pantaleoni, Hewitt. 1985. *On the Nature of Music.* Oneonta, N.Y.: Welkin Books.

Pearson, Roger. 1974. *Introduction to Anthropology.* New York: Holt, Rinehart and Winston.

Potter, Pamela. 1998. *Most German of the Arts.* New Haven, Conn.: Yale University Press.

Powers, Harold S. 1970. "An Historical and Comparative Approach to the Classification of Ragas." *Selected Reports of the Institute of Ethnomusicology, UCLA* 1 (3): 1–78.

Prajnanananda, Swami. 1973. *Music of the Nations.* New Delhi: M. Manoharlal.

Racy, Ali Jihad. 1991. "Historical Worldviews of Early Ethnomusicologists: An East-West Encounter in Cairo 1932." In *Ethnomusicology and Modern Music History,* edited by Stephen Blum, Philip V. Bohlman, and Daniel Neuman, 68–91. Urbana: University of Illinois Press.

Randel, Don Michael. 1992. "The Canons in the Musicological Toolbox." In *Disciplining Music: Musicology and Its Canons,* edited by Katharine Bergeron and Philip V. Bohlman, 10–22. Chicago: University of Chicago Press.

Reck, David. 1977. *Music of the Whole Earth.* New York: Scribner's.

Redfield, Robert. 1953. *The Primitive World and Its Transformations.* Ithaca, N.Y.: Cornell University Press.

Reese, Gustave. 1954. *Music in the Renaissance.* New York: Norton.

Reinhard, Kurt. 1963. "The Demonstration Collection." Booklet accompanying the LP album *The Demonstration Collection of E. M. von Hornbostel and the Berlin Phonogramm-Archiv.* Ethnic Folkways Library FE 4175.

———. 1968. *Einführung in die Musikethnologie.* Wolfenbüttel, Germany: Mosiler.

Rice, Timothy. 1987. "Toward the Remodeling of Ethnomusicology." *Ethnomusicology* 31:469–88.

———. 2003. "Time, Place, and Metaphor in Musical Experience and Ethnography." *Ethnomusicology* 47:151–79.

Riemann, Hugo. 1882. *Musik-Lexikon.* Leipzig: Verlag des bibliographischen Instituts.

———. 1887. *Opernhandbuch.* Leipzig: C. A. Koch.

———. 1904–13. *Handbuch der Musikgeschichte.* 5 vols. Leipzig: Breitkopf und Härtel.

———. 1967. *Riemann Musik Lexikon. Sachteil.* 2d ed. Edited by Willibald Gurlitt and Hans Heinrich Eggebrecht. Mainz: Schott.

Rigdon, Susan. 1988. *The Culture Facade: Art, Science, and Politics in the Work of Oscar Lewis.* Urbana: University of Illinois Press.

Ringer, Alexander L. 1991. "One World or None? Untimely Reflections on a Timely Musicological Question." In *Comparative Musicology and Anthropology of Music,* edited by Bruno Nettl and Philip V. Bohlman, 187–200. Chicago: University of Chicago Press.

Roberts, Helen H. 1936. *Musical Areas in Aboriginal North America.* Yale University Publications in Anthropology, no. 12. New Haven, Conn.: Dept. of Anthropology, Yale University.

Roberts, Warren E. 1958. *The Tale of the Kind and the Unkind Girls.* Berlin: De Gruyter.

———. 1964a. *Log Buildings of Southern Indiana.* Bloomington, Ind.: Trickster.

———. 1964b. *Norwegian Folktale Studies.* Oslo: Universitetsforlaget.

Roland-Manuel, Alexis. 1960. *Histoire de la musique I: Des origines à Jean-Sébastien Bach.* Encyclopédie de la Pléiade. Paris: Gallimard.

Rose, Arnold M. 1968. "Minorities." In *International Encyclopedia of the Social Sciences,* 10:365–71. New York: Macmillan.

Rosenberg, Neil V. 1993. *Transforming Tradition: Folk Music Revivals Examined.* Urbana: University of Illinois Press.

Rouget, Gilbert. 1970. "Transcrire ou décrire: Chant soudanais et chant fuegian." In *Échanges et communications: Mélanges offerts à Claude Lévi-Strauss,* edited by J. Pouillion and Pierre Maranda, 1:677–70. The Hague: Mouton.

———. 1985. *Music and Trance: A Theory of the Relations between Music and Possession.* Chicago: University of Chicago Press.

Rousseau, Jean-Jacques. 1768. *Dictionnnaire de musique.* Paris.

Royce, Anya. 1982. *Ethnic Identity: Strategies of Diversity.* Bloomington: Indiana University Press.

Sachs, Curt. 1918. "Die Streichbogenfrage." *Archiv für Musikwissenschaft* 1:3–9.

———. 1929. *Geist und Werden der Musikinstrumente.* Berlin: Bard.

———. 1937. *World History of the Dance.* New York: Norton.

———. 1940. *The History of Musical Instruments.* New York: Norton.

———. 1943. *The Rise of Music in the Ancient World, East and West.* New York: Norton.

———. 1953. *Rhythm and Tempo.* New York: Norton.

———. 1959 [1930]. *Vergleichende Musikwissenschaft: Musik der Fremdkulturen.* 2d ed. Heidelberg: Quelle und Meyer.

———. 1962. *The Wellsprings of Music.* The Hague: M. Nijhoff.

Salmen, Walter. 1954. "Towards the Exploration of National Idiosyncracies in Wandering Song-Tunes." *Journal of the International Folk Music Council* 6:52–56.

Sammelbände für vergleichende Musikwissenschaft. 1922–24. Munich: Drei-Masken Verlag.

Samson, Jim. 2001. "Canon III." In *The New Grove Dictionary of Music and Musicians,* 2d ed., edited by Stanley Sadie and John Tyrell, 5:6–7. London: Macmillan.

Sapir, Edward. 1910. "Song Recitative in Paiute Mythology." *Journal of American Folklore* 3:455–72.

Sarana, Gopala. 1975. *The Methodology of Anthropological Comparisons: An Analysis of Comparative Methods in Social and Cultural Anthropology.* Tucson: University of Arizona Press.

Saygun, Ahmed Adnan. 1951. "Authenticity in Folk Music." *Journal of the International Folk Music Council* 3:7–10.

Schaeffner, André. 1936. *Origine des instruments de musique.* Paris: Payol.

Schinhan, Jan Philip. 1937. *The Music of the Ballads.* Durham, N.C.: Duke University Press.

Schmidt, Wilhelm. 1939. *The Culture Historical Method of Ethnology.* New York: Fortuny's.

Schneider, Albrecht. 1976. *Musikwissenschaft und Kulturkreislehre.* Bonn: Verlag für systematische Musikwissenschaft.

———. 1979. "Vergleichende Musikwissenschaft als Morphologie und Stilkritik: Werner Danckerts Stellung." *Jahrbuch für Volksliedforschung* 24:11–27.

———. 2001. "Sound, Pitch, and Scale: From 'Tone Measurements' to Sonological Analysis in Ethnomusicology." *Ethnomusicology* 45:489–520.

———. 2006. "Comparative and Systematic Musicology in Relation to Ethnomusicology: A Historical and Methodological Survey." *Ethnomusicology* 50:236–58.

Schneider, Marius. 1934. *Geschichte der Mehrstimmigkeit.* Vol. 1. Berlin: Bard.

———. 1957. "Primitive Music." In *Ancient and Oriental Music,* edited by Egon Wellesz, 1–82. Vol. 1 of *The New Oxford History of Music.* London: Oxford University Press.

Seeger, Anthony. 1987. *Why Suyá Sing*. Cambridge: Cambridge University Press.

Seeger, Charles. 1977. *Studies in Musicology 1935–1975*. Berkeley: University of California Press.

Sharp, Cecil J. 1932. *English Folk-songs from the Southern Appalachians*. London: Oxford University Press.

Shelemay, Kay Kaufman. 2001a. *Soundscapes: Exploring Music in a Changing World*. New York: Norton.

———. 2001b. "Towards an Ethnomusicology of the Early Music Movement." *Ethnomusicology* 45:1–29.

Shiloah, Amnon. 1979. *The Theory of Music in Arabic Writings*. Munich: Henle.

———. 1992. *Jewish Musical Traditions*. Detroit, Mich.: Wayne State University Press.

Simon, Artur. 1978. "Probleme, Methoden, und Ziele der Ethnomusikologie." *Jahrbuch für musikalische Volks- und Völkerkunde* 9:8–52.

Singer, Milton. 1972. *When a Great Tradition Modernizes*. New York: Praeger.

Slobin, Mark. 1992a. "Ethical Issues." In *Ethnomusicology: An Introduction*, edited by Helen Myers, 329–36. New York: Norton.

———. 1992b. "Micromusics of the West: A Comparative Approach." *Ethnomusicology* 36:1–87.

[Society of Jesus]. 1959. *Jesuit Relations and Allied Documents: Travels and Explorations of the Jesuit Missionaries in New France 1619–1791*. Edited by Reuben Gold Thwaites. New York: Pageant Books.

Solie, Ruth A. 1993. *Musicology and Difference: Gender and Sexuality in Music Scholarship*. Berkeley: University of California Press.

Stevenson, Robert. 1960. *The Music of Peru: Aboriginal and Viceroyal Epochs*. Washington, D.C.: Pan-American Union.

Steward, Julian H., ed. 1949. *Comparative Ethnology of South American Indians*. Vol. 5 of *Handbook of South American Indians*. Bureau of American Ethnology Bulletin 143. Washington, D.C.: Smithsonian Institution, Bureau of American Ethnology.

———. 1955. *Theory of Culture Change*. Urbana: University of Illinois Press.

Stock, Jonathan. 2007. "Alexander J. Ellis and His Place in the History of Ethnomusicology." *Ethnomusicology* 51:306–25.

Stocking, George W., Jr. 1968. *Race, Culture, Evolution: Essays in the History of Anthropology*. Chicago: University of Chicago Press.

Stockmann, Doris, and Jan Steszewski eds. 1973. *Analyse und Klassifikation von Volksmelodien*. Kraków: Polskie wydawnictwo muzyczne.

Stockmann, Erich. 1988. "The International Folk Music Council/International Council for Traditional Music—Forty Years." *Yearbook for Traditional Music* 20:1–10.

Stokes, Martin, ed. 1994. *Ethnicity, Identity and Music: The Musical Construction of Place*. Oxford, U.K.: Berg.

Stone, Ruth. 2008. *Theory for Ethnomusicology*. Upper Saddle River, N.J.: Prentice Hall.

Stumpf, Carl. 1886. "Lieder der Bellakula Indianer." *Vierteljahrschrift für Musikwissenschaft* 2:405–26.

———. 1892. "Phonographierte indianische Melodien." *Vierteljahrschrift für Musikwissenschaft* 8:127–44.

———. 1911. *Die Anfänge der Musik*. Leipzig: J. F. Barth.

Symonette, Lys, and Elmar Juchem, eds. 2000. *Kurt Weill: Briefe an die Familie (1914–1950)*. Stuttgart: Metzler.

"Symposium on Transcription and Analysis: A Hukwe Song with Musical Bow." 1964. *Ethnomusicology* 8:223–77.

Szabolcsi, Bence. 1935. "Über Kulturkreise der musikalischen Ornamentik in Europa." *Zeitschrift für Musikwissenschaft* 17 (2–3): 65–82.

———. 1959. *Bausteine zu einer Geschichte der Melodie*. Budapest: Corvina.

Tagore, Sourindro Mohun. 1963 [1896]. *Universal History of Music, Compiled from Divers Sources*. Varanasi: Chowkhamba Sanskrit Series Office.

Tang Yating. 2000. "Influence of Western Musicology in China: An Historical Evaluation." *Journal of Music in China* 2 (1): 53–67.

Tappert, Wilhelm. 1890. *Wandernde Melodien*. 2d ed. Leipzig: List und Francke.

Taruskin, Richard. 2005. *The Oxford History of Western Music*. New York: Oxford University Press.

Taylor, Ronald. 1991. *Kurt Weill: Composer in a Divided World*. Boston: Northeastern University Press.

Temperley, Nicholas. 1998. *Hymn Tune Index: A Census of English-Language Hymn Tunes*. Oxford: Oxford University Press.

Thompson, Stith. 1929. *Tales of the North American Indians*. Cambridge, Mass.: Harvard University Press.

———. 1951. *The Folktale*. New York: Dryden.

———, ed. 1952. *Four Symposia on Folklore*. Bloomington: Indiana University Press.

———. 1953. "The Star-Husband Tale." *Studia Septentrionalia* 4:93–163.

———. 1996. *A Folklorist's Progress: Reflections of a Scholar's Life*. Special Publications of the Folklore Institute, no. 5. Bloomington: Folklore Institute, Indiana University.

Titon, Jeff Todd, gen. ed. 1984. *Worlds of Music*. New York: Schirmer Books.

Tsuge, Gen'ichi. 1970. "Rhythmic Aspects of the Avaz in Persian Music." *Ethnomusicology* 14:205–27.

Turino, Thomas. 2000. *Nationalists, Cosmopolitans, and Popular Music in Zimbabwe*. Chicago: University of Chicago Press.

———. 2008. *Music as Social Life*. Chicago: University of Chicago Press.

Turino, Thomas, and James Lea, eds. 2004. *Identity and the Arts in Diaspora Communities*. Warren, Mich.: Harmonie Park Press.

Turnbull, Colin. 1961. *The Forest People*. New York: Simon and Schuster.

Tylor, Edward B. 1881. *Anthropology*. New York: Appleton.

Vander, Judith. 1988. *Songprints: The Musical Experience of Five Shoshone Women.* Urbana: University of Illinois Press.

Vega, Carlos. 1966. "Mesomusic: An Essay on the Music of the Masses." *Ethnomusicology* 10:1–17.

Voegelin, Carl F. 1945. "The Influence of Area on American Indian Linguistics." *Word* 1:54–58.

Voegelin, Carl F., and Florence M. Voegelin. 1977. *Classification and Index of the World's Languages*. New York: Elsevier.

Voegelin, Carl F., and Erminie Wheeler-Voegelin. 1944. *Map of North American Indian Languages*. American Ethnological Society Publication 20. New York: American Ethnological Society.

Wachsmann, Klaus. 1971. "Universal Perspectives in Music." *Ethnomusicology* 15:381–84.

Wallaschek, Richard. 1893. *Primitive Music*. London: Longmans, Green. German-language ed., *Anfänge der Tonkunst* (1903).

Wallin, Nils L., Björn Merker, and Steven Brown, eds. 2000. *The Origins of Music*. Cambridge, Mass.: MIT Press.

Walther, Johann. 1732. *Musikalisches Lexikon oder musikalische Bibliothek*. Leipzig: W. Deer.

Warwick, Donald P., and Samuel Osherson, eds. 1973. *Comparative Research Methods*. Englewood Cliffs, N.J.: Prentice-Hall.

Washburne, Chris, and Maiken Derno, eds. 2004. *Bad Music: The Music We Love to Hate*. New York: Routledge.

Waterman, Christopher Alan. 1990. *Jùjú: A Social History and Ethnography of an African Popular Music*. Chicago: University of Chicago Press.

Waterman, Richard A. 1951. "Gospel Hymns of a Negro Church in Chicago." *Journal of the International Folk Music Council* 3:87–93.

Wells, Evelyn. 1951. "Some Impressions of the Conference." *Journal of the International Folk Music Council* 3:2–3.

Weltfish, Gene. 1965. *The Lost Universe: The Way of Life of the Pawnee*. New York: Basic Books.

White, Leslie. 1949. *The Science of Culture*. New York: Farrar, Strauss, and Cudahy.

———. 1959. *The Evolution of Culture*. New York: McGraw-Hill.

Whitten, Norman E., Jr. 1976. *Sacha Runa: Ethnicity and Adaptation of Ecuadorian Jungle Quichua*. Urbana: University of Illinois Press.

Wilber Donald N. 1976. *Iran, Past and Present*. 8th ed. Princeton, N.J.: Princeton University Press.

Wiora, Walter. 1949. "Concerning the Adaptation of Authentic Folk Music." *Journal of the International Folk Music Council* 1:14–19.

————. 1953. *Europäischer Volksgesang.* Das Musikwerk no. 4. Köln: Arno Volk Verlag.

————. 1956. "Älter als die Pentatonik." In *Studia Memoriae Bélae Bartók Sacra,* edited by Zoltán Kodály and László Lajtha, 185–208. Budapest: Academia Scientiarum Hungaricae.

————. 1965. *The Four Ages of Music.* New York: Norton.

————. 1975. *Ergebnisse und Aufgaben vergleichender Musikforschung.* Darmstadt, Germany: Wissenschaftliche Buchgesellschaft.

Wissler, Clark. 1912. *Social Organization and Ritualistic Ceremonies of the Blackfoot Indians.* American Museum of Natural History Anthropological Papers, vol. 7, pt. 1. New York: American Museum of Natural History.

————. 1917. *The American Indian.* New York: McMurtrie.

Wissler, Clark, and D. C. Duvall. 1909. *Mythology of the Blackfoot Indians.* American Museum of Natural History Anthropological Papers, vol. 2, pt. 1. New York: American Museum of Natural History.

Witmer, Robert. 1982. *Musical Life of the Blood Indians.* Ottawa: National Museum of Man.

Wong, Isabel K. F. 1991. "From Reaction to Synthesis: Chinese Musicology in the Twentieth Century." In *Comparative Musicology and Anthropology of Music,* edited by Bruno Nettl and Philip V. Bohlman, 37–55. Chicago: University of Chicago Press.

Zemp, Hugo. 1971. *Musique dan: La Musique dans la pensée et la vie sociale d'une société africaine.* Paris: Mouton.

————. 1979. "Aspects of 'Are'are Musical Theory." *Ethnomusicology* 23:5–48.

Zonis, Ella. 1973. *Classical Persian Music: An Introduction.* Cambridge, Mass.: Harvard University Press.

Index

the term, 160; three myths of history in, 160–65; and time, 224–26; in the 21st century, 55–56; varieties of, 55–56
evolutionary musicology, xxv, 87, 108–18
Excursions in World Music (B. Nettl et al.), 37

Feld, Steven, 113, 220
Fewkes, Walter, 19
fieldwork, 64–66
Fletcher, Peter, 38
folklore studies, 93, 96, 100, 140
folklorists, 99, 139
folk music: collecting and scholarship of, 14–16; comparative study of, 84; distribution of, 77; IFMC/ICTM's definition of, 151–52; national schools of, 25; the study of, 41–43, 148–51, 153–54
folk opera, 212–14
folksong: collections of, 198–99; in opera, 213
Folk Song Style and Culture (A. Lomax), 175
Foundations of Social Anthropology, The (S. Nadel), 124
Four Symposia on Folklore (S. Thompson, ed.), 139
French ethnomusicology, 24–26

Garfias, Robert, 37–38
Garland Encyclopedia of World Music, 50
Gebrauchsmusik, 212
Geist und Werden der Musikinstrumente (C. Sachs), 175
genetic interpretation, 83
geographic distribution, 77, 173–78
Geschichte der Mehrstimmigkeit (M. Schneider), 115, 179
Gesellschaft zur Erforschung der Musik des Orients, 141
Gourlay, Ken. A., 64
Grauer, Victor, 68, 86–87
Greve, Martin, 56

Handbuch der Musikgeschichte (G. Adler), 4, 44
Handbuch der Musikgeschichte (H. Riemann), 46
Handbuch der Musikwissenschaft (E. Bücken), 47–48
Herder, Johann Gottfried, 40–42
Herskovits, Melville J., 84, 121, 164
Herzog, George: and authenticity, 205; and comparative study, 75, 94; course taught by, 15, 49; and the founding of SEM, 168–69; and fundamental issues of ethnomusicology, 105; among Hornbostel's students, 23; on Native American ideas about music, 63; and the 1950 conferences, 100; paradigm of, 140–42; and popular music, 153
Histoire de la Musique (Roland-Manuel), 48–49
Historical musicology: 1885 origins of, 5; and ethnomusicology, 3–8, 58, 163, 173; and folklore, xxv
History of ethnomusicology: alternative views, 23–32; conventional view, 22–23
Hood, Mantle: Concept of ethnomusicology of, 67, 96, 142–43, 168; critique of comparative musicology by, 84–85; and UCLA, 83, 143
Hornbostel, Erich M. von: on the basic tasks of ethnomusicology, 59, 73, 111; evolutionist view of history of, 114; in the history of ethnomusicology, 161; as leader of European school, vxii, 23
How Musical Is Man? (J. Blacking), 64

Indiana University, 93–94, 99, 138–40, 147, 212–14
instrument classification, 8–9
International Council for Traditional Music (ICTM): Bloomington conference of, 100–101; Copenhagen conference of, 167; history of, xxvi, 144–45, 146–58; M. Karpeles and,

BRUNO NETTL is professor emeritus of music and anthropology at the University of Illinois Urbana-Champaign and the author of *The Study of Ethnomusicology: Thirty-One Issues and Concepts* and many other books.

The University of Illinois Press
is a founding member of the
Association of American University Presses.

. . . .

University of Illinois Press
1325 South Oak Street
Champaign, IL 61820-6903
www.press.uillinois.edu